INDIGENOUS AFFINITIES

Indigenous Affinities

TOWARD SOLIDARITY ACROSS THE GLOBAL SOUTH

Amal Eqeiq

FORDHAM UNIVERSITY PRESS   NEW YORK 2025

Fordham University Press gratefully acknowledges financial assistance and support provided for the publication of this book by Williams College.

Copyright © 2025 Fordham University Press

All rights reserved. No part of this publication may be reproduced, stored in a retrieval system, or transmitted in any form or by any means—electronic, mechanical, photocopy, recording, or any other—except for brief quotations in printed reviews, without the prior permission of the publisher.

Fordham University Press has no responsibility for the persistence or accuracy of URLs for external or third-party Internet websites referred to in this publication and does not guarantee that any content on such websites is, or will remain, accurate or appropriate.

Fordham University Press also publishes its books in a variety of electronic formats. Some content that appears in print may not be available in electronic books.

Visit us online at www.fordhampress.com.

For EU safety / GPSR concerns: Mare Nostrum Group B.V., Mauritskade 21D, 1091 GC Amsterdam, The Netherlands, gpsr@mare-nostrum.co.uk

Library of Congress Cataloging-in-Publication Data available online at https://catalog.loc.gov.

Printed in the United States of America
27 26 25   5 4 3 2 1
First edition

To my beloved parents,
To the children of Gaza.

Contents

NOTE ON TRANSLITERATION   ix

Introduction: On Conversations Yet to Be Had   1

1 On Affinity and Affiliative Comparison   19

2 Topographies of Affinities: Writing Erasure and Borderlands   51

3 Border Crossers and City Dwellers: Narratives of Indigenous Urban Culture   94

4 Murals, Marches, and Metaphors: Performative Commemoration in Rural Chiapas and Palestine   119

Conclusion: Unveiling with Affinity   153

Postscript: *Indigenous Affinities* after the Gaza Genocide   157

ACKNOWLEDGMENTS   167

GLOSSARY   179

NOTES   181

BIBLIOGRAPHY   211

INDEX   225

Note on Transliteration

This work uses the standard *International Journal of Middle East Studies (IJMES)* method for transliteration of words in Arabic and Hebrew. However, I have opted not to follow the *IJMES* convention when it comes to indicating the difference created by a silent *h* at the end of words that end in a "*tā' marbūṭa*" (tied *t*) in Arabic. For instance, I write *'ulfa* instead of *'ulfah*. That said, I have retained the final *h* in *kuffiyeh* to align with the commonly used English spelling in Palestinian cultural productions and to reflect the phonetic inflection of the Palestinian *fallāḥīn* (fellaheen) speech. While in most cases the final *h* is unstressed and therefore omitted, in *kuffiyeh* (often transliterated as *keffiyeh*) it is included because it receives stress following the geminated semivowel *y* in rural Palestinian dialects.

For greatest ease of reading, personal names are transliterated using the most common English spelling. Along similar lines, this work uses English spelling in reference to words in Tsotsil and Spanish. Hence, Maya literature and culture as well as the Maya peoples are jointly referred to as Mayan. All names of Palestinian and other Arab authors are presented in their Latinized forms; however, in the bibliography, they are also listed in Arabic to assist readers interested in consulting the original works in Arabic.

Regarding place names, Jovel, the Tsotsil name for San Cristóbal de las Casas, is rendered as Jobel—the more commonly used spelling—while Oventik, the Tsotsil name of an autonomous Zapatista community, is retained in its original spelling. Names of Palestinian villages and cities that do not have widely recognized English equivalents—unlike Jaffa or Haifa—are transliterated according to the Palestinian vernacular pronunciation. Along these lines, I choose to transliterate the word *Kafr* as *Kufur* in quoted material in Arabic to reflect the pronunciation in the Palestinian rural dialect, rather than the more common *Kufr*.

INDIGENOUS AFFINITIES

Introduction
On Conversations Yet to Be Had

Chiapas and Palestine are far apart, but they share familiar political landscapes. When Mayans in Chiapas, the southernmost state of Mexico, staged the Zapatista uprising in 1994—an armed rebellion that was described as the first postmodern revolution[1] against the neoliberal Mexican state—Chiapas, the poorest state in the country at the time, became a synonym for the anticolonial and anti-globalization struggle of Indigenous Peoples in Mexico and beyond. The quest for Indigenous autonomy, together with the Mayan rebels' reaffirmation of the right of Indigenous Peoples for self-determination and their resistance to the militarized settler Mexican state that deployed a third of its military force to suppress the uprising, resembled the revolutionary spirit of the Palestinian Intifada in 1987, a pivotal moment in the ongoing struggle in Palestine against Zionist settler colonialism, military occupation, and an apartheid ethno-nationalist Jewish state.

Since the early 2000s, the subtle similarities between these two geographies of struggle have become more visible to scholars, activists, and artists alike. A growing body of scholarship—led by Mark LeVine, Sylvia Marcos, and Linda Quiquivix—has drawn parallels between the Zapatista and Palestinian resistance movements, highlighting their shared opposition to neoliberalism, patriarchy, and colonialism. Both movements have built grassroots networks that challenge the very idea of the state, whether the settler or the postcolonial. LeVine uses the term "global intifada" to underscore the interconnectedness of the uprisings in Chiapas and Palestine against global systems of oppression.[2] Meanwhile, Marcos and Quiquivix emphasize that the struggles in both geographies are led by Indigenous Peoples defending themselves against the violence of the capitalist systems. They evoke the decolonial and anticapitalist vision of the Zapatista framework of "together and side by side" to emphasize its power as a radical model of solidarity and an emancipatory strategy for circulating power in a dispersed way, thus "creating the world anew."[3] Within this framework, the liberations of Chiapas and Palestine are not only interconnected, but also co-constitutive in reimagining political and social relations from below.

Increasing attention among activists and artists to the long-standing histories of *ṣumūd* (steadfastness) in both Chiapas and Palestine is another recent development that has contributed to fomenting the connection between the Indigenous struggles in these two places. The nascent transnational network of Indigenous activists, artists, community organizers, youth movements, and immigration and human rights advocates in Mexico, Palestine, Latin America, the United States, and beyond has brought together the iconographies of *ṣumūd* in Chiapas and Palestine by placing them side by side in various visual expressions of global solidarity, specifically in murals opposing the construction of militarized border walls.[4]

Notable examples of this trend include the weaving together of the Zapatista ski mask with the Palestinian *kuffiyeh* and the merging of the imagery of *nopal* and cactus as well as maize and the olive tree. The incorporation of these four sacred motifs of Mayan and Palestinian rootedness in the land in murals has also featured prominently in slogans, banners, chants, and marches[5] protesting the border walls built in Palestine, along Mexico's northern border with the US, and to a lesser extent, on its southern border with Guatemala. In fact, we can observe a boom in such artistic expressions in the Indigenous-Palestinian-Mexican solidarity movement against border walls. This growing movement has produced a plethora of visual artwork from graffiti to murals that display a sophisticated fusion of Zapatista, Mesoamerican, and Palestinian iconography of *ṣumūd* not only in areas along the US-Mexico borderland, but also in other parts of the US. The Bay Area World Without Walls Coalition in Northern California, for example, has organized annual collective paintings of solidarity murals since its foundation in 2018. The collective painting of these murals, which brought together artists and members from Chicano/a/x, Latinx, Palestinian American, Arab American, and Muslim American communities, created a rich tapestry of images from the Palestinian and Mexican landscapes blended with Indigenous revolutionary cultural symbols, flags, and colorful shapes. In another example from Providence, Rhode Island, Jess X. Snow (an Asian Canadian public artist, poet, and filmmaker) and Gavriel Cutipa-Zorn (a Peruvian American academic and immigrant rights / Palestine solidarity activist) painted a two-story portrait mural of two queer women of color, a Guatemalan and a Palestinian, both well-recognized activists in their communities. In the mural the two women face each other as a mutual reflection, while flora and fauna from their respective lands appear in the background as natural elements of their parallel universes. Mirroring and contact are key motifs of the mural: two women of similar age, facial features, and shade of brown skin color; equal juxtaposition of the Central and Latin American condor and cactus vis-à-vis the Palestinian quetzal and carob tree; a deep gaze in the same direction toward the common roots of a plant growing between them; and an exchange of gentle touch on each other's cheeks. The symmetry in the mural is extended further in its edges, where images of the US-Mexico border fence and the Apartheid Wall in Palestine loom over the heads of the two women. Captions in Arabic and English are also carefully balanced on both sides of the mural: "*Tabda' al-thawra fī al-'arḍ, fī al-nafs*/The revolution begins in the earth, in the self." The dual invocation of the word *al-'arḍ*/الأرض, which in Arabic means both land and earth, and the visual anchoring of the captions at the bottom of the mural highlight interconnectedness of mutual liberation and connection to the land/Mother Earth.

Against the historical backdrop of this coalescing relationship of familiarity between Chiapas and Palestine and the multivalent solidarity unfolding between Mexico and Palestine more broadly, I set out in this book to put Chiapas and Palestine in a South-South conversation through a comparative reading of contemporary Mayan and Palestinian texts. While the different parallels and overlaps pointed out above illustrate the complexity of the geopolitical ground on which the links between Chiapas and Palestine are drawn, the conversation that I am curating here shifts the attention to a less visible terrain of this ground: the comparable context of internal colonialism that Mayans in Chiapas and Palestinians in Israel (henceforth, '48 Palestinians, or simply Palestinians), have in common. As minoritized, subalternized, and racialized second-class citizens in militarized settler colonial states, Mayans and Palestinians share similar material conditions of internal colonialism, which is essentially a system of inequality, subordination, and oppression that transcends majority/minority numbers ratios.[6] Indeed, scholars such as Pablo González Casanova[7] and Elia Zureik[8] have used the term "internal colony" to describe the territorial dispossession, economic exploitation, cultural and linguistic oppression, and racial segregation of Mayans and Palestinians. Internal colonialism is also a salient topic in Mayan and Palestinian literatures. In both traditions, there is a thematic focus on the ongoing struggle against the settler colonial domination of the Mexican and Israeli states. While settler colonialism in Mexico is manifest in the state's encroachment on Indigenous lands and the formation of "a nationalist whitening project rooted in hierarchical colonial race relations that stem from a celebrated *mestizaje* that erases indigeneity by absorbing it into the body politic,"[9] Israeli settler colonialism is evident in the encroachment on the territory of Palestine both within the 1948 border and in the West Bank and Gaza. The structures of coloniality in both states involve control over Mayan and Palestinian citizens through technologies of surveillance, the demarcation of internal borders that relegate them to racially segregated peripheries, alongside a set of racist and discriminatory practices that adhere to the logics of dispossession and elimination, which, as Patrick Wolfe reminds us, are key tenets of settler colonialism, whose primary motive is access to territory. After all, as Wolfe aptly puts it, "territoriality is settler colonialism's specific, irreducible element."[10]

In light of this context and the overlap of familiarity and solidarity that trace the connection between Chiapas and Palestine, I posit the concept of affinity as a lens that can help us gain a deeper insight into the fine threads that link the two landscapes and the relational connection between Mayan and Palestinian texts. As a native speaker of Arabic and a Palestinian comparatist who was born and raised in Al-Taybeh in *al-muthallath* (The Triangle), an area in central Palestine/Israel located on an invisible border, or the so-called Green Line, which demarcated the partition of Historic Palestine in 1947, I arrived at the conclusion that *'ulfa* (affinity in Arabic) is a heuristic comparative framework to explore the intricacies of the structural and thematic convergence between Mayan and Palestinian texts. My observation of the vivid representation of linguistic minoritization, territorial enclosure, internal borders, racism, and the militarized encounter with the state in contemporary Mayan texts, from the decade leading to the Zapatista uprising in 1994 to the present moment, corresponds to the imagery of Indigenous resistance against the surveillance of the Israeli military rule, land theft, and police brutality we see in Palestinian literature in the 1960s throughout the 1970s, and that resurfaced again in the early 2000s with the outbreak of the Second Intifada.

This organic emergence of affinity as an appropriate frame to illuminate these echoes of familiarity and my observation of the resonances between Mayan and Palestinian texts were approved by my Mayan interlocutors. Throughout my five research stays and educational trips in Chiapas over the past decade, my interlocutors in both rural and urban settings have expressed their own sense of *'ulfa* with Palestine. Although they acknowledged that *la Tierra Santa*—or *PachaPalestina* (a play on the Quechua word *Pachamama*, which refers to the revered deity of Mother Earth in Andean cultures), as some Zapatista activists called it—is indeed *muy lejos* (far away), I was warmly welcomed and received as a *compañera* who came *from far away*. The Mayan writers, artists, language teachers, translators, and cultural promoters whom I interacted with and interviewed generously shared their work, insights, and archives. They also inquired about the situation in Palestine, how their

Palestinian peers responded to it, and what Palestinians planted in their *milpas*. My mestizo host families, Zapatista activists, and their local and international supporters facilitated my research through recommendations for people to contact, resources to consult to deepen my understanding of Mayan literature, and the shortcuts to take to arrive at the street in San Cristóbal de las Casas (San Cristóbal, or "Jobel" henceforth) where pro-Palestinian graffiti was scribbled in Arabic. Likewise, they made sure to inform me about the existence of members in the local community in San Cristóbal / Jobel who might be related to me, such as a Palestinian artist who has been living in Chiapas for over a decade painting the Lacandon jungle, nebulous mountains, and green landscapes. He was introduced to me as *"tu paisano"* (your fellow countryman).

The neighborhood of El Peje de Oro at the outskirts of San Cristóbal / Jobel is another space where I was warmly welcomed not only as the Palestinian *compañera*, but also as the *hermana* (sister) from *la ciudad sagrada de Jersualén* (The Holy City of Jerusalem). These were the terms that members of the Chamula Muslim community would use to introduce me to their family and friends. Initially, I was introduced to the community by the Mexican American poet Ámbar Past during my first trip to Chiapas in 2010, and since then I have been regularly invited to attend Friday prayers in the local mosque and to participate in communal Eid celebrations.

A short drive from the mosque, I encountered Palestine again. This time, Palestine was present in the library and the administrative office of El Centro Indigena de Capacitación Integral (CIdeCi)-UNITIERRA, an Indigenous residential school and community affiliated with the Zapatista movement, where books by Edward Said rested on the shelves near the Palestinian *kuffiyeh* and flag that adorned the walls of the office. In summer 2018, Palestine had a special presence during one of the weekly Thursday seminars when the community gathers for a public debate and educational activities. Sitting around a large table at the center of the library, a diverse audience composed of a large group of local and international Zapatista activists, both young and elderly, listened patiently as a Mayan man and a *ladina (non*-Indigenous) woman read aloud in Tsotsil and Spanish a report about the release from Israeli prison of Ahed Tamimi, a Palestinian activist and writer who was incarcerated as a child for slapping an Israeli soldier, before proceeding to read more breaking news from the global revolution, including the obituary of Samir Amin, the Marxist economist and world-systems analyst who coined the term Eurocentrism. In the discussion following the reading, I was invited to provide some remarks on the news from Palestine, which led to an exchange with the audience in Spanish about hope and the various possible translations of its meaning. Hearing the phrase *abrigar la esperanza* (to harbor hope), I was reminded of the line *"Nurrabī al-ʾamal*/الأمل نُرَبِّي" (to cultivate hope) from the poem "Ḥālat ḥiṣār" ("State of Siege," 2002) by the Palestinian poet Mahmoud Darwish. In my attempts to find the adequate verb in Spanish to preserve the poetic quality of this metaphor and to render its ethos of *ṣumūd* legible, I contemplated *sembrar* (to plant) or *cultivar* (to cultivate). My interlocutors concluded that given the semantic rootedness of both verbs in the land, they are not only grammatically correct, but also politically sound. This collective translation of the joint faith in hope and *ṣumūd* enhanced my sense of the deep affective resonance of *ʾulfa* that brings Chiapas and Palestine together. It also confirmed my impression that the warm reception that I enjoyed, which extended beyond hospitality into familial solidarity, was but a glimpse of a human expression of this *ʾulfa*.

This impression, however, is not surprising. As Cecilia Baeza points out, since the early 2000s, Indigenous movements in Latin America have been among the most vocal supporters of the Palestinian people's right to self-determination. The impetus behind this, Baeza argues, has arisen because of the parallels that these movements have drawn between the settler colonial condition in Palestine and the similar patterns of legal and illegal settlements in their own Indigenous territories, including the continuous invasion by agribusiness, mining and logging companies, and projects to build dams and oil and gas pipelines.[11] While state repression, racism, and the murder of Indigenous persons by non-Indigenous settlers, militias, or police are additional factors that explain this solidarity with Palestine, Baeza asserts that "what gives the Palestinian issues such a powerful resonance among Indigenous movements is the way that Latin American states have labeled these movements as 'terrorist' and the inspiration of Palestinian resistance that is internationally known and has perdured despite hardship."[12]

Given the multifaceted web of connections between Chiapas and Palestine, as elucidated above, and the centrality of affinity for the Mayan-Palestinian conversation, I have divided the book into two sections: the conceptual and the empirical. Whereas I dedicate the first chapter to conceptualizing a bilingual Arabic-Tsotsil modality of affinity, and thus create a common philological ground to examine the asymmetrical relationship between these different geographies of struggles, I devote my attention in the following three chapters to conducting a comparative close reading of Mayan and Palestinian narratives through the lens of affinity. In addition to examining parallel articulations of linguistic resistance vis-à-vis configurations of indigeneity, *ṣumūd* and land struggle, settler colonial spatiality, and commemorations of colonial violence, I illuminate the similarities and resonances between Chiapas and Palestine that remain otherwise concealed or unknown. Each empirical chapter has been written independently of the other, but together they are connected by the thread of internal borders.

My approach to affinity as a concept that embodies relationality is in conversation with current models of relational comparisons that literary scholars in comparative Indigenous studies have developed to conduct a comparative analysis of texts, whether alphabetical, pictorial, or oral, that are produced in distinctive colonial and settler colonial circumstances and articulations of indigeneity. In this respect, my conceptualization of affinity builds on the foundational work of Chadwick Allen and Steven Salaita and their respective uses of the categories trans-Indigenous and inter/national to capture similarities, without neglecting differences or overlooking the political significance of the interconnectedness of Indigenous struggles. For Allen, the *trans-Indigenous* approach is highly relevant for the context of ongoing (post)colonial relations for the following reasons. First, it attests to the complex, contingent asymmetry of different juxtapositions of Indigenous literatures. Second, it contributes to expanding globally Indigenous fields of inquiry. Precisely for these reasons, Allen contends, scholars should place texts "across genre and media, aesthetic systems, and worldviews, technologies and practices, tribes and nations, the Indigenous-settler binary, and historical periods and geographical regions" and explore them as "together (yet) *distinct*."[13] As for Salaita, who was among the pioneering comparatists[14] to conduct a comparative study of Native American and Palestinian literatures, the existing inter/national tradition of inquiry in American Indian studies that focused on the comparative study of "intertribal" relations and pan-national affinities paved the road for developing methodological and institutional connections with Palestine despite the fact that Natives and Palestinians "have no other historical connection to speak of."[15] Nevertheless, Salaita argues that a comparative analysis of Native American and Palestinian literatures is possible because of the theological dimension of their respective colonization, namely the biblical justification for settler colonialism in both lands, and the transfer of Holy Land themes to the Americas and, later, back to Palestine. This circular movement, he concludes, provides an exploratory model for a comparative interpretation of injustice in profoundly institutional contexts.[16]

From my vantage point, the affinity between Mayan and Palestinian literatures that this book elucidates stems from a similar line of thinking. My comparative reading of Mayan and Palestinian texts does not dismiss the structural differences between their dissimilar historical contexts, although it considers the genocide of Mayans in Mesoamerica during the Spanish conquest in 1519–24 and the ethnic cleansings of Palestinians and the destruction and partition of Historic Palestine in 1948 at the hands of Zionist settlers as two similar Nakbas. The demographic and spatial minoritization in both geographies, in addition to the demarcation of internal colonial borders, resulted in establishing two analogous systems of racial, cultural, and linguistic domination: *Ladinos* and mestizos over Mayans in Chiapas; Israeli Jews over Palestinians in Palestine. The internal structure and dynamics of these different systems of domination produced different configurations of indigeneity, nationalism, ethnicity, religion, and identity. My comparative reading of Indigenous literary traditions against this backdrop applies the particularities of these different trajectories and their ramifications to highlight the formation of different cultures of writing, modes of literacy, and notions of the literary.

My concept of affinity draws on the philosophical tradition of relationality in Indigenous studies. As Lauren Tynan defines it, relationality is foundational to "how the world is known and how we, as Peoples, Country, entities, stories and more-than-human kin know ourselves and our responsibilities to one another."[17] In illuminating the invisible thread that connects Mayan and Palestinian texts, affinity recognizes the significance of developing the relationship between two people in parallel geographies of Indigenous struggle for both mutual and collective liberation. Moreover, going beyond recognition, this affinity propels us to imagine future relations in the Global South as a web of connections informed by a multilingual perspective that emerges from a political landscape where Mesoamerican and Levantine topographies mirror each other beyond colonial cartographies.

Essentially, affinity is interlinked with solidarity; it embodies relationality. In this respect, I build on Matt Wildcat and Daniel Voth's distinction between inter-Indigenous relationships and global or pan-Indigenous accounts. Inter-Indigenous relationships seek to create new spaces involving traditions from numerous nations.[18] They are creative by nature and inform our critical thinking about linkages across Indigenous communities. Therefore, relationality is "potentially transformative without being deterministic. It can bring about change without having to pre-determine what a proper outcome or decision looks like prior to understanding the contexts we find ourselves in."[19] At the same time, I am keenly aware of the limitations of expecting solidarity as a given or inevitable outcome of relational frameworks. While such approaches can illuminate resonances and mutualities across struggles, they can also run the risk of obscuring the specificities of settler colonial formations and the localized forms of violence enacted against Indigenous Peoples. As Dana M. Olwan demonstrates in her analysis of the complex dynamics surrounding queer activism for migrant justice—and the critique of queer inclusion in nation-state projects—embedded in the 2012 Palestinian statement of support for the Idle

No More movement in Canada, such alliances can overlook unequal power dynamics and rest on false assumptions about reciprocity. Despite the political significance of these gestures, they often perpetuate historical erasures and flatten differences in the pursuit of unity. Olwan refers to these forms of engagement as "assumptive solidarities."[20] While well-intentioned, alliances as such, she argues, remain romantic and comfortable, reduce the complexity of relationships among allies, and ultimately fail to transform either those relationships or their connection to the land on which they live.

Because this book is the first to bring Mayan and Palestinian literatures together in a South-South conversation, I tap into the generative possibilities of affinity and its affective meaning and ethical dimension to foster future bidirectional relations of solidarity between Chiapas and Palestine. To pave the way for this solidarity, however, I believe that we must take a different route than the older Third World solidarity road that connected Palestine with Latin America.

The strong international connections of Third Worldism that developed between Palestine and Latin America in the 1960s are widely circulated in the popular archive of the global left, though they remain largely undocumented.[21] For example, Cuban artists and designers who were committed to promoting the discourse of Third Worldism paid special (if not the most) attention to the Palestinian resistance in photography, posters, and other types of visual media that they produced within the initiative of the Organization of Solidarity with the Peoples of Asia, Africa, and Latin America (OSPAAAL) in the 1960s throughout the 1980s. Operating under the auspices of the Cuban state, OSPAAAL advanced a broader Cuban strategy aimed at building a revolutionary alliance against imperialism and colonialism. The literary solidarity of major Latin American writers with Palestine is another example of Third World alliances. In a special issue on Latin America that dates to 1981, the Palestinian literary journal *Al-Karmel* published interviews with Gabriel García Márquez and Julio Cortázar. Both novelists, who opposed military dictatorship and US imperialism, expressed their unequivocal support for the Palestinian Revolution and the Palestinian people in their struggle for liberation.[22]

The current contemporary moment of the shared struggle for self-determination and the role of the state in the repression of its own Indigenous citizens, however, is a different historical moment. In orienting myself toward mapping out the Mayan-Palestinian South-South conversation, I had first to stop and ask: On what ground did I stand? Is the Third World geography that brought the armed Palestinian struggle together with revolutionary Latin America in the 1960s in a joint front against imperialism a solid enough ground to sustain the internal colonial condition and second-class citizenship of

Mayans in Chiapas and Palestinians in Israel? The answer is simply: No. The anticolonial and national liberation movements that brought Latin America and Palestine together in the 1960s obscured the struggle of Indigenous movements in Mesoamerica for liberation and the coloniality of the idea of Latin America. The direction that I needed to take required making a shift to the political landscape of the Global South, a space of resistance not only against the domination of the Global North, neoliberal capitalism, and other forms of global hegemonic power, but also an increasingly decolonial project focusing on the persistence of racial inequalities and systemic domination across the globe.[23] In other words, to go to Chiapas from Palestine, I had to follow a deeper and marginalized path that did not go through Mexico—as a place that is politically considered part of Latin America—but rather through trails drawn on an Indigenous map that led to Abya Yala:[24] the land before colonial invasion. This also meant that the literary and cultural connections that I was looking for or the solidarity networks that I was envisioning were not necessarily concerned with exalting the nation or celebrating nationalism. In this regard, it is important to mention here parallel initiatives and visions of solidarity that are being undertaken in Mexico over the past decade. The creative collaborative project of translating Mahmoud Darwish's emblematic poem of Indigenous solidarity, "The Red Indian's Penultimate Speech to the White Man" (1992), into Spanish and several Indigenous Mexican languages (Mazatec, Chinantec, Mixe, Yucatec Maya, Náhuatl, Totonaco, and Zapotec, among others), is a striking example. The project was a cross-linguistic collaboration between Indigenous students at the Universidad Nacional Autónoma de México (National Autonomous University of Mexico, UNAM), Professor Silvana Rabinovich, and Mexico City–based Palestinian translator and scholar Shadi Rohana. The translated poem traveled to Palestine in 2015 and was performed at the Mahmoud Darwish Museum in Ramallah. Reflecting on this project, Rabinovich emphasizes the heteronym of justice that inspired the translations and the ethics of solidarity.[25] It is my hope that *Indigenous Affinities* will inspire both Mayan and Palestinian translators to collaborate on translating the poem into Tsotsil and to consider future joint projects that would yield translations of Tsotsil poems into Arabic and other Indigenous languages in the Arabic-speaking world and beyond. Such collaborative projects embody the conceptual framework of affinity underlined here and broaden the seeping connections between the two places and their language(s).

As noted earlier, the Mayan and Palestinian texts were developed in divergent historical contexts of Spanish conquest and Zionist settler colonialism. This temporal and structural asymmetry presented two major methodological challenges: linguistic and material. In terms of language, I had to reckon with the distinct strands of bilingualism that inform Mayan and Palestinian literatures. Whereas contemporary Mayan literary and cultural production is commonly conducted in Mayan languages and Spanish, or in translation between the two, Palestinian literature in Israel is written predominantly in Arabic despite the fact that Palestinian writers in Israel are bilingual in Hebrew and Arabic. To address the Indigenous language aspect of this study, therefore, I tried to focus mainly on texts that were originally written in Mayan and Arabic. That said, it was almost impossible to ignore the common practice of the resort to bilingualism in Mayan texts. Therefore, I included some bilingual texts by Mayan authors who tend to write mainly in Mayan languages and analyzed their work in light of what Gloria Chacón theorizes as *kab'awil*, a double gaze that counteracts colonial forgetfulness through linguistic maneuvers between Mayan languages and Spanish, thus becoming a reminder that memory is constantly activated by the seemingly erased "Indian" body.[26]

In contrast, a decision not to include work by bilingual Palestinian authors presented less of a challenge. Indeed, the exclusionary nature of Hebrew as the language of the Jewish state does not motivate Palestinian writers to pursue creative writing in it. Nonetheless, those who did transgress this divide and were well-received within Hebrew literature, notably the novelists Anton Shammas and Sayed Kashua, have spoken openly about the unresolved challenges of this pursuit, if not its ultimate impossibility, as some critics argue.[27] In fact, both authors who ended up in the US for different reasons have adopted English as a third, albeit exilic, language in which to write.[28] In a recent essay titled "Can the Bilingual Speak?," Shammas confesses that as "a retired bilingual desperado," his "alleged" bilingualism survived longer in his trajectory as a translator of and between Arabic and Hebrew. He writes:

> When I think about my own bilingual past, a past in which whenever I wrote in Hebrew, Arabic would always be its unconscious, and vice versa ... having a third language to discuss the adversarial, mutually exclusive relationship between Arabic and Hebrew adds a spin of sanity to that act, making the linguistic and political entanglements of my Arabic and Hebrew, and the asymmetrical power relation between the two, seem easier to handle, easier to unravel. Still, who knows, maybe that is yet another illusion.[29]

Kashua, on the other hand, who attributes his choice to write in Hebrew to his early teens in the 1980s when he studied in a Jewish boarding school in Jerusalem where the library had no books in Arabic and he had no familiarity with the writing of Frantz Fanon,[30] concludes that for a Palestinian who writes in Hebrew, "it's better to be clearly foreign, to be exiled, voluntarily or otherwise, rather than live under a forced exile in the heart of one's homeland."[31] This core difference between the scope of bilingualism in Mayan and Palestinian literatures is one of the reasons why comparative reading of Mayan and Palestinian texts focuses primarily on monolingual texts written originally in Tsotsil and Arabic.

The Mayan-Palestinian conversation presented in this book is supported by illustrative materials that have been gathered over the past ten years. Given the rapidly growing interest in Palestinian and Mayan literatures, there have been more available resources in English translation. That said, a substantial portion of the material examined here is an assemblage of original primary resources that are unstudied, unarchived, and largely undocumented. Some texts were available for purchase only at local stationery stores and bookshops in Chiapas and Palestine, and therefore required transportation across different lands and borders. Other materials, primarily those used in Chapter 4, include a collection of personal interviews, records of oral testimonies from community gatherings, and pamphlets of local histories, alongside brochures and activity programs performed at the memorial sites in rural villages in Chiapas and Palestine. Engaging with this assemblage of what I identify as *small books* revealed two critical insights.

First, contrary to the relatively visible presence of Chiapas and Palestine on the global level as critical geographies of Indigenous struggle, Mayan literature in Chiapas and Palestinian literature in Israel remain relegated to the periphery. In a way, their status as minoritized literatures is evident in this form of marginality and invisibility. Put differently, they dwell at the margin of international and global literary spaces akin to literatures of small nations, thus emerging as what Pascale Casanova calls "small literature."[32] Second, to access, gather, and assemble this various written (alphabetical and other forms of written texts), oral, visual, and performative material, I had to conduct ethnographic fieldwork and engage closely with literary ethnography as a medium to situate these resources in their relevant context. It is crucial that I point out here that my ethnographic engagement with the material is driven by the structural marginalization of these resources. Moreover, the verbal form of some other texts, such as oral testimonies, voice recordings at memorial sites, and personal interviews to document the stories of memorial sites in Mayan and Palestinian villages necessitated an ethnographic examination. In a way, I engaged with ethnography in two overlapping forms: as an encounter and as an approach. None of these forms of engagement were straightforward or free of tension.

As a Palestinian scholar who, under the influence of Edward Said, is keenly aware of the colonial gaze embedded in an anthropological reading of texts written by minoritized, subalternized, and racialized people, I am centering

Mayan texts and focusing on their aesthetics. Although I have studied Tsotsil to deepen my knowledge of Mayan texts, my proficiency in the language is still basic. Therefore, I have consulted regularly with my Tsotsil language teacher and other Tsotsil-speaking interlocutors to verify the meaning of particular words and accuracy of translations. Moreover, I resorted to Mayan secondary resources to provide as much detailed information as possible about previously unpublished Mayan texts. By doing so, my goal is to amplify the decolonial shift in the field of Mayan literary studies. In this regard, I concur with Rita M. Palacios's assertion that the field is moving away from ethnographic approaches that relegate Indigenous Peoples to the position of informers and texts to artifacts and toward a more just approach that privileges the voices of those who create poems, stories, and other narratives and of those whom they represent.[33] In the case of Palestinian literature, I followed a similar ethnographic approach, although as a Palestinian scholar and a native speaker of Arabic I was able to gain easier access to local resources and translate previously unpublished texts, anecdotes, or secondary resources, in addition to interviewing authors and local activists and community members. This web of close relationships and personal encounters provided me with the insights of critical intimacy that allowed me to put Mayan and Palestinian literatures in a polyphonic conversation. To describe these encounters, I turned to auto-ethnographic reflections that weave the personal with the critical. The presence of these reflections throughout the book illuminates how the I/eye that facilitates the conversation sees the affinity between Mayan and Palestinian literatures. They are an integral part of my analysis and are conspicuous in every chapter.

Terminology is another methodological challenge that I encountered. The Mayan-Palestinian conversation that shapes this book has been coalescing over the past ten years across multiple fields of knowledge that extend from academic settings to personal encounters, archival research, and translation across languages and fields of inquiry. Likewise, the decolonial turn of the past decade has resulted in sweeping changes in various disciplines, including Indigenous studies, Latin American studies, Middle East studies, and Palestine studies. Maintaining a consistent use of words and terminology to describe the connection between Mayan and Palestinian narratives against the backdrop of these shifting sands across disciplines was truly challenging. While it could have been more decolonial to adhere to a constant use of "Mesoamerica" or "Abya Yala" instead of "Mexico" when referring to the geography of Mayan literature, the necessary engagement with Mexican and Latin American scholarship from earlier periods prevented me from making such a choice. Additionally, I alternate between using the terms "Indigenous," "Indian," "*indígena*," and "Amerindian" to refer to the Mayans as the Originative People of

Mesoamerica, not because these terms are interchangeable or free from racial undertones and colonial taxonomies but, on the contrary, because they allow me to emphasize how they are used in academic scholarship and how Mayan writers and scholars have responded to them. In respect to Palestinian literature in Israel, however, it was easier to make a decolonial move by refusing the colonial territorial fragmentation of Palestine and referring to the geography of '48 Palestine simply as Palestine. As for names of Mayan and Palestinian places, I opted to use their original precolonial names, and thus honor naming practices used by Mayans and Palestinians and their way of preserving the ancestral names and stories of these places. However, my sporadic use of a slash to represent some of these places, such as San Cristóbal/Jobel and Yāfā/Yaffa/Jaffa, aligns more with the interchangeable approach that some Mayans and Palestinians, respectively, follow. This choice is also motivated by an occasional necessity to streamline my analysis by following the accepted generic naming conventions across the different fields.

Book Structure

Indigenous Affinities commences with the conceptual anchor of the book: affinity. In the first chapter, "On Affinity and Affiliative Comparison," I develop the relational modality of comparison between Mayan and Palestinian narratives by conceptualizing a bilingual Arabic-Tsotsil modality of affinity. Through a comparative etymological and philological examination of affinity in Arabic and Tsotsil from the Quran to contemporary Mayan philosophy, respectively, I demonstrate the fact that there are unquestionably certain similarities in how both languages convey the inherent link between affinity and solidarity. Building on this conceptualization and the collective communal translation process that led to it, I then introduce *'ulfa–kuxlej/kuxlejal* as an innovative kaleidoscopic lens to examine relational comparison. My main argument in this chapter is twofold. First, it affirms that affinity is particularly pertinent for South-South connections, as it highlights shared histories of anticolonial resistance and decolonial aspirations. In this context, affinity underscores resonances and brings forth the different aspects of familiarity and solidarity that are grounded in a shared struggle. Second, by centering relationality, affinity serves as a critique of traditional models of comparison rooted in the Eurocentric structures and methodologies of comparative literature. As a field, comparative literature has historically approached cross-cultural relationships through horizontal and linear paradigms shaped by colonial cartographies and temporalities. These frameworks have produced skewed conceptions of literature and its circulation, thus limiting our understanding of how texts move across national, linguistic, and cultural boundaries.

Chapters 2 to 4 constitute the second and empirical part of the book. Although they contain different thematic concerns and different sets of illustrative materials that include poems, short stories, novels, murals, and commemorative practices, these chapters share a common line of inquiry: the border. The demarcation of colonial racialized borders—both external and internal—in Chiapas and Palestine created linguistic, spatial, and territorial boundaries that remain until today an integral part of the experience of Mayans and Palestinians. These boundaries, however, continue to be contested and challenged through physical and figurative border crossing and other similar transgressive acts of resistance. This is why borders and border crossing are key characteristics of Mayan and Palestinian literatures. They undergird the structural formation of these traditions, shape their literary history, and inform their aesthetics. The border and border crossing are brought together in these chapters in order to demonstrate how Mayan and Palestinian poets, writers, artists, and villagers, in both rural and urban settings, construct narratives of indigeneity vis-à-vis parallel processes of settler colonialism and dispossession, linguistic domination, racial segregation, and state terror.

As the first empirical chapter demonstrating the affinity between Mayan and Palestinian literatures, Chapter 2, titled "Topographies of Affinities: Writing Erasure and Borderlands," focuses on the question of Indigenous language and its relationship to the land. Starting with the assumption that Tsotsil and Arabic are two minoritized languages that share commonalities in their position as subalternized and racialized languages vis-à-vis the respective spatial segregation and colonial dominance of Spanish and Hebrew, this chapter sets out to unveil the affinity between written Mayan narratives in Chiapas and their Palestinian counterparts in Israel by revealing their similar struggle for the survival of the native language. Given the targeted erasure of Tsotsil and Arabic in both geographies and the respective settler colonial encroachment on the lands where they are spoken, the deployment of these languages for writing Mayan and Palestinian narratives, I argue, plays a pivotal role in articulating a linguistic resistance to coloniality, and at the same time, asserting indigeneity. While this battle for Tsotsil and Arabic emerges from divergent processes, particularly revitalization for Mayan writers and preservation for Palestinian writers, I further argue that writers in both contexts deploy an intentionally heightened affect in the use of their native languages as rooted in the land. To elucidate this argument, the chapter charts first the numerous ways in which Mayan and Palestinian writers, critics, and poets have conceived, framed, and positioned written Tsotsil and Arabic in relation to indigeneity, coloniality, and racialized borders. Then, I turn my attention to a comparative analysis of Mayan and Palestinian literary criticism alongside a comparative reading of poems by Mayan and Palestinian poets who belong to the generation that launched the battle for linguistic and cultural ṣumūd (steadfastness): Mariano Reynaldo Vázquez López (1974–), Xun Betan (1982–), Tawfiq Zayyad (1929–1994), and Mahmoud Darwish (1941–2008). The political consciousness underpinning the use of Tsotsil and Arabic as endangered languages in this representative sample of poems, I conclude, speaks to a converging sense of ṣumūd and a renewed kinship with this very land that is being systematically fragmented and dispossessed by the settler colonial militarized states of Mexico and Israel.

Building on this linguistic topography of affinity, Chapter 3, "Border Crossers and City Dwellers: Narratives of Indigenous Urban Culture," proceeds to address another aspect of the parallels between Mayan and Palestinian literatures: the colonial spatial divide. The demarcation of colonial borders in Chiapas and Palestine created geographical and demographic divides between the rural and the urban. As interior borders, these material boundaries upheld racial segregation and socioeconomic apartheid between Mayas and non-Mayas (ladinos) in Chiapas, on the one hand, and Jews and non-Jews in Palestine, on the other hand. This chapter focuses on how Mayan and Palestinian narratives cross these borders. Drawing on Chicana theorist Gloria Anzaldúa's conception of the border as "an open wound,"[34] I investigate the border as a physical barrier and a colonial psychic wound that reinforces the rural-urban divide. To gain a deeper understanding of this divide, I propose reading contemporary Mayan and Palestinian narratives in the parallel historical context of local "migration" of Mayan and Palestinian writers from their villages in the late 1980s and early 1990s into the cities in their respective homelands. Given the prevalence of the border and the city as motifs across different genres, this chapter examines a range of Mayan texts, written originally in Tsotsil, including a play by the collective of La FOMMA, a novella by Mikel Ruiz, and a poem by Manu Pukuj, alongside a collection of Palestinian texts written in Arabic, featuring two short stories by Sheikha Helawy and Majd Kayyal, and a novella by Ibtisam Azem. In addition to centering the colonial spatial aspect of interior borders and Indigenous urbanity as key thematic concerns, these texts share a common interest in the liminal world of Mayan and Palestinian border crossers and city dwellers, notably, labor migrants, urbanized students, dispossessed villagers, displaced returnees, peripheralized individuals, and other marginalized figures. Through comparative analysis and close reading of this assemblage of fictional, theatrical, and poetic texts, I interrogate the parallel preoccupation with a reclamation of an Indigenous urban landscape, resistance to racial segregation, and a decolonization of internalized walls/borders, thus elucidating another aspect of the affinity between Mayan and Palestinian narratives.

Although connected to the previous chapters in its concern with borders, Chapter 4, "Murals, Marches, and Metaphors: Performative Commemoration in Rural Chiapas and Palestine," the final empirical chapter in the book, sets out to reveal and tell the story of a hidden episode that illuminates the connection between Mayan and Palestinian Indigenous struggles, namely the militarized encounter of minoritized Indigenous communities with the settler state. Despite the transcontinental spatial divide and the forty-one-year temporal gap between the massacres of Kafr Qasem in Palestine (1956) and Acteal in Chiapas (1997), the local commemorative memorials constructed in both sites showcase an analogous history of colonial violence committed by the Israeli and the Mexican militaries, respectively, against Indigenous peasants in border villages. This chapter is dedicated to telling the stories of these massacres and their aftermath as narrated by survivors and the extended bereaved communities in Kafr Qasem and Acteal. Drawing on extensive archival research, literary ethnography, personal testimonies, and translations of previously unexamined original material, I explore the aesthetics of commemorative practices in memorial sites, primarily murals, that the communities in each village employ to express their grief, and to tell the stories of their ongoing quest for justice. In a way, I perform in this chapter the double task of documenting these murals and curating a conversation between Kafr Qasem and Acteal. In bringing the stories of these massacres together as a tale of kindred memories, I illuminate how the affinity between them can create a new connection that invites the readers to imagine a future sister village kinship between Kafr Qasem and Acteal.

In addition to providing an overview of the South-South comparison that unfolded throughout *Indigenous Affinities* and discussing its major findings, my concluding analysis in "Unveiling with Affinity" revisits the title of the book. I reflect on the pursuit of affinity as a concept that can lift the veil of unknowability and untranslatability, and therefore comparability. In this respect, I discuss the merits of affinity as a methodological practice to unveil past, present, and future South-South connections. I also elaborate on the outcome of the Mayan-Palestinian conversation presented in this book to affirm that, despite the particularities of Indigenous struggles in Chiapas and Palestine, the affinities between Mayan and Palestinian narratives of *ṣumūd*, borders, and embodied memories of the land invite us to think more broadly about convergences and overlaps of different Indigenous struggles within the larger framework of global indigeneity.

The conceptual framework of affinity that underpins the Mayan-Palestinian South-South conversation unfolding in this book is inherently linked to borders. It acknowledges, celebrates, and fosters the multilayered border-crossing relation between Chiapas and Palestine. However, even within this affinity, which bridges the distance between these two far-apart landscapes, there is a new border that is being traced. This border, however, is neither territorial nor hermetic. It is a vast and porous borderland where the polyphony of a South-South speculative vision of decolonial futures, vernacular forms of thinking together from the periphery, and shared planting of seeds of hope thrive. To enter the conversation, therefore, I invite the reader to imagine the experience of breaking free from the limitation of real and imagined colonial boundaries. In other words: to *cross* the border(s).

1
On Affinity and Affiliative Comparison

"To exist is to resist" is the assertive message painted above two nearly identical murals in two places that are so geographically distant, yet politically resonant: Mexico and Palestine. Echoing the Palestinian ethos of *ṣumūd* (steadfastness), this motto, which affirms the symbiosis of survival and resilience, appears in big, bold, red letters in two strikingly different sites: a community center in one of the major autonomous Zapatista municipalities in the highlands of Chiapas called *caracol* Oventik, and the Apartheid Wall in occupied Bethlehem. In the Zapatista context, a *caracol* (Spanish for "snail") refers to a regional hub of Mayan self-governance, grassroots solidarity, and Indigenous resistance—symbolizing both collective autonomy and the slow, deliberate pace of building from below a world where many worlds fit. In stark contrast, the Apartheid Wall stands as a towering militarized barrier—an architectural manifestation of racial segregation, territorial fragmentation, Zionist settler colonial expansion, and the ongoing occupation of Palestine. Gustavo Chávez Pavón, an artist from Mexico City and a cultural promoter in the Zapatista muralist movement, co-painted both murals in 2004.[1] Each of the almost identical murals has at its center a portrait of a Zapatista rebel masked with a black-and-white *kuffiyeh*, a Palestinian cultural icon of resistance. The captions under the determined eyes of the rebel, however, are different. At the mural in Bethlehem, under the English-language motto "To exist is to resist" in large red letters, a Spanish subtitle in smaller black letters reads: *"Viva Palestina Libre abajo el muro facsista [sic]"* (Long live Free Palestine under the facsista[2] wall). At the mural in Oventik, the motto appears in several languages in this order: Tsotsil, Spanish, English, and Italian, hence: *"Ts'ik vokol ja' kuxlej / Resistir es Existir /* To exist is to Resist */ Resistere é [sic] Esistere."* At the bottom, a Spanish subtitle states:

Figure 1. To Exist Is to Resist mural, Chiapas, Mexico. Photo by Amal Eqeiq, 2013.

"*De Chiapas a Palestina, la lucha por la libertad nos hermana*" (From Chiapas to Palestine, the struggle for liberation makes us kin). Displaying the vivid aesthetics of affinity by camouflaging the *kuffiyeh* with the Zapatista *pasamontaña*,[3] both murals offer a visual testimony to common struggles and transnational connection between the Mayans in the southeast of Mexico and the people of Palestine. The ubiquitous adage of "To exist is to resist" articulates the shrinking distance between Mexico and Palestine.

In 2016, another representation of this unfolding bridge between Mexico and Palestine emerged at the northern border of Mexico. Right in the heart of the US-Mexico borderlands at the *border* (or imagined border, more accurately) between El Paso and Juárez, Palestinian artist Khaled Jarrar anchored a metal ladder to protest the planned Trump Wall. Evoking the material and symbolic significance of the ladder in Palestine as a tool of crossing and jumping over the Apartheid Wall, Jarrar installed a freestanding ladder sculpted from an 18-foot rail dismantled from the border wall in Tijuana. In this open-air installation, titled *Khaled's Ladder*, Jarrar enacts a direct analogy between the 25-foot-tall Apartheid Wall that stretches for 440 miles and Trump's border wall, which was designed to stretch 35–55 feet high alongside the entire 1,989 miles of the US-Mexico border. As an expression of a shared strategy of resistance to these walls, the ladder stands vertically, or as Jarrar puts it: "a monument somewhere to where people can *see*."[4] Hence, to cross over the wall establishes a mental bridge that defies the very purpose of the Wall: separation.

As the ladder defies separation by enabling movement across a divided land, it alludes to the parallel history of ongoing border crossing across the borderlands of Mexico and Palestine since 1848 and 1948, respectively.

The rap song "Border Ctl / طلبوا الهوية" ("*Ṭalabū al-huwīya*" [They asked for the I.D.]) performed by the Palestinian hip-hop group 47Soul in collaboration with the Palestinian British rapper Shadia Mansour and the Jamaican British rapper Fedzilla in 2021 is another very recent example of the trans-hemispheric expression of the burgeoning connection between Mexico and Palestine. Akin to the transborder makeup of the group, the videoclip spans different borders: Mexico, Palestine, Jordan, and the United Kingdom. Presented as a united call of Palestinian-Latino-Andean solidarity, images emerge and fade across three themes that touch on topics related to border walls, such as travel permits and freedom of movement, fighting the shared injustices of militarized states, and border crossing as an act of anticolonial resistance. These tropes are conveyed in a trilingual asymmetrical text in which vernacular Palestinian Arabic, Spanish, and rap English converge to express distinct aspects of similar struggles against militarized borders:

"Border Ctl / طلبوا الهوية"
(Original trilingual text, left, and English translations of verses 1 and 3, right.)

بإختصار مش احنا عبرنا الحدود لا
يابا بلعكس الحدود عبرتنا
من غزة الضفة القدس للمكسيك، حنسقط
جدار الخرساني ونبني محله جدار بشري

In brief, we didn't cross the border
But the border crossed us
From Gaza, the West Bank, Jerusalem to Mexico
We will bring down the concrete wall
And rebuild in its place a more human one

This border control
Congesting our soul
Taking its toll on us all
we gonna dissolve
this Mexico Bethlehem wall
If you hear us heed the call

Documento estampado, permiso rechazado
Juntos enfrentamos injusticias del Estado
Palestino Latino Andino no será callado
Palestino Latino Andino no será callado

Stamped documents, rejected permits
Together we face the injustices of the state
Palestinian Latino Andean will not be silenced
Palestinian Latino Andean will not be silenced[5]

Though interwoven, the trilingual lyrics of the song as well as the bilingual title playfully juxtapose the similar antiborder struggles that Palestinians, Latinos/as, and Latin Americans—in this case, Andeans—have in common. Rather than delineating an equal map of this struggle, the song weaves a thread between a coalescing connection of brotherhood and sisterhood. The trans-hemispheric collectivity of this nascent kinship is alluded to in the salient repetition of "we" across Arabic, English, and Spanish as a motif of a joint struggle and the repeated code-switching between the three languages.

These contemporary murals, installations, songs, and performative texts are vivid representations of a border-crossing and expansive trans-hemispheric solidarity that originated between Chiapas and Palestine and circulated later from Palestine to Mexico across its southern and northern borderlands. Together, they form the kernel of a growing repository of multidirectional South-South solidarities that transcend borders and develop beyond, but not totally outside, the colonial binaries of East and West. Moreover, they are saturated with similar aesthetics of exchange and mutuality through a playful deployment of duality, camouflage, mirroring, translation, adaptation, and fusion of Palestinian, Mayan, Chicano/a, Mexican, and Latinx iconography of cultural resistance. In a way, this polyphonic repository displays a kaleidoscopic reflection of the multivalent relational connection between Mexico and Palestine, or to put it succinctly, the affinity between them.

Where this polyphonic repository, which remains largely undocumented, shows us the different shapes and formats that the affinity between Palestine, Chiapas in particular, and Mexico more broadly, has taken, it also offers us both critical insight and a methodological challenge. On the one hand, it invites us to pay attention to the radical possibilities that are emerging from the periphery to produce a new form of South-South cultural encounters. These encounters are still unfolding and are linked to the political geography of the Third World. At the same time, they engage in a collective cultural production of a global network of solidarity that goes beyond national frameworks to imagine a joint engineering of decolonial anti-capitalist futures. In the process, they have produced a particular language that speaks to the inherent connection between solidarity, familiarity, and similarity. Affinity is a constitutive element of this configuration. On the other hand, this solidarity is revitalized by a multivalent and transregional juxtaposition of different genres, media, and artifacts from popular culture that defy normative definitions of a traditional literary text. The question that arises then, is, How can we read them together? To answer this question, I argue, we must return to the language that weaves the texture of this South-South solidarity. In other words, we must examine affinity closely—its semantics, its discursive frames, and the potential of its epistemic reach.

In this chapter, I posit affinity as an innovative concept to approach the South-South connection between Chiapas and Palestine. Drawing on the emotive connotations of affinity, primarily, its philological rootedness in the epistemology of the heart in both Arabic and Tsotsil, I posit that affinity, as a method of relation, is an optimal lens to examine the link between Indigenous struggles in Chiapas and in Palestine. Precisely because the Mayan and Palestinian thread of solidarity vivifies and validates South-South connections that are not categorically similar, yet *familiar,* it is crucial to consider relationality rather than the more conventional path of comparison and contrast that presumes symmetry or horizontal pairing. I find it fruitful to think about this relationality through affinity because it foregrounds the affective dimensions of solidarity, while propelling us to imagine relations beyond social ties formed by proximate connections, biological bloodlines, or self-evident kinships. Hence, as a concept of relational comparison, affinity allows us to observe relational connections across analogous cases that are familiar, but not belonging to similar categories. In the context of this book, it enables us to discern the invisible thread between Chiapas and Palestine embedded in the commonalities between how Mayan and Palestinian narratives configure indigeneity vis-à-vis racialized minoritization, the role of native languages in shaping a critical Indigenous consciousness, representation of dispossession, steadfastness and land struggle, crossing internal and external borders, the ongoing militarized encounter with the state, and embodied memories of peasant communities that were victims of state-sanctioned violence. As such, affinity unveils moments of convergence between Chiapas and Palestine without dismissing the structural dissimilarities between these two geographies of struggle, which, despite being territorially and historically unconnected (at least visibly), nevertheless share common ground in the anticolonial and decolonial imaginary of the Global South.

Taking this common ground as a point of departure, I conceptualize affinity from a combined Arabic and Tsotsil perspective. In doing so, my goal is to elucidate how bringing these two languages together to co-construct a conceptual framework offers us a South-South language that is neither Anglophone nor Eurocentric to converse about kindred connections of shared histories of Indigenous subalternization and racialization in the Global South. That said, I am keenly aware of the limits of spelling out this bilingual model in English—the language of my academic and professional training in the US—and thereby contributing to the consolidation of the hegemony of Anglophone scholarship on global indigeneity, which, institutionally speaking, continues to exclude and marginalize indigeneities outside the North American context, including those that have already developed a fully fledged discourse of indigeneity, such as Amazigh.[6] Likewise, I am aware of the problematic subsuming of Chiapas and Palestine, and thereby of Mayan and Palestinian narratives, into a respective monolingualism of Arabic and Tsotsil. After all, Palestinian literary and cultural production, mainly in the post-Nakba era, is polylingual, constituting texts in Arabic, English, Hebrew, Spanish, and Nordic languages, among others.[7] Moreover, as Refqa Abu-Remailah aptly observes in retracing the dismembered literary history of post-Nakba Palestinian literature, "a large portion of Palestinian literary production took place and continues to take place outside historic Palestine."[8] Keeping in mind that these productions also include texts written by refugees, people in exile, and their descendants, alongside non-Palestinians who self-identify as Palestinian—such as the Lebanese novelist Elias Khoury, whose fictional work, namely the novel *Bāb al-Shams* (1998) (*Gate of the Sun*, translated by Humphrey Davies, 2006) is seen as the ultimate epic that narrates the story of the Nakba—Abu-Remailah invites us to think about Palestinian narratives through a more open framework that takes into consideration multivocality and hybridity of identities and languages regardless of the legal status, nationality, or origin of those involved in the making of Palestinian literature. As for Tsotsil, it is only one of the twelve[9] Mayan languages spoken in Chiapas, though it is recognized among the top three most spoken languages. A question that we may ask at this point is, What about Mayan narratives produced in the other languages, particularly the neighboring Tseltal and Ch'ol, which, like Tsotsil, derive from the Western Cho'lan (Classic Maya)?[10]

My response to this question and the aforementioned limitations is the following: First, while a future translation of this book in both Arabic and Tsotsil will be needed to provide a better picture of its merit as a South-South model of conversation, my default reliance on English is more in line with my use of it as a language of mediation and translation, rather than an ideological endorsement of a US-centered Anglophone perspective. Despite the recently growing number of calls made by emerging collectives of activists, artists, and scholars to establish a space for conversations about global struggles that privilege local and regional perspectives instead of abiding by a US-centered frame of analysis,[11] the rigid disciplinary boundaries and identity politics in academic institutions in the US tend to block routes to thinking about struggles that exist elsewhere, let alone the affinities between them. The point that I am stressing here is the inherent tension in the process of thinking in Arabic and Tsotsil while writing in English about a conversation that exists outside the borders of a US Anglophone geography of knowledge.

With this in mind, the practice of conceptualizing a bilingual model of affinity in Arabic and Tsotsil that I follow in this current book is less interested in pursuing bilingualism for its own sake. What I am concerned with is rather the decolonial potential of border thinking steeped in this transcultural model, particularly the epistemologically generative possibilities of thinking together about indigeneity and relational connections in two languages that remain, together with American Indian languages and other Indigenous languages, on the periphery of knowledge production in the Global North. In this respect, I build on Walter Mignolo's notion of bilanguaging and dialogical thinking—which he develops from the works of Paulo Freire, Abdelkebir Khatibi, Gloria Anzaldúa and Cherríe Moraga—as practices that contribute to outdoing hegemonic power, and "[recasting] cultures of scholarship by the recognition of diversity of knowledge which outshines monothinking and monolanguaging."[12] To conceptualize affinity in Arabic and Tsotsil, therefore, is to create a dialogue between two traditions of thought and, thus, to generate a philological and epistemic exchange in thinking about relationality.

Second, the reason that I focus mainly on Arabic and Tsotsil in thinking about affinity to analyze Palestinian and Mayan narratives is straightforward. In considering the parallel histories of minoritization and racialization of subalternized Indigenous Peoples in Palestine and Chiapas, the focus on the geography of Palestine '48, in what is now modern-day Israel, is the most relevant. Like Mayans in Chiapas, Palestinians in Israel are treated as second-class citizens and are dominated by similar structures of internal colonialism, racialization, and borders. In this geography, Arabic is the major language. Apart from a fairly small number of literary and cultural productions in Hebrew and an even smaller portion in English, the majority of Palestinian narratives from this geography are produced primarily in Arabic. In Chiapas, in comparison, Tsotsil and Tseltal have a relatively similar number of speakers, but it was Tsotsil that was used in the mural "To Exist Is to Resist." Moreover, the initial steps of contemporary writerly Mayan narratives date to *El Taller Tzotzil* (The Tsotsil workshop) in 1976, which from then until 2002 published more than thirty Tsotsil Maya booklets by Indigenous authors, some of whom cofounded the first autonomous collective of Mayan writers, *Sna Jtz'ibajom* (The Writer's House), in 1983.[13]

Toward an Arabic-Tsotsil Concept of Affinity: The Affective Attributes of *'Ulfa*

The struggles in Chiapas and Palestine are far from being identical, but the various degrees of resemblance between the two make it almost impossible not to see the unequivocal resonance of familiarity between the political forces behind them: the fight for liberation, the surveillance of border walls, a militarized encounter between Indigenous Peoples and the state, and the coloniality of neoliberalism and racial capitalism. The striking collectivity that runs across the imagery in the repository unveils for us the intersection of solidarity, the familiar, and the familial. This intersection is neither abstract nor arbitrary. Conversely, it is philologically and metaphorically embodied in the notion of affinity and the ethos of the communal that informs its meaning in both Arabic and Tsotsil.

In the Arabic lexicon, affinity is a significant concept. The interconnectedness of affinity and solidarity is embedded in the morphology of the word ألفة/*ʾulfa*. Both the verb and noun forms of ألفة/*ʾulfa* convey the inherent correlation between familiarity and union. This interlink is established in Islamic theology, love theory, and modernist poetics alike. According to the Arabic lexicon, affinity, ألفة/*ʾulfa*, originates from the root ف ل أ /*ʾalf*, and it simply means: to be intimately familiar with something or someone. The second form of the verb, ألّف/*ʾallafa* —note the double "l"—emphasizes the interconnectedness between intimate familiarity and affective unity. It describes the act of reconciling people with others, of joining separate entities and creating harmony, affection, and concord between them. In the Quran, the second form, ألّف/*ʾallafa*, is mentioned twice. The verb is evoked to exalt the sacredness of bringing people's hearts together:[14]

وَأَلَّفَ بَيْنَ قُلُوبِهِمْ ۚ لَوْ أَنفَقْتَ مَا فِى ٱلْأَرْضِ جَمِيعًا مَّآ أَلَّفْتَ بَيْنَ قُلُوبِهِمْ وَلَـٰكِنَّ ٱللَّهَ أَلَّفَ بَيْنَهُمْ ۚ إِنَّهُ عَزِيزٌ حَكِيمٌ.

(سورة الأنفال / ٦٣)

Whose hearts He has brought together: [for,] if thou hadst expended all that is on earth, thou couldst not have brought their hearts together [by thyself]: but God did bring them together. Verily, He is almighty, wise. (Surat Al-Anfal, 8:63)[15]

This attribution of a divine miraculous essence to affinity and its ability to foster social bonds is reiterated in two other verses. In Surat Al-'Imran, the verb ألّف/*ʾallafa*, to bring hearts together, elucidates the blessed act of creating brotherhood:

وَٱعْتَصِمُوا۟ بِحَبْلِ ٱللَّهِ جَمِيعًا وَلَا تَفَرَّقُوا۟ ۚ وَٱذْكُرُوا۟ نِعْمَتَ ٱللَّهِ عَلَيْكُمْ إِذْ كُنتُمْ أَعْدَآءً **فَأَلَّفَ** بَيْنَ قُلُوبِكُمْ فَأَصْبَحْتُم بِنِعْمَتِهِۦٓ إِخْوَٰنًا وَكُنتُمْ عَلَىٰ شَفَا حُفْرَةٍ مِّنَ ٱلنَّارِ فَأَنقَذَكُم مِّنْهَا ۗ كَذَٰلِكَ يُبَيِّنُ ٱللَّهُ لَكُمْ ءَايَـٰتِهِۦ لَعَلَّكُمْ تَهْتَدُونَ.

(سورة آل عمران / ١٠٣)

And hold fast, all together, unto the bond with God, and do not draw apart from one another. And remember those blessings which God has bestowed upon you: how, when you were enemies, *He brought your hearts together so that through his blessing you became brethren*; and [how, when] you were on the brink of a fiery abyss and He saved you from it. In this way God makes clear His messages unto you, so that you might find guidance. (Surat Al-'Imran, 3:103)

The third form of the verb / آلَفَ /*'alafa* describes the act of befriending someone or providing companionship, whereas the eighth form of the verb, إئتَلَف /*'i'talafa*, refers to the act of creating a coalition. In Surat Al-Tawba, moreover, the use of the passive participle, المؤلفة قلوبهم /*wa-al mu'allafati qulūbuhum*, which denotes the reconciliation between new Muslims and friends of the Muslim community, is evoked as a category for classifying those who are eligible for the reception of alms, Zakat:

إِنَّمَا ٱلصَّدَقَـٰتُ لِلْفُقَرَآءِ وَٱلْمَسَـٰكِينِ وَٱلْعَـٰمِلِينَ عَلَيْهَا **وَٱلْمُؤَلَّفَةِ قُلُوبُهُمْ** وَفِى ٱلرِّقَابِ وَٱلْغَـٰرِمِينَ وَفِى سَبِيلِ ٱللَّهِ وَٱبْنِ ٱلسَّبِيلِ ۖ فَرِيضَةً مِّنَ ٱللَّهِ ۗ وَٱللَّهُ عَلِيمٌ حَكِيمٌ.

(سورة التوبة/٦٠)

The offerings given for the sake of God are [meant] only for the poor and the needy, and those who are in charge thereof, and *those whose hearts are to be won over*, and for the freeing of human beings from bondage, and [for] those who are over burdened with debts, and [for every struggle] in God's cause, and [for] the wayfarer: [this is] an ordinance from God—and God is all-knowing, wise. (Surat Al-Tawba, 9:60)[16]

Thus, the principle of solidarity in *'ulfa* has animated the religious and philosophical texts of various Muslim jurisprudents, exegetes, and Sufis from the seventh through the eleventh centuries.[17] In their commentary and interpretations of the verses that evoke *'ulfa* in the Quran, scholars such as Abu al-Faraj al-Isfahani (897–967) and Mahmoud ibn Omar al-Zamashkhari (1074–1143), for example, drew connections between affinity, justice, and brotherhood. For al-Isfahani, the significance of affinity, as a virtue of love, exceeds that of justice and equity. When love is absent, he concludes, equity becomes necessary. In the exegesis of al-Zamashkhari, *'ulfa* appears as a synonym for the strong bond of love and brotherhood that developed among the Arabs who embraced Islam. He refers to the nascent collective solidarity that developed among Muslim converts. The Aws and the Khazarj, for instance, were two prominent Arab tribes whose relationship before Islam was characterized by conflicts and mutual enmity. Al-Zamashkhari describes the solidarity that resulted from their conversion to Islam as a special favor that God bestowed on the new Muslims.[18] In the commentary on his translation of the Quran, Yusuf Ali refers to the union of the hearts produced among the jarring warlike ties between the tribes as "the greatest miracle and most wonderful working of Allah's grace."[19]

In the work of the great Sufi Abu Hamed al-Ghazali (1058–1111), affinity is an essential characteristic of good Muslim conduct and ethics. In fact, *'ulfa* features prominently in his notable book *Iḥyā' 'Ulūm al-Dīn* (*The Revival of the*

Religious Knowledge), in which he dedicates an entire chapter to the theme of affinity within the context of norms of daily life. In "On the Duties of Brotherhood," affinity is listed among a set of practices of relief from discomfort and inconveniences that Muslims should perform to fulfill their *brotherly duties.*[20] "It has been said that if you drop your *kulfa* (formality) your *'ulfa* (friendship) will last, and that if your burden is light you will have lasting affection."[21] Al-Ghazali here highlights the contradiction between formality and friendship by juxtaposing the phonetic similarity of *kulfa* and *'ulfa.*

In modern Arabic literature and poetics, *'ulfa* is evoked in nonreligious terms. It centers the heart and underlines the ethos of love. To give a classical example, consider the seminal text of 'Ali ibn Ahmad ibn Hazm, *Ṭawq al-Ḥamāma fī al-'Ulfa wa-l-'Allāf (The Ring of the Dove: A Treatise on the Art and Practice of Arab Love)* (published posthumously in 1022). This book is a foundational text in the theory of profane love, a genre of its own in modern Arabic literature that includes poems, essays, and books that center upon profane earthly love and the emotional, spiritual, social, and physiological aspects of being in love. The intertwining of ألفة /*'ulfa* and its derivative الآلاف /*al-ālāf* in the title recurs throughout the book. It also underwrites Ibn Hazm's theorization of affinity in terms of the alchemy of souls, a supernatural reunion between kindred spirits:

> For my part I consider Love as a conjunction between scattered parts of souls that have become divided in this physical universe, a union effected within the substance of their original sublime element. I do not share the view advanced by Muhammad ibn Dawud—God have mercy on his soul!—who followed certain philosophers in declaring that spirits are segmented spheres; rather do I suppose an affinity of their vital forces in the supernal world which is their everlasting home, and a close approximation in the manner of their constitution. We know the secret of commingling and separation in created things to be simply a process of union and disassociation; every form always cries out for its corresponding form, like is ever at rest with like. Congeniality has a perceptible effect and a visible influence; repulsion of opposites, *accord between similars, attractions of like for like*—these are facts taking place all round us.[22]

For Ibn Hazm, harmony between people who are similar and mutual attraction across similitude are core conditions for love. Here, affinity, which stands for an "accord between similars," is conceptualized as a primordial need for reunion with a kindred spirit, or the "attractions of like for like," as he puts it. According to Ibn Hazm's philosophy of love, affinity is about forming an affectionate union with a similar Other. This connection between the primal desire to seek linkages and love is reinforced again in the book in the metaphor of "affinity of heart:"

> Thou the primeval Spirit art,
> As I undoubtingly believe,
> Which an affinity of heart
> Made our souls worthy to receive.[23]

The affective connotation of *'ulfa* is elucidated further in two canonical texts of Butrus al-Bustani (1819–1883) and Faris al-Shidyaq (1804–1887). In the writings of these two literary figures—who were influential in modernizing Arabic letters during the Arab *Nahda,* which literally means the "awakening," and refers to the project of Arab cultural and political modernity from the early nineteenth to the early twentieth century—*'ulfa* designates concord and friendship. What stands out about the conceptualization of *'ulfa* here is the association of the term with humanism. Indeed, in a historical period characterized by sectarian conflict, political factionalism, and the formation of Arab nationalism against the competing forces of a declining Ottoman Empire, an intensifying European colonialism in the Levant and the Maghreb, and a rising expansive Zionist settler colonialism in Palestine, *'ulfa* emerged as a pivotal ethos of union and harmony.

Amidst the unprecedented violence that marked the mid-nineteenth century in Greater Syria, a period that many historians now consider as the first Lebanese Civil War, al-Bustani published a series of pamphlets (1860–61) under the title *Nafīr Sūriyā* (*The Clarion of Syria*). Addressing his fellow countrymen in the hybrid form of a sermon and an invitation to a dialogue, he called for *'ulfa.* The term is repeated several times throughout the texts. It is conjured up as concord and harmony, which he puts forward as the basis for a much-needed universal brotherly love and national unity to counter the religious fanaticism and sectarian violence that engulfed the region:

> For concord, unlike discord, is a natural instinct of mankind that denotes companionship—as opposed to estrangement—and not forgetfulness, as some claim. Concord was indispensable for the rise of mankind and the promotion of the interests and well-being of human existence. This is why our hopes for a return to concord are high, in the long run at least.[24]

In *Kitāb al-Sāq 'alā Sāq fīmā huwa al-Fāryāq* (*Leg over Leg, or The Turtle in the Tree Concerning the Fariyaq*; 1855) al-Shidyaq draws upon the humanism of *'ulfa.* Obsessed with Arabic, he sets out in this literary masterpiece to innovate a modernist language that speaks to the cultural transformation of the *Nahda*. Through extensive reflections on social and political issues expressed in an encyclopedic style and a thick glossary of modern Arabic vocabulary, al-Shidyaq seeks to break taboos and to imagine Arab universalism. He writes:

> He said, therefore, to the Bag-man, "Sir, I heeded everything with which you've filled my ears and believe the truth to lie with you alone. I am your partisan, your follower, and the co-carrier of your bag. Just protect me from these undercapitalized parasites. They think that destroying a soul out of zeal for religion will earn them a place close to Him. They hold tight to such exterior meanings of the words of the gospel as they believe are in keeping with their aims and will increase their standing and authority. They say for instance, that Christ's words 'I came not to send peace, but a sword' license them to apply the said instrument to people's necks to make them return to the true path. They have cast behind them the essence, substance, and consequences of religion, which are *friendship among all men*, affection, assistance, and a proper certitude as to the existence of God Almighty."[25]

In speaking about the essence of religion in terms of *'ulfa*, which in Humphrey T. David and Michael Cooperson's English translation is translated as a synonym for "friendship among all men," al-Shidyaq's strong political position against the religious discord that engulfed Greater Syria at the time becomes clear. This translation amply resonates with the spirit of al-Shidyaq's book, above all, his vision of freedom as a prerequisite condition for Arab modernity.

Modernist and postmodernist Arab writers proceeded to reiterate the sense and practice of intimacy encompassed in *'ulfa*. In his self-elegy, *Fī Ḥaḍrat al-Ghiyāb* (*In the Presence of Absence*, 2006), for example, the Palestinian poet Mahmoud Darwish (1941–2008) evokes *'ulfa*, in the sense of the familiar, as a redemption of the existential loneliness and estrangement of exile. In Darwish's poetics of exile, the survival of the exiled becomes conditioned on their ability to adjust to alienation by training themselves in accepting the familiar. He writes: "But the regimen of *familiarity* is what ultimately makes *life* possible."[26]

In aggregation, these different interpretations of *'ulfa* in Arabic underscore the social and political significance of creating communities based on solidarity among strangers. As an antithesis of estrangement and alienation, *'ulfa* has the power to dissolve the unfamiliar, and thus can catalyze the formation of intimate and communal unions. More importantly, *'ulfa* aligns with a universal notion of affection that engenders both friendship and kinship beyond bloodlines and faith.

Looking for 'Ulfa in Tsotsil

In comparison with the linear and textual path that I followed to deduce the philological roots and the cultural trajectory of affinity in Arabic, my decade-long attempts to identify an accurate translation for it in Tsotsil involved a series of journeys across unwritten resources and personal encounters with speakers, readers, writers, orators, teachers, and translators. These meanderings revealed two key contradictions. On the one hand, Tsotsil bears the distinctive features of a language "salvaged" from colonial erasure. Its current revitalization necessitates bringing together recuperated folktales and myths; unwritten records of historical and scientific accounts; truncated sacred texts, such as the *Pop Wuj (Popol Vuh)*, the Mayan book of creation, which was originally recorded in Maya Quiché and transcribed into Latin script in the sixteenth century; and the *Chilam Balam*, the collection of twelve books that preserved Mayan traditions in the 1700s in Yacatec Maya written in the Latin alphabet; as well as other forms of cultural memory preserved in living archives. These fragments encapsulate the historical deterritorialization of Tsotsil as a minoritized Mesoamerican language. On the other hand, as a living native mother tongue undergoing a vibrant process of textual revitalization and cultural awakening fueled by the formalization of writing Mayan languages in Latin alphabet in 1970s, Tsotsil is witnessing a reterritorialization. This expanding territorial and linguistic movement emerges from beneath the accumulated rubble of five centuries of epistemic violence, which has long perpetuated the devaluation of Tsotsil as merely another "dead" Mayan language. That is to say, Tsotsil is being reclaimed not as a symbolic relic of an ancient mute past, the silent language of uninhabited Mayan pyramids, but rather as a contemporary language that speaks to the present and opens portals toward the future. This living Tsotsil is asking us to reorient our understanding of the shifting power dynamics within the present-day linguistic tapestry of Mexico, which includes sixty-eight living Indigenous languages resisting marginalization vis-à-vis the colonial dominance of Spanish. Yásnaya Elena Aguilar Gil's manifesto "The Indigenous Languages Write Their Letters to the Three Kings" is a vivid example of this shift. In outlining the six demands of Indigenous languages in Mexico, Aguilar makes a poignant remark about the significance of de-Othering these languages and affirms their relevance to contemporary times: "We want to have the gift of ubiquity. We'd like to be everywhere—in hospitals, classrooms, town squares, on TV and on the radio, but above all, we always want to be in the mouths of children and of all the people who want to get to know us."[27]

If tracking the philology of *'ulfa* in Arabic revealed a salient and continuous textual presence of the word from the oral revelation of the Quran to postmodern

Arab cultural discourses, looking for a translation of *'ulfa* in Tsotsil was anything but linear. On the contrary, the process entailed making historical leaps across textual fragments and temporal gaps. The limited resources available for consultation featured an anthropological lexicon in English by Robert M. Laughlin and John Beard Haviland from the late 1980s—which is a translation of a surviving copy of an anonymous manuscript published originally in Spanish in the sixteenth century[28]—a multilingual Spanish-Mayan miniature dictionary published in 2005, which I found on the travel section shelf at a local bookstore in San Cristóbal / Jobel, an online version of a Tsotsil translation of the Bible completed in 2014, alongside a chain of personal encounters and virtual exchanges from 2018 through 2023, including WhatsApp messaging and voice notes with Tsotsil-speaking acquaintances and interlocutors in Chiapas, namely Ibrahim Chechev, the Tsotsil-speaking Imam of the Chamula Muslim community, and Maestro Jose Mendoza Lopez, my Tsotsil language teacher. The search also continued by correspondence via email and social media with Paul M. Worley, a US-based scholar of Latin American and Mesoamerican literatures and a prolific translator of contemporary Mayan poetry from Chiapas and Guatemala, who also facilitated a personal introduction to other Tsotsil speakers, including a coordinator of Mayan language classes who goes by the name Nico, and the poet, translator, and Tsotsil language promoter Xun Betan.[29]

Given the personal nature of these interactions and the informal medium through which they were sustained, both code-switching and auto-ethnography inevitably surfaced as integral practices. Whereas the former emerged as a natural outcome of the orality and fluidity of our discussion of possible translations, the latter highlighted the need to reflect on the dynamics of our encounter and my positionality in relation to my interlocutors. And so, my search led me down a less formal and less institutionalized path, one that reflected the medium of communication in our modern and globalized world beyond the borders of academia. Ultimately, it is because of these virtual encounters and exchanges that the translation of *'ulfa* in Tsotsil reflects not simply the search for a single linguistic equivalent, but the very process of navigating its meaning across different contexts. This journey of translation mirrors the essence of *'ulfa* itself—an evolving, relational experience—thus intertwining the meaning of the word with the translational quest it inspired.

When it comes to translating Indigenous languages, following a zigzag path to the construction of a glossary in a foreign language and engaging in a collective process of meaning-making are not exceptional. As Worley and Ellen Jones have described in what they term "*tequio literario*," literary translation from Indigenous languages is rarely done by one individual alone.[30] Rooted in an Indigenous understanding of communal labor, this notion refers to collective translation practices common in current translations of Mesoamerican Indigenous literatures, mainly into Spanish and English. One of the characteristics of *tequio literario* is the collaboration between the translator and the author, other translators, and community members in a network of mutual support that operates across multiple languages.[31] Indeed, in addition to proposing several potential translations of *'ulfa* based on my explanation of its different contextualized meanings in Arabic and its literal translation in Spanish as *afinidad*, some of my interlocutors suggested that I consider looking into the meaning of *'ulfa* in the sister Mayan language, *Bats'il k'op*, Tseltal. Whereas my Tsotsil teacher brought to my attention the distinction between the written Tsotsil in our textbook and the spoken variants across the different communities, Imam Chechev, who studied Arabic in Spain,[32] asked me to be mindful of the fact that the Chamula Muslim community adheres to the Ahmadiyya branch of Islam, and thus it relies on the Spanish translation of the Quran issued by the International Ahmadiyya in Islam press in the UK in 2003. Eager to assist in finding the best translation for *'ulfa* in Tsotsil, he welcomed an invitation to conduct a comparative reading of two Spanish translations of the Quran on a WhatsApp call. And while he was in San Cristóbal / Jobel looking into the verses in the Quran where *'ulfa* and its derivatives are mentioned, I was on the other end of the line in Williamstown in western Massachusetts reading the parallel verses from the Spanish translation of the Quran done by Abdel Ghani Melara Navio in 2005. It did not take long before both of us realized that our joint effort to deduce a possible translation was in fact a cross-cultural, cross-linguistic, and trans-hemispheric interpretation exercise. Unable to identify a single encompassing translation in Tsotsil, Imam Chechev concluded: "Give me a chance to find more approximate words. I will ask my father."[33]

The *tequio literario* with the Imam and the Maestro yielded different meanings of *'ulfa* in Tsotsil that subsequently led to developing an overarching encompassing definition, as I will elaborate in the following section. Reflecting on this process, I observed two pivotal trends pertinent to the idiosyncrasies of juxtaposing an Indigenous Mesoamerican language with a non-Euro-American language. First, although the default dependence on Spanish—including Mayan Chiapanecan Spanish—and to a lesser extent, English, as mediation languages to facilitate the translation between Arabic and Tsotsil did not dismantle colonial Anglo-European cultural hegemony, it became clear that Spanish and English remain, for the time being, instrumental for creating a South-South translation. To link Arabic and Tsotsil through the mediation of Spanish, nonetheless, is to risk contamination with the fossils of the imperial encounter between Spanish and Tsotsil. The violence of this encounter is manifest in the clash and grapple with dynamics that result from the highly asymmetrical relations of power between both languages. As in Mary Louise Pratt's theorization of the contact zone,[34] this violence is pervasive in other encounters between colonial European languages and Indigenous languages in the Americas. Precisely for this reason, forging a direct path between Arabic and Tsotsil strikes me as a viable alternative. Released from the historical colonial burden that Spanish carries, the relationship between Arabic and Tsotsil can follow a decolonial route. Put differently, the collaborative translation of *'ulfa* is a fertile ground to establish future mutual influence between Arabic and Tsotsil that is free from "the infiltration and contagion of each side by the other"[35] that characterize Spanish and other European cultural translations of Indigenous customs in the Americas and that ultimately codify the Otherness of Indigenous Peoples. My vision of a decolonial relationship between Arabic and Tsotsil draws on Ngũgĩ wa Thiong'o's assertion that there are two ways by which different languages and cultures can relate to one another: the imperial way, resulting in hierarchies of unequal power relations; or the democratic way, based on a network of equal give and take.[36] Clearly, the second way is the path opening up for Arabic and Tsotsil.

Second, given the fact that to date there is no historical proof of a previous nonreligious linguistic encounter between Arabic and Tsotsil, the collaborative translation of *'ulfa* in Tsotsil in this study offers a starting point for developing a reciprocal contemporary literary and cultural connection between the two languages. That said, it is important to mention here another unfolding encounter. Over the past decade, an indirect relationship between Arabic and Tsotsil has developed through translations of Zapatista communiques and educational material that were widely circulated in Palestine and the leftist technosphere of social movements across the Arabic-speaking world. In fact, in Palestine some of these translations became available within the framework of the Zapatista solidarity with Palestine. In this regard, the pioneering work of Linda Quiquivix, a critical geographer and a long-term committed Zapatista educator from California who descends from Mayan origins in Guatemala, must be acknowledged. Quiquivix initiated translations of Zapatista materials into Arabic to support a course on the movement that she taught in Palestinian refugee camps in the Occupied West Bank in the early 2010s. In 2013, she chaperoned a Palestinian delegation to La Escuelita Zapatista (The Little School) in Chiapas. As a member of that delegation and a reader of the translated materials, I witnessed the vital role Quiquivix played as a participant in the *tequio literario* by being both an interpreter and a witness to the deepening ties between the Zapatistas and Palestinians. Her powerful reflections on this experience appear in her recent book *Palestine 1492: A Report Back* (2024), where she eloquently writes:

> I often mention Chiapas whenever I mention Palestine and I often mention Palestine whenever I mention Chiapas. I encountered the two resistances at around the same time when I was first learning about the global struggles from below and against capital; when I was first learning to listen to the pains and the dignity of the below. There are many similarities between the two; there are many differences. Pains and dignity are constants in both. *I prefer to die on my feet than to live on my knees*, the Zapatistas are famous for saying. *Like trees, we die standing*, the Palestinians are famous for saying. Dying in order to live is a famous saying for both Palestinians and the Zapatistas.
>
> Palestinian *compas* say they don't get to hear too much about the Zapatistas and have asked me to say more about them in this report back. I offer my interoperations of the Zapatistas here in the hope readers will listen directly to them rather than to me. The Zapatistas speak for themselves. Parts of my offering might be more helpfully understood as witness testimony from someone raised by the world of Columbus and Them who can testify that the world teaches Palestinians have never existed and that Maya no longer exist.[37]

As for the production and promotion of the translated Zapatista texts in Arabic, it is worth mentioning the formative work of Shadi Rohana, a Mexico City–based Palestinian translator and scholar, and Nusair Abdullah, a Saudi writer and political activist. Whereas Rohana has played a major role in translating from Spanish to Arabic a set of Zapatista declarations and manifestos, some of which were originally written in Tsotsil and then translated to Spanish, Abdullah translated from English several Zapatista statements. In 2021, he published on the website *al-Hamesh* (*The Margin*) Rohana's translations from Spanish and his own translation from English in a special dossier in honor of the twentieth anniversary of the Zapatista uprising.[38]

The religious encounter between Arabic and Tsotsil also took place in a Zapatista-related context. It dates to 1995 when several Tsotsil-speaking families, namely Chamulas, converted to Islam. The conversion began when a group of proselytizing Spanish Muslim converts who belong to the Murabitun Movement arrived in Chiapas to spread the message of Islam among Zapatista-affiliated Mayan communities. Believing that the Zapatista agenda shared important similarities with their own politico-religious agenda, namely, the liberation from market and state oppression, the group approached first the leadership of the Zapatistas in the jungle, including Subcomandante Marcos, who turned down the solicitation. Despite this initial failure, the group, determined to continue its proselytizing mission—*daʿwa* ("invitation" in Arabic)—settled at the rural-urban margins of San Cristóbal / Jobel and lived next to landless Mayan peasants who settled earlier in the area after being expelled from their original communities due to political and religious conflicts that began in the 1970s.[39] Since this encounter, the size of the Muslim community in Chiapas has increased, and currently there are several Muslim communities divided across ethnic and religious branches from Sunnis to Shiites, Sufis, and Ahmadiyyas. Nevertheless, the Tsotsil-speaking Mayans from Chamula who were the first to convert remain the most cohesive and visible. In addition to building a new mosque, they have forged their own path toward defining themselves as Ahmadiyya Muslims. This process began when members of the Spanish group demanded that the recently converted Mayas relinquish their Indigenous cultural practices, including eating tortillas and wearing traditional outfits, to assimilate as Muslims. Perceiving these demands as a poignant reminder of the colonialist attitudes, spiritual superiority, and cultural racism of the Spanish Christian missionaries from the Conquista, the Tsotsil-speaking Mayans from Chamula refused to conform and thus separated from the growing Muslim community led by the Spaniards.[40] This split was formalized after the return of Chechev from Granada, Spain, where he had gone to study Islam and Arabic together with his younger brother and sister. Curiously, this split is architecturally evident in the current structure and location of the community's main gathering place, which is a humble two-room mosque located in a single-floor cement family-style building standing across the street from the grand Andalusian-style mosque established by the Spaniards in 2014. In terms of social ties, though, the extent of this split is not clear, as Chechev is married to the daughter of one of the Spaniards' missionaries.

Having visited regularly with the Tsotsil-speaking Mayans from Chamula over the past decade[41] and having witnessed firsthand the cultural and religious transformation of the community, I have observed that, apart from the advanced proficiency of Chechev, the vast majority in the community has a basic knowledge of Arabic. Despite taking Arab names in addition to their Spanish and Tsotsil names, members of the Ahmadiyya Muslim community's use of Arabic is limited to memorized Quranic verses and a set of phrases pertinent to prayers and religious rituals. It is for this reason that Chechev became the chief collaborator in the translation of *ʾulfa* into Tsotsil. Nonetheless, our joint effort to find an equivalent of *ʾulfa* to capture my conceptualization of the South-South connection between Chiapas and Palestine was made possible because of *ʾulfa* in the first place.

Indeed, for Chechev I was a *familiar* translator. Admittedly, I was privileged by my position as a native speaker of Arabic and a Palestinian Muslim woman who was welcomed into the Tsotsil-speaking Chamula Muslim community since the first personal encounter I had with his mother, Juana Gómez Hernandéz, who is widely recognized among Muslims in Chiapas as the matriarch of the Chamula Muslim community and the first Tsotsil-Mayan woman to perform Hajj. Since our encounter in 2010, I have regularly visited with Gómez Hernandéz, or *Hajja* Nora, her adopted Arabic name, and accepted invitations to her house to attend family celebrations of Muslim holidays that coincided with my research trips in Chiapas. The personal relationship that developed between us over the past decade positioned me as a *familiar* person. It also solidified the trust that the community had in me as a translator of the meaning of Arab names, religious codes in Arabic, and Islamic cultural references. Considered *familiar,* I was often called *la hermana de Palestina* (the sister from Palestine). During my visits, I was also allowed to bring with me guests, including an *indigène* decolonial thinker from Belgium, members from my mestizo host family, Mexican American friends who live between the US and Chiapas, Maestro Mendoza Lopez, and his family too. The generosity of this welcoming hospitality fostered an informal atmosphere of a multilingual cultural exchange that took place around a big table on the patio of the mosque where everyone gathered to share home-cooked festive meals and freshly baked tortillas. Topics discussed during these gatherings covered a range of political issues and personal anecdotes, from Marxism and liberation theology to US-Mexico relations; the difference between religious and cultural practices among Catholics, Pentecostals, and Muslims; in addition to familial stories about ancestors, grandchildren, and relatives from places near and far. It is in the spirit of this communal context that Chechev and I engaged in a cross-cultural translation of *'ulfa* beyond its religious connotations. Certainly, my personal background allowed me a critical intimacy that fostered the informality of this interaction with the community. Chechev's keen interest in bridging the linguistic and cultural distance between Arabic and Tsotsil enhanced this interaction as well. Being acutely aware of the gap between Arabic and Tsotsil as an imam who delivers the weekly Friday sermon in Spanish and Tsotsil, while at the same time striving to convey the different interpretative meanings of the Quranic Arabic scripture, he approached the translation with an equal degree of devotion and caution. Our consistent communication and back-and-forth exchanges over Messenger and WhatsApp—mediums that inadvertently bridged the distance between Arabic and Tsotsil in inventive ways—unveiled how the translation of *'ulfa itself* generated *'ulfa.* In sum, this embodied experience of *'ulfa* played a key role in providing a tangible definition and a lived meaning of affinity.

If my position as a *familiar* translator facilitated the collaborative translation of *'ulfa* in Tsotsil with Chechev, it was the *familiarity* of my questions about translating Tsotsil that crystallized the *'ulfa* in the *tequio literario* that Mendoza and I engaged in. Throughout my Tsotsil classes and the exchange with Mendoza, my inquiries about the linguistic rationale for borrowing grammatical structures of written Tsotsil from the lexical attributes of Spanish, the correct way to use the Mayan concept of *ch'ul* (the sacred) in another language, and the gap between the different approaches in spelling practices of written Tsotsil vis-à-vis the regional variants of spoken Tsotsil were instantly recognizable. Indeed, more than once, Mendoza shared his similar preoccupation with these questions as a student of literary Tsotsil and an instructor of Tsotsil who works closely with bilingual native speakers and foreign students like me. Yet, when it came to translating Tsotsil into Arabic, and particularly to a Palestine-related context, addressing these questions set in motion a series of doubts and reflections about the translatability of words and worlds that required a deeper thinking about the linguistic encounter between Arabic and Tsotsil and the configuration of the Palestinian-Mayan conversation.

For example, we grappled with the basic question of how to write Palestine in Tsotsil. Since the word does not exist in Tsotsil morphology, it falls under the category of neologism. Given this, Mendoza suggested writing it in an italicized form similar to the treatment of words such as *Honduras, football, department,* and *gas*.[42] Likewise, in postulating the connection between the meaning of the single word *ṣumūd* and the phrase *Ts'ik vokol ja' kuxlej* (To exist is to resist), we had to break down the latter to dissect how the affirmative article *ja'*, which solidifies the interlink between enduring suffering and life, allegorizes the motto of "To exist is to resist." As for using *ch'ul* to refer to Palestine as the Holy Land, Mendoza proposed the formula *Palestina ja' jun ch'ul osil balumil* (Palestine is a Sacred Land), thus centering the significance of land by adding the word *balumil* (land) and expanding further the two-word definition of *ch'ul osil* (Holy Land) in Laughlin and Haviland's dictionary.[43]

In a similar vein, finding the Tsotsil equivalent for the Spanish phrase *el pueblo palestino* (the Palestinian people)—a popular idiom canonized in the manifestations of solidarity with Palestine in Spanish-speaking Latin America and in Chiapas, where it is conjured up by both the Zapatista and the Tsotsil-speaking Muslim community[44]—foregrounded the three-way tension, or pull, of a kind, in the juxtaposition of Arabic, Tsotsil, and Spanish. It further highlighted the complex dynamics of translating across a chain of languages and different epistemologies.

To coin a Tsotsil expression for *el pueblo palestino*, Mendoza and I had to reach a consensus on what the terms *el pueblo* and *Palestino* mean in the first place. My cotranslator posed these simple, yet critical, questions: "When you say *pueblo*, do you refer to a territory or a people?" and "When you say *Palestino*, do you refer to a state or a country?"[45] The answer to these questions and the conclusion based on them, nonetheless, were far from straightforward. Unconvinced by the direct answer to the former question regarding "people," Mendoza proposed several possible translations that revealed not only the Tsotsil-Mayan logic of conceptualizing the relationship between people and land, but also a strange familiarity between Tsotsil and Arabic. In Tsotsil, *yosilal*, which corresponds with the Spanish *pueblo*, denotes both territory and township. It is analogous to the words *al-balad* and *al-balda* in Arabic, which designate both country and small town. In Palestinian vernacular Arabic, the plural form of both, *liblad*, is a popular endearing nickname for the country of Palestine. Inspired by this discovery of the resemblance between *yosilal* and *liblad*, Mendoza and I devoted a special time in class for a fun activity that involved identifying words that could potentially have similar patterns of affinity. In fact, we were both equally intrigued (and amused!) to encounter a hidden linguistic *'ulfa* between Arabic and Tsotsil while trying to translate the word *'ulfa* from Arabic to Tsotsil. As for the latter question, I resorted to a method of elimination, which unintentionally laid bare the inherent paradox of translating the political reality of Palestine. After all, Palestine is *not* a state, but a country, though its territory is geographically shrinking and politically fragmented because of the ongoing expansionist Zionist settler colonialism. Given the fact that in Tsotsil, *muk'ta yosilal* signifies both state and country, opting for *yosilal* did not make sense. A better alternative, Mendoza suggested, would be: *Bats'i vinik antsetik jnaklejetik Palestinoetik* (The true men and women inhabitants of Palestine). While the word *jnaklejetik*, which originates from the root *nak*, meaning "to reside," solidifies indigeneity by establishing a connection between inhabiting the land and being the true people of the land, it excludes the stateless Palestinian refugees and exiles who inhabited the land before and remain dispersed in the *shatāt* (diaspora) since 1948 while being denied the right of return by the settler colonial Israeli state.

It is against this double context of finding *'ulfa* in Tsotsil that we must understand the unknown *'ulfa* between Arabic and Tsotsil. Intriguingly, as the *tequio literario* illustrated, the affective resonance of *'ulfa* enhanced the task of *familiarizing* Arabic and Tsotsil with each other, thus underscoring Walter Benjamin's assertion that "translation ultimately has as its purpose the expression of the most intimate relationships among languages. Translation cannot possibly reveal or produce this hidden relationship; however, translation can represent this relationship insofar as it realizes it seminally or intensively."[46] This familiarity can't be established without adhering to an ethics of translation, as Samah Selim, translating Moroccan philosopher Hassan Wahbi's French words, argues. Wahbi reminds us that

> translation reveals a virtual universality, a silent reciprocity, which is to say it makes us understand that the elements that are present in the other—through languages and symbolic or artistic codes—are also present in ourselves and vice versa; they are not identical but posit a presumed equivalence, a promise of filiation that calls forth shared meanings.[47]

Here, we can observe again that Arabic and Tsotsil are not identical but "posit a presumed equivalence, a promise of filiation that calls forth shared meaning" that transcends their difference without "falling into the illusory trap of 'cultural dialogue,'" as Selim observes.[48] In this respect, the innovative, collaborative, multi-border-crossing model of finding 'ulfa in Tsotsil offers us an alternative framework for translatability; one that escapes this trap entirely. By emphasizing borderlands rather than cultural dialogue in its liberal, depoliticized sense, this model not only traverses linguistic boundaries but actively seeks to remake them. This act of world-making and border crossing involves a subversive dimension that challenges and transgresses the colonial cartographies that have historically separated Arabic from Tsotsil.

Deriving from a decolonial notion of border crossing, the Arabic–Tsotsil translational encounter moves beyond the current material realities of borders in Palestine and Chiapas, offering us a vision of translatability rooted not in closure, but rather in the fertile relational space of a South-South borderland. This space, shaped by the juxtaposition of the Arabic and Tsotsil side by side, is profoundly generative and open. The virtual absence of Hebrew and Spanish from this space releases Arabic and Tsotsil from their entanglements with these colonial languages, ultimately creating possibilities for linguistic liberation and future translations between the two languages as well as between Arabic and other Indigenous languages too.[49]

Additionally, the collaborative translation of 'ulfa within the South-South borderland, constructed by the encounter between Arabic and Tsotsil, performs an anticolonial act of traversing territorial and militarized borders, thus reclaiming the porousness of borders. The liberatory subversive dimension of this act is more acutely visible in the context of Arabic in Palestine, where Arabic is subjected to the regulatory mechanisms of surveillance and control, or what Emily Apter identifies as the "checkpointization" of translation.[50] Drawing on the Palestinian experience, Apter uses the term "checkpoint" as a metaphor for biopolitical patrols, translational identity checks, and the enforcement of borders as mechanisms of discipline. Her reservations about the fluidity of borders stems from this context, where Palestinian movement, whether it is physical, artistic, or linguistic, becomes a matter of survival under constant scrutiny.

It is important to recognize, however, that the widespread presence of checkpoints in Palestine represents real structures of surveillance and territorial colonialism. The Arabic-Tsotsil encounter constructs a South-South *borderland* that is essentiality a *counter-border* space. In contrast to Apter's contention that translation has been compromised by its association with the metaphor of fluid borders and her critique of the general language of border crossing, which she argues obscures the real violence of state surveillance at the border, such as checkpoints and racial profiling (both of which exist in Palestine, and to a lesser extent, in Mexico, along its northern and southern borders), the solidarity-informed translation of Arabic and Tsotsil in this borderland demonstrates how both languages infiltrate this violence by reclaiming border crossing as a symbolic and material act of resistance. Although the Arabic and Tsotsil model of translation, performed mainly by those who are held at the border, does not erase the reality of militarized borders, or the racialization and policing of both languages at the checkpoint as Indigenous languages, it defies the colonial logic of confinement. Whether it is the checkpoint in Palestine that violently prevents Arabic from moving beyond the control of Hebrew, or the colonial boundaries that have historically confined the translation of Indigenous languages to the Euro-American circuits, the borderland formed by Arabic and Tsotsil disrupts and challenges these geopolitical structures. As a crack in the wall, this borderland allows infiltration, thus enabling a linguistic diffusion of Arabic and Tsotsil into new routes.

From the Epistemology of the Heart to a Relational Model of Life: The Prism of 'Ulfa in Tsotsil

In Robert Laughlin and John Beard Haviland's *Great Tzotzil Dictionary of Santo Domingo Zinacantán* (1988)—the first dictionary to canonize Tsotsil writing in Roman alphabets by documenting the variety of Tsotsil spoken in the late sixteenth century and described as "one of the greatest dictionaries ever published on an American Indian language"[51]—the words *friend, kin, companion*, and all things familiar are classified under the entry *chi'il*. The recent translation of the Bible into Tsotsil, which came out in 2014 after twenty-five years of collaboration between Mayan communities and Evangelical missionaries, evokes *chi'il* as a synonym for "helper" (Genesis 2:18) and "brother" (Genesis 33:9).[52]

Although Chechev and Mendoza agree with this translation, each considers other words that uphold the principal affective attributes of *'ulfa:* companionship, unity, and similarity. For Chechev, to extrapolate *'ulfa* in Tsotsil while integrating this interpretive framework relies on prioritizing its morphological and semantic deployment in the Quran over the impulse to find a grammatical analog for it in Mayan languages. With this in mind, he proposes: *Jchi'iltik* (companions, or we are the same), *jpuntasik kontontik* (to unite our hearts), and the uncommon version *jmojotik* (all united). Mendoza finds that *jmojotik* is rarely used. What is most used, however, is *tsoboltik*, which also means "we are similar."

Observant of the divergence between alphabetical and spoken variants across different Tsotsil-speaking communities, Mendoza, who originates from Venustiano Carranza, on the opposite side of the mountains from Chamula, where Chechev's family has its roots, suggests *x'ko'olajik* for *'ulfa*, a derivative of the word, *ko'ol*, which means "similar" or "equal to."

Reflecting on these various possible translations, Xun Betan, who is also from Venustiano Carranza, concludes that the closest word in Tsotsil for *'ulfa* is *ko'olajel*. Like Mendoza, Betan concurs that the difference between *jmojotik* and *jchi'il* (and its plural *jchi'iltik*) speaks more to the vernacular variations in Tsotsil than to a discrepancy in meaning. That being said, Betan asserts that the word *jchi'iltik* refers solely to friendship among people who are similar or who are from the same community. Interestingly, this connotation resonates with the affiliative sense of *'ulfa* in the Quranic verse "*wa-al mu'alafati qulūbuhum*" (9:60),[53] which underscores the amicable solidarity bond among old and new Muslims. In the context of Chiapas, however, apart from affirming kinship, this definition draws a clear line between the colonized and the colonizer. Betan asserts: "We use *jchi'iltik* to say that we are from the same community or that we are the same Mesoamerican people . . . but when we speak, for example, about *kaxlanes* or *mestizos/as*, we don't use *jchi'iltik*."[54] This explicit political distinction between who belongs to the community and who is considered a threat is fortified by the use of the Tsotsil and Tseltal word *kaxlan* (plural *kaxlanes*), which literally means "hen" and is often used to make fun of mestizos/as. Above all, it is a pejorative idiom for foreigners, namely *ladinos/as* (non-Indigenous), mestizos/as, and Europeans.

The advantage of using the phrase *ko'olajel* (favored by Betan), which derives also from *ko'ol*, provokes valuable thinking about familiarity and solidarity through the implication of similarity, equality, and sameness. Another reason why I opt for this translation is syntax driven. If *chi'il* is to be used, it would be necessary to insert an agent to create a more specific meaning. According to Betan, to convey the idea of a shared struggle along the lines of, for instance, "we suffer from the same situation," one would say "*jchi'il jbatik ta vokolil*," which literally means, "we are companions in suffering."[55] Although this construction embodies the spirit of affinity between Chiapas and Palestine, it is not a single word, but a composition.

Given the above, if we were to use *ko'olajel* as an equivalent of *'ulfa*, we would arrive at a semantically correct translation, because both words underscore the possibility for drawing a connection between similar things. To adopt this translation, thus, is useful for framing the affinity between Chiapas and Palestine as similar geographies of struggle. Epistemologically speaking, however, the *'ulfa–ko'olajel* equation is imbricated with a thorny asymmetry. To illustrate the connection between Mayan and Palestinian narratives, I approach *'ulfa* as a concept of relationality, and not simply as a word that exists in both Arabic and Tsotsil. In this respect, *ko'olajel* in Tsotsil does not possess the same expressive function that *'ulfa* has in Arabic. This distinction brings forth two crucial issues related to the philosophical and conceptual conditions for comparison. First, the *'ulfa–ko'olajel* asymmetry echoes Gilles Deleuze and Félix Guattari's assertion that concepts are neither discursive nor universal, because "every concept has a history and bits or components that come from other concepts, which corresponded to other problems and presupposed other planes."[56] Second, this asymmetry highlights a certain incommensurability, emphasizing both the importance of relationality as a decolonial approach in comparative literature and the need to develop relational frameworks for intercultural inquiry in contexts without preestablished rules of comparison—such as trans-Indigenous and transnational comparisons. In this case, we are presented with a conceptual challenge that calls for the intervention of a reflexive comparatist as articulated in Ming Xie's notion of critical comparativity.[57] Eschewing a conventional model of comparison, which focuses on identifying similarities and differences, this approach is more concerned with how meaning is constituted, and thus puts an emphasis on the epistemological conditions of comparison. Seen in this light, attending to the divergent meanings and usage of *'ulfa* and *ko'olajel*—and the distinct ways relationality is conceived in Arabic and Tsotsil—not only reveals the limits of direct equivalence, but also exemplifies why concepts must be situated within their respective epistemic and cultural contexts. In doing so, we do not overlook incommensurability. On the contrary, we directly confront it by embracing a decolonial and critically comparative methodology that rejects flattening differences and instead foregrounds the complexity of trans-Indigenous frameworks and relational approaches in comparative literature.

Although *ko'olajel* is not deployed as a conceptual understanding of relationality, relationality is a pivotal concept in Tsotsil: It constitutes a Mayan philosophy of life. Anchored in a Mayan cosmology that centers the heart and its way of knowing and relating, this philosophy posits solidarity, pluriversality, communalism, and interculturalism as the guiding principles of a dignified and autonomous existence. It is not *ko'olajel* (similar) that animates this philosophy, but rather the words *kuxlej* (sustenance) and *kuxlejal* (life, or "life-existence"). These two words remain intertwined in their meaning and usage, in both Tsotsil and Tseltal, to demonstrate the emotive attributes of *'ulfa* and its call for solidarity and unity. Moreover, they epitomize a political vision of *ṣumūd*, thus providing another reason for the affinity between Chiapas and Palestine.

In contemporary Mayan philosophy and poetics, *kuxlej* and *kuxlejal* are conjured up as significant concepts that speak to the theories and practices of a Mayan cosmovision. In the post-Zapatista rebellion years, Mayan philosophers, writers, and activists have drawn extensively on these concepts to assert *ṣumūd* and Indigenous autonomy. The vision statement of the New Chiapanecan School,[58] published in 2017, for example, foregrounds the construction of a sustainable humanity following the communal design of *Buenvivir*, which literally translates as Well-Being or Good Living. Key to this process is a return to Mayan cosmogonies, gnoseologies, territories, and social models that promote dignity, solidarity, intercultural dialogue, and biocultural diversity that recognize the intimate relationship between the human and the nonhuman. Whereas these principles are instrumental for creating an autonomous Indigenous world vision, or more precisely a Mayan utopia, they are essentially decolonial, because they assume a disciplinary and rationalist epistemic framework that exists outside European colonial modernity. At the same time, they are ontologically rooted in the wisdom of the heart, and embody a collective social Well-Being / Good Living by enacting the relational model of *ser-estar-pertencer* / to be–to exist–to belong.[59] Put in the words of one of the cofounders of this vision, Felipe Reyes-Escutia, utopia is "interculturality, to exist and progress in a loving dialogue between cultures, histories, and territories as an inalienable principle."[60]

It is interesting to point out here that by drawing on the concept of *Buenvivir*, Mayan philosophers in Chiapas situate their political vision within a broader worldview of Indigenous Peoples in Abya Yala. Arising from the *People's Conference on Climate Change and the Rights of Mother Earth* in Bolivia in 2010, the concept of *Buenvivir* emphasizes the plurinationalism of Indigenous Peoples and the abundance of anticapitalist community practices that take place at the local and regional level across Abya Yala. In her analysis of the praxis of *Buenvivir* in Chiapas, María Eugenia Santana Echeagaray observes that since the last quarter of the twentieth century Mayan communities of the Jungle of the Las Margaritas and Tsotsil-speaking Mayan women weavers from Zinacantán rejected the Mexican government's development project. Instead, they promoted the core elements of *Buenvivir*, which includes land, housing, freedom, autonomy, and Indigenous identities, to privilege an Indigenous relationship to Mother Earth over profit. When it came to the Indigenous perception of land, for example, the preservation of harmony with land superseded taking advantage of the government's push to commercialize access to food and natural resources. This is also true regarding the notion of freedom. For Mayan farmers, for instance, good living was associated with the refusal to be forced to enter the labor market of a dependency economy by working as farm laborers in government programs that subjugate them. What mattered for these Mayan farmers, Santana Echeagaray remarks, was living in open spaces where they could appreciate their broad horizons and have the freedom to work on their own terms.[61]

Elaborating on the primacy of the heart in this philosophy and its praxis of a Mayan cosmovision based on the affiliative belonging of and between the individual, the communal, and the natural, the Tsotsil-speaking philosopher and poet Manuel Bolom Pale uses the term *k'anel*, a key concept of relationality in Pan-Mayan thought. As an ethical category, this term, which means "to want," links the knowledge from the heart as a prime issue for thought. When thinking from the heart, Bolom Pale states, "the subject establishes social relations with the entire community, thus establishing a balance within it, whereby all individuals presuppose their belonging first and foremost to the community."[62] This understanding of *k'anel* extends also to the realm of writing, reading, and reception. As Paul M. Worley and Rita M. Palacios suggest, *k'anel* highlights the social dimension of the collective production of *ts'íib*, a Tsotsil word denoting alternative literacy based more on a tradition of performance and reperformance of text than in text itself.[63] Because *k'anel* exists on three distinct interrelated planes, the intrapersonal (within a single person); the interpersonal (between individuals); and the extrapersonal (across the community at large), it plays a pivotal role, they contend, in the (re) production of knowledge. Additionally, *k'anel* underscores the significant connection between artists, writers, publics, and even the natural world as active coproducers of micro- and macrohistories.[64]

As a bottom-up model of communal learning and relating to the land, *lekil kuxlejal*, Bolom Pale argues, undermines the dehumanization and the systems of competition put in place by neoliberal development projects that continue to dispossess Indigenous lands, Peoples, and resources:

> In an extractivist vision, respect for the mountains, the water, the trees, the wind, the animals, and the spirits does not add to their value, but from the affective (feeling/sense) point of view of the Tsotsiles, the Tseltales, or the native people it means everything. . . . The philosophies of *lekil kuxlejal* survive in the communities as other forms of relationship and are offered as collaborative learnings that maintain the communal autonomy of the peoples with the land. In this way, the Tsotsiles and Tseltales maintain that whoever defends the ancestral seeds defends the self-determination of the people. This [lesson] is learned in the community from the early days of childhood.[65]

A similar concern with the knowledge of the heart as a pillar of a relational philosophy of a good, dignified life permeates Tseltal social practices and philosophy of history. In some Tseltal-speaking communities, for instance, collective calls to return to the heart were mobilized as a social code to assert communal unity in the face of the Mexican state colonial violence. Lola Cubells, a non-Mayan feminist activist and Indigenous rights defender who worked closely with Tseltal-speaking communities, points out that after the counterinsurgency war declared by the Mexican government against the Zapatistas in 1996—a period that came to be known as the years of low-intensity war—leaders in Mayan communities turned to the ethical paradigm of *kuxlej* and *kuxlejal* to restore harmony and justice within their communities that were facing a growing wave of interethnic conflict. Indigenous peasants across Mayan communities revived the tradition of *cargo comunitario* (community duty)—a voluntary unremunerated rotating service—by assuming the role of *jMeltsa'anwanej*, the person who fixes conflicts or solves problems.[66] Despite not being trained as professional judges or legal mediators, these Indigenous peasants evoked the inherent significance of rights to life and social organization. In Tseltal communities, for example, they evoked terms like *jun pajal o'tanil* (a single heart) and *suhtesel o'tanil* (return to the heart) to create reconciliation and restore harmony within Indigenous territories. The term *slamalil k'inal* (tranquility in the environment) was also deployed to emphasize the reciprocal connection between restoring peace in the community and harmony in nature.

The notion of return to the heart is also featured in the Tseltal understanding of memory as embodied history. In this regard, Tseltal-speaking philosopher Xuno López Intzin asserts the link between the concepts of *sujtesel o'tan* (to go back to the heart or walk back to the path) and *stalel jkuxlejaltik* (the becoming of our life, the life that has been) and how they jointly define a Tseltal-Maya perception of the past, or more precisely, memory:

> *Stalel jkuxlejaltik* should be understood as the becoming of history and the becoming of our life as a people. You have to look at what that becoming actually is, how the present feeds on the past. There's also the other term *Stalel kuxlejal*, which is like the way of being of our ancestors, it's both a mother and a father, so there is an ancestral mother-father figure from one generation to the next. This lived experience is kept in the heart of certain people who reproduce this path, this way of being and living. Some also call it tradition, this knowledge of the past and the present that is kept within the heart.[67]

All in all, *kuxlej* and *kuxlejal* outline a model of relationality that entails affective and affiliative dimensions akin to those embedded in *'ulfa*. Additionally, both concepts epitomize everyday-and-lived praxis of *ṣumūd*. The epistemological, philosophical, and political convergence between these different concepts crystallizes their belonging to an overlapping symbolic universe and practice. Herein lies the bedrock on which the Arabic-Tsotsil concept of affinity is based.

As mentioned earlier, the Mayan-Palestinian comparison is neither linear nor symmetrical. At this point, one must wonder about the application of the Arabic-Tsotsil concept of affinity to conduct a relational comparative reading in Mayan and Palestinian narratives. If there is no single definition of *'ulfa* in Tsotsil, which lens of the *ko'olajel, kuxlej,* and *kuxlejal* prism then should be used to understand the connection between Mayan and Palestinian narratives? My response to this question is the following: Considering that the comparative model I use is meant to illustrate an emphatic resistance to oppression and erasure, and a clear demarcation of Indigenous struggle, there is a definite reliance on the concept of *ṣumūd*, and the philosophical, spiritual, and affective underpinnings of indigeneity and land-based relationalities that shape it. Therefore, the more appropriate option is *'ulfa–kuxlej/kuxlejal*. On the one hand, it eschews the inclination to think of these two cases as similar, thereby erroneously flattened on an equal plane. On the other hand, while drawing on affinity and *'ulfa* as a comparative lens to illustrate the narratives of both Chiapas and Palestine, we should clearly remember that affinity does not create equality, but maintains the autonomies and complexities of each culture, history, and geography, while bringing closer seemingly disparate struggles. For ultimately, we should undoubtedly strive to portray the autonomy of two peoples whose lifelong goal is to assert it.

On Affinity, Relationality, and Affiliative Comparison

Recent scholarship in comparative literature, subaltern studies, and Indigenous studies has already established the potency of relationality as a decolonial form of inquiry that disavows center-periphery binaries and symmetrical grids constructed by the logic of European coloniality and perpetuated in its contemporary extension: US imperialism and its global militarized systems of colonization, settlement, racialization, and dispossession. Drawing on Édouard Glissant's Antillean archipelagic imaginary, which generated the poetics of relation—a theoretical analytical model that resides in spatial and temporal movements that spur shrinking geographical distances for the sake of an integrative reading of world history from the margins—theorists have put the spotlight on how thinking through relationality, instead of models of comparison that conceive of geographies of struggle (the racialized, the minoritized, the colonized, and so forth) as absolute, separate, or atomic, provides a deeper and more acute understanding of the interconnectedness of seemingly disconnected subalternized histories.

Shu-mei Shih, for instance, points out how relational comparison opens up a new area, perhaps even a new life, for comparative literature.[68] In reformulating relations as a verb, Shih calls for an active examination of archival and other research work on texts from different traditions that have been loosely related to better understand their relationalities in a decolonial historical context. The ultimate goal of this endeavor, which enables us to "especially [discern] the suppressed relationalities that uphold the status quo," Shih concludes, is not to arrive at the universal, but to arrive at interconnections and the singularity of each text.[69]

Tracing the genealogy of relationality in Indigenous millenarian cosmology, Walter D. Mignolo concurs that in Indigenous Amerindian philosophies dichotomies never existed. On the contrary, relationality is everything in the universe and in daily life.[70] Much like Shih's disavowal of a predetermined universal outcome of relational comparisons, Mignolo's understanding of relationality asserts its opening to pluriversality, or what he describes as "the coexistence of *vincularidad* with the ontology of relations."[71] For Mignolo, the concept of *vincularidad*—a derivative of the Spanish verb *vincular*, "to link," denoting the state of being linked with all the living—is neither matter nor ontology, but movement and flow. It has always been like that, he goes on to argue, from before Western interventions. Nonetheless, the false newness that theories of New Materialism attach to relationality is nothing but a projection of the modernity/postmodernity frame of mind put in place by Western thinkers who imposed a colonial view on the world based in dichotomies before proceeding to demand the dismantling of such dichotomies.

Recasting decolonization as relationality, Cutcha Risling Baldly and Melanie K. Yazzie call for radical relationality.[72] Their definition of the term in the North American context bears a remarkable similarity to *vincularidad*. Centering the multifaceted ongoing material struggle of Indigenous Peoples, radical relationality expands on previous definitions that confined decolonization to the transformation of consciousness within the realm of research and knowledge. Building on Linda Tuhiwai Smith's five dimensions of decolonial struggle,[73] both seek to attend to the interconnecting and variously scaled decolonial practices, including the human-land-water connection fostered in Indigenous feminism. Rooted in the dynamics of a decolonial struggle, radical relationality, Baldly and Yazzie contend, is instrumental for building "the kind of mass movements that are necessary for staging a serious counterhegemonic challenge to the *status quo* of death that currently structures [Indigenous] existence."[74] What stands out about this model of relationality is its emphasis on an expansive interconnectedness that embraces the kinships forged in the shared promise for mutual care and protection between mountain, human, animal, and water relatives, the collective commitment to liberation movements across the world, and the endorsement of far-reaching relational politics of life.

Notwithstanding the generative decolonial possibilities of relationality as noted above, it is important to keep in mind that relationality is not mechanically harmonious. Fraught with frictions and incommensurability, relationality can be oppositional. It can negate and dismiss certain aspects of relatedness too. The Afro-Indigenous encounter in the Americas is an illustrative example of such dynamics. Whereas scholars in North America have questioned the possibility of addressing Black geographies, dispossession, and other racialized propriety violence as incommensurate with, yet not apart from, Indigenous land sovereignty,[75] their peers in South America who investigated how the uneven colonial legislative reforms influenced Black and Indigenous interactions[76] pointed out the intercommunal tensions and conflicts that resulted from the denial by Latin American states of Afro-descendants' land claims.

Whereas the Arabic-Tsotsil concept of affinity is attentive to these articulations of similitude and relationality, it is tailored to focus particularly on the emotive conditions of familiarity and relatedness that make relation-making between Palestinian and Mayan narratives possible. Grounded in the equation of unity in similarity embedded in *ko'olajel* and the joint affective and relational elements of *'ulfa* in *kuxlej* and *kuxlejal,* this concept seeks to show not only how Palestine and Chiapas can be united in their Indigenous land struggle and quest for liberation through an exchange of their sense of *ṣumūd*, but also how they could create connectedness by recognizing the similarities that bring them together in a kinship of familiar brothers and sisters. Certainly, this orientation is not oblivious to the turbulence in forging this connection ensuing from the disparity between the history of Zionist settler colonialism and its ongoing project of building an exclusive Jewish state, on the one hand, and the thriving legacy of Spanish conquest that contributed to establishing a modern Mexican state on a homogenizing national imaginary of *mestizaje*, that is, de-Indianization as a form of whitening, on the other hand.

For this reason, affiliation is a vital component of the Arabic-Tsotsil concept of affinity. By seeking a South-South link beyond familial lines or more immediate networks of solidarity, this concept emerges as an affiliative model of comparison that abounds with a type of relation-making that extends from within the echoes of resemblance in *ṣumūd*; familiarity with resistance to minoritization, subalternization, racialization, and borders; similitude in the performance of commemorating the colonial state execution of Indigenous peasants; and the co-building of South-South solidarity-based sisterhood and brotherhood. In a way, affinity shows how the nonbinary juxtapositions of Palestinian and Mayan narratives from the geographically disconnected grounds of Palestine and Chiapas reinforce the need to think beyond bloodlines and nationalism, by opting for affiliations, or chosen kin. If we read Mayan and Palestinian narratives in light of this relationality between Chiapas and Palestine, we gain a glimpse of how a periphery–periphery interconnected Global South front can contribute to decolonizing the present and to imagining alternative futures fueled by encounters that are born alongside solidarity, yet aspire to go beyond it. In other words, the Arabic-Tsotsil bilingual concept of affinity invites us to contemplate the future on the other side of the mural of "To Exist Is to Resist"; to imagine Mayan and Palestinian unity beyond the struggle for liberation, beyond resistance, beyond borders, and beyond, simply, existence. Are we free enough to see beyond the wall?

2
Topographies of Affinities: Writing Erasure and Borderlands

In the summer of 2018, I accompanied my Tsotsil language teacher, Jose Bartolomé Mendoza Lopez, to his creative writing and translation workshop at the center of Unidad de Escritores Mayas-Zoques (UNEMAZ), an independent collective of Mayan writers based in San Cristóbal de las Casas, or Jobel in Tsotsil.[1] In the classroom dedicated to Tsotsil, my teacher sat next to other native learners of Tsotsil who were, like him, seeking to advance their linguistic and literary competency in their mother tongue, or *Bats'i k'op (La verdada lengua, the language of the true people)*, as they referred to it. As a guest and a novice Tsotsil learner, I sat in the corner, but not too far from my teacher, who split his attention between taking notes and facilitating my learning alongside him. Following his instructions, I took notes on vocabulary, phonetics, and grammatical structures. Professor Juan López Gonzáles stood at the center of the classroom with a set of colorful markers and a white board behind him: green was for writing words in Tsotsil, red for words in Spanish, and black for visual explanations that would ultimately provide a vivid illustration of the translation back and forth between Tsotsil and Spanish. His hands moved dynamically between the different colors, the dialogue with the students in front of him, and the two large paper pads that were taped on opposite sides of the board. The pad on the right was in Spanish, entitled: Indigenous culture. Underneath, a circle with a list: wisdom/knowledge, memory, cultural memory, historical memory, oral tradition. Below the circle, a nameless quote: "Not to follow the footprints of the other writers, but to seek what they sought."[2] The pad on the left side of the board was in Tsotsil. It was a numerical list of the communities represented in the room and their Tsotsil variation: eight in total. The colorful board with the two pads on the sides projected a conceptual map of Tsotsil that was inviting the students to engage in an open brainstorming exercise. Moreover, the relaxed positive atmosphere that dominated the classroom challenged long-held assumptions concerning the proliferation of local dialects by viewing it as an expression of parochialism and internal border-making resulting from the internalization of forceful isolation and segregation caused by colonial administrative policies, settlement patterns, and civil and religious organizations.[3]

The polyphonic linguistic and cultural Mayan landscape of the Tsotsil creative writing workshop was reflected in the spatial layout of UNEMAZ and its geographical location. The center had two floors: the lower had several classrooms marked by a paper sheet indicating the Mayan language taught in each class, and the upper where a library displayed bilingual Spanish and Mayan publications alongside a wide collection of monolingual books in Tsotsil, Tseltal, Cho'l, Tojolabal, Zoque, and Lacandon, in addition to other Mayan languages, by contemporary Mayan writers from Chiapas and Guatemala. An open patio with a colorful mural inspired by precolonial classical Mayan iconography and abstract modern shapes shaded by a row of green fruit trees connected the two floors. After the classes were over, a multigenerational group of Mayan poets, writers, musicians, and teachers gathered on the patio to read selections from their poems, to rehearse songs, to provide feedback, and to discuss formal, linguistic, cultural, and political aspects of writing contemporary Mayan literature. The discussion was conducted in what seemed like an effortless transition and mixing between Spanish, Tsotsil, Tseltal, and other Mayan languages.

The cacophony of UNEMAZ reverberated through its black iron gate, opening to a side street that connected it to the Mercado Viejo, the oldest open market in San Cristóbal / Jobel. The market bustled with a variety of Mayan languages and fragments of Spanish among the diverse members of the speech community that was composed of vendors, shoppers, workers, farmers, and craft artists, as well as commuters who were hopping in and out of crammed *combis*, the cheapest mode of public transportation and the only one that connected the city with the Mayan villages in the bordering mountains. In this soundscape, Mayan languages mediated personal conversations, commercial exchanges, and discount announcements. A salient presence of Tsotsil and Tseltal, handwritten in the Latin alphabet, was visible on advertisement boards announcing the availability of homemade corn tortillas, milpa-grown vegetables, traditional medicinal herbs, and directions to the small central bus station where *colectivos* (shared vans) carried passengers to San Juan Chamula, the largest Tsotsil-speaking town in Chiapas and a gateway to numerous Mayan villages in the highlands.

Between UNEMAZ, the market, and the communal transport hub, the strong presence of Mayan written words and sounds was sending a clear message: Mayan languages and cultures are *still* here. Although located on the periphery of this colonial capital, namely on the colonial border that demarcates the rural-urban divide, or more precisely the socioeconomic and cultural boundary that segregates the area of impoverished Mayan villages scattered in the mountains from the more affluent *ladino* (Non-Indian, an assimilationist mestizo, or European) and *kaxlan* (a Tsotsil word for a Spanish speaker or a mestizo) urban space, Mayan languages and their native speakers continue to *exist*. Their existence is a material manifestation of collective survival and resistance to the domination of the Spanish language and the ongoing cultural genocide that the Spanish conquistadors started in the sixteenth century and the Mexican settler colonial state perpetuates in the twenty-first century. Unquestionably, the vibrancy of Mayan languages and their speakers in both the interior space of UNEMAZ and its immediate surroundings are only a glimpse of what five hundred years of Mayan *ṣumūd* look like.

The commitment of Professor López Gonzáles and his students to expanding the Tsotsil dictionary by eliciting words from each region while simultaneously negotiating accurate translations of metaphors to capture the profound poetics of everyday Mayan languages in the Latin alphabet was more than an exercise in literary translation. In paying close attention to the dexterity and patience with which the class collectively attended to this complex task, I observed the following. First, a deep political quest to create an autonomous linguistic, textual, and philological space for Tsotsil. Second, a collective attempt to subvert the epistemic hegemony of Spanish by tapping into ancestral knowledge and Mayan cultural memory. To achieve this goal, the class followed an integrative pedagogy that absorbed family stories, reflections on the ways Tsotsil is used in various oral texts, comparative analysis of regional differences in dialects, and a fragmentary bilingualism that served as a strategy to undo the colonial hierarchy between Spanish and Tsotsil.

Leaving UNEMAZ to return to my Spanish-speaking mestizo host family, who lived in a residential working-class neighborhood less than a fifteen-minute ride away, I was struck by the limited spatial scale of the encounter between Tsotsil and Spanish that I had just witnessed. The further the *combi* drove away from UNEMAZ, the more predominantly monolingual and racially homogenous the streets became. The need to speak, think, and write in Tsotsil or to address its asymmetrical relationship with Spanish faded gradually as Spanish increasingly took over street signs, advertisement boards, and small family-owned bodegas. That said, the absence of Tsotsil was not total. Fragments of

Tsotsil could be heard on the sidewalks in exchanges between Mayan street vendors and housekeepers. Frictions of the atmosphere at UNEMAZ also trickled into the central avenues of San Cristóbal/Jobel, namely the touristy plazas of the city where popular artisanal markets, Zapatista-owned cooperatives, and luxurious boutiques competed in selling Mayan "authenticity" and Zapatista-inspired paraphernalia to an ever-increasing mass of Mexican and international tourists.[4] In this space, Tsotsil could be heard in conversations among the Mayan traders. It was also written on a handful of bilingual signs, some of which had appropriated the script through sensational and exotic graphic representation to attract shoppers seeking to consume a "local cultural flavor." In sum, whether reclaimed by its native speakers, or culturally appropriated by commercial tourist agencies operating within the neoliberal Mexican economy, Tsotsil was clearly disrupting the seemingly absolute dominance of Spanish.

Although the status of Tsotsil in the current linguistic landscape of Indigenous languages in Mexico was a topic that my teacher Mendoza Lopez and I discussed extensively in Spanish during our one-on-one classes, our joint visit to UNEMAZ was an exemplary illumination of the affinity that I observed between Tsotsil in Chiapas and Arabic in Israel. The rhythm of Professor López Gonzáles's hand movement on the board and his color-coordinated writing evoked a familiar use of code-switching and fragmented bilingualism. Trying to keep up with the pace of his alternation between spoken and written Tsotsil and Spanish, I found myself drawn into a déjà vu of my high school literature and social sciences classes in my border hometown of Al-Taybeh. I was reminded of a parallel multifaceted linguistic entanglement that shaped my overall colonial educational formation as a Palestinian in Israel from elementary school through high school where the language(s) of learning and instruction created a mélange of oral regional Palestinian colloquial vernaculars, modern Standard Arabic, and modern Hebrew (written in the Hebrew alphabet and pronounced with an Arabic accent). Despite being habituated to this mélange—a distinctive feature of the educational Arab Palestinian educational system, which is segregated from that of the Jewish Hebrew-speaking majority[5]—being reminded of it in Chiapas in a creative writing class in Tsotsil heightened my awareness of the rugged linguistic terrain that underpins fragmented bilingualism in a minoritized context. Once again, I was reminded of the unresolved tension between Arabic and Hebrew in my classes and the firmness of my teachers, mainly those who taught Arabic, history, and geography, who insisted, albeit sometimes unsuccessfully, that we speak in Arabic only. I was nudged as well by the commanding voice of my late Hebrew teacher, *ustādha* Mariam Massarwah (*Allāh yerḥamhā*), who urged us to pronounce the Hebrew letters according to the phonetics of Arabic, and thus to roll our "*Rs*" emphatically, to glottalize the "H," and to articulate the *'ain* correctly from the pharynx, because, as Arabic speakers, she stated, we were capable of doing so. After all, she insisted, we were not Ashkenazis.

More importantly, the Tsotsil class visit at UNEMAZ illuminated a parallel saliency of borders, both conspicuous and invisible, in Chiapas and Palestine. The geographical and cultural separation between minoritized and dominant languages was marked not only by a sociolinguistic spatial divide, but also by the presence of particular racialized bodies in particular places. As much as the Tsotsil-Spanish bilingualism in UNEMAZ was mainly concentrated in the periphery of the *ladino*-dominant Spanish-speaking city, the Arabic-Hebrew bilingualism in my classroom was confined to the five-mile Arabic-speaking radius that surrounded the school. It did not extend to the Jewish-dominant Hebrew-speaking adjacent Jewish towns, settlements, and kibbutzim that were spread across both sides of the so-called Green Line—which were strategically built between Palestinian villages and on top of hills to tower over Palestinians to exert geographical domination. Moreover, it did not cross the so-called Green Line border into the Palestinian villages in the Occupied West Bank across the fence, where Arabic was not only the language of a Palestinian majority, but also the national language of the homeland. If Hebrew were to be found there, it would be printed on road signs indicating the way to the illegal settlements or scribbled with spelling errors on some Palestinian-owned mechanic and service shops along the way. It would also be found at the checkpoint reminding everyone of its dominating power. In this hyper-militarized zone, Palestinians on both sides of the fence engaged with Hebrew as a language of colonial surveillance. They developed a particular proficiency in what became widely known as "checkpoint Hebrew" by recognizing the signage that specifies who can cross and how, the terminology of racial profiling, the warning signs, the vocabulary detailing punitive measures against transgressors, and the abusive military orders of Israeli soldiers. Whereas the vast majority of Palestinians from the Occupied West Bank had a very basic knowledge of Hebrew that did not exceed the limited proficiency of the "checkpoint Hebrew" lexicon, a fairly large number of Palestinians, primarily academics interested in Israeli studies, laborers who worked in Israel, businessmen who traded with Israelis, and prisoners detained in Israeli jails, had a more advanced level. Due to their daily interactions with Hebrew beyond the checkpoint, they developed a deeper familiarity with the language and to a certain extent Israeli culture and society.

Taking as its point of departure this affinity between Tsotsil and Arabic as two minoritized languages that share commonalities in their position as subalternized and racialized languages vis-à-vis the respective spatial segregation and colonial dominance of Spanish and Hebrew, this chapter unveils the features of the *'ulfa–kuxlej/kuxlejal* between written Mayan narratives in Chiapas and their Palestinian counterparts in Israel by revealing a similar struggle that Mayan and Palestinian writers have undergone to safeguard the survival of their native languages. In this struggle, which entails the resort to divergent defensive measures, namely revitalization of Tsotsil for Mayan writers versus preservation of Arabic for Palestinian writers, we can detect, I argue, an analogous configuration of indigeneity. What constitutes indigeneity in this context is the deep bond that Mayan and Palestinian writers construct between Tsotsil and Arabic as native languages and the corresponding ancestral lands of Chiapas and Palestine. Given the ongoing targeted erasure of Tsotsil and Arabic in both geographies, and the settler colonial encroachment on the lands where they are spoken, Mayan and Palestinian writers, I further argue, deploy a persistent intentionally heightened affect in the use of their native languages as rooted in land.

To elucidate this argument, this chapter charts first the many ways in which Mayan and Palestinian writers, critics, and poets have conceived, framed, and positioned written Tsotsil and Arabic vis-à-vis this configuration of indigeneity. Then, I turn my attention to a comparative analysis of key moments in Mayan and Palestinian literary history alongside a comparative reading of poems by Mayan and Palestinian poets who belong to the generation that launched the battle for linguistic and cultural *ṣumūd* (steadfastness): Mariano Reynaldo Vázquez López (1974–), Xun Betan (1982–), Tawfiq Zayyad (1932–1994), and Mahmoud Darwish (1941–2008). The political consciousness underpinning the use of Tsotsil and Arabic as endangered languages in this representative sample of poems, I conclude, speaks to a converging sense of *ṣumūd* and a renewed kinship with this very land that the settler colonial militarized states of Mexico and Israel continue to systematically appropriate and fragment.

Bilingualism is not uncommon in the literary, cultural, and political landscapes of Mayan and Palestinian writers. This chapter, however, does not address the dynamics of bilingualism[6] in Mayan and Palestinian texts, or works by Mayan authors who write only in Spanish, or Palestinian writers who write in Hebrew. My concern is not the linguistic encounter between colonial and colonized languages in texts, but rather an examination of the comparable political landscapes of Tsotsil and Arabic. In the pages that follow, therefore, I focus primarily on a comparative reading of revindication of Tsotsil and Arabic. By gaining a deeper understanding of this emancipatory political project, I not only highlight the linguistic battlefields that shaped Tsotsil and Arabic as Indigenous languages, but also shed light on similar modes of linguistic resistance to deterritorialization, which is a defining element of indigeneity.

The Literary Revitalization of Tsotsil: A Historical Overview

Historically, contemporary Mayan literature written in Tsotsil dates back at least to the mid-1950s when a group of US anthropologists from the Harvard Chiapas Project arrived in Chiapas. Under the leadership of Evon Z. Vogt (1957–75) and Robert M. Laughlin, the project conducted a series of ethnographic studies and linguistic anthropology research in Mayan villages in the Highlands. In addition to designing questionnaires in Tsotsil, the project offered special training programs in Tsotsil aimed at preparing the participants for ethnographic fieldwork. It also used Tsotsil in its pilot orthological research in Zinacantán[7] and employed local bilingual linguist informants to aid in conducting personal interviews in rural communities. The publication of Laughlin's annotated dictionary, *The Great Tzotzil Dictionary of San Lorenzo Zinacantán* in 1975, was a definitive turning point in the revival and preservation of Tsotsil. Described as the most complete American Indian–language dictionary ever published,[8] Laughlin's dictionary, which contains more than thirty-five thousand Tsotsil words and took twelve years to elicit, compile, and edit, canonized the alphabetical writing of Tsotsil. Donald Frischmann considers this linguistic and cultural revival of written Tsotsil a catalyst for the establishment of the first Indigenous writers' collective, *Sna Jtz'ijabom* (The Writer's House) in 1983. In fact, some of the Tsotsil informants—as Frischmann describes them—who worked with Vogt and Laughlin would ultimately be among the cofounders of the collective.[9]

The Taller Tzotzil (Tsotsil Workshop) (1976–2002) is another initiative that played a pivotal role in the revival and dissemination of written Tsotsil narratives. Mobilized by members of one of the earliest international coalitions for solidarity with Mayan communities and commitment to Indigenous autonomy, the workshop published collectively written booklets in Tsotsil—and later in Spanish and Tsotsil—that document the reflections of Tsotsil speakers who gained literary skills in Tsotsil. Following the model of Paulo Freire's pedagogy of the oppressed, the workshop aimed at fostering *concientización* (consciousness raising or empowerment)[10] through writing testimonials about communal labor, revitalization of local fiestas, educational rights, and other issues of concern for Mayan communities. A notable feature of this workshop, which by 2002 had published more than thirty booklets by Indigenous authors in Tsotsil, is the intercultural collaboration between the Tsotsil writers, the majority of whom were Tsotsil adult Christian converts interested in gaining literacy in Tsotsil in order to read the Bible in Tsotsil,[11] and their Francophone, Hispanophone, and Anglophone supporters, including the following individuals: Andrés Aubry, a French sociologist, activist, and cofounder of the workshop in 1974 who later would serve as adviser for the Zapatistas; Angélica Inda, a Mexican anthropologist and cofounder of the workshop; alongside Jan Rus, Diane L. Rus, John Burstein, Amber Past, and Carlota Duarte. This latter group of anthropologists, poets, and artists moved from the US to Chiapas in the 1970s and since then have been actively involved in the emerging Mayan cultural movement. Equally as important as the *Tsotsil Workshop* was the outgrowth of different literary collaborations in the 1980s and early 1990s with Carlos Montemayor, the first Mexican poet and journalist to ally himself with Indigenous poetry, and Frischmann, a professor of Spanish with teaching positions in the US, that eventually led to the publication of *Words of the True Peoples / Palabras de los Seres Verdaderos: Anthology of Contemporary Mexican Indigenous-Language Writers* (2004–7). In this seminal multivolume trilingual anthology, original works of poetry, short stories, and drama in Tsotsil appeared for the first time alongside their translations in Spanish and English.

What is compelling about this recent history of written Tsotsil narratives[12] is the fact that it provides unequivocal evidence of the survival of Mayan literacy and literary cultures despite the catastrophic destruction of Mayan books in the sixteenth century during the Inquisition, ordered by the Franciscan friar Diego de Landa in the Yucatán Peninsula in 1562[13] and in Chiapas[14] in 1554. In both events, the Spanish missionaries carried out rituals of public penance that involved the massive burning of Mayan codices and religious documents and at the same time torturing Mayans who continued to perform their traditional religious ceremonies. If we were to be oblivious to this cultural *Nakba* we would not fully grasp the scope of the written Mayan literature that emerged in the second half of the twentieth century nor appreciate its rapid proliferation in the twenty-first century. Indeed, the expansive contemporary corpus of Mayan texts written in various Mayan languages, which also contains a wide array of genres, themes, and forms, is a vivid proof of the *ṣumūd* of Mayan civilization and the vibrancy of Mayan languages and their speakers. This five-hundred-year-old *ṣumūd* is steeped in a long-standing tradition of preservation, at times clandestine, of Mayan languages throughout the era of Spanish colonial rule. Moreover, it is the backbone of the literary and cultural movement that coalesced in the 1980s thanks to a written revitalization of pre-Columbian Mayan folktales, fables, myths, oral accounts, dream narratives, and philosophical texts. This movement, often described as the Mayan Renaissance, or the Mayan Awakening, flourished due to and despite the persisting domination of Spanish in Mexico, a national imaginary that subordinates the Indigenous as the unmodern racialized Other, and a settler colonial Mexican state that continues to displace and dispossess its Indigenous citizens.

Although it is paramount to be mindful of the established record of the *ṣumūd* of written Mayan culture, we cannot overlook the more recent history of structural suppression of Mayan literacy. This also applies to Tsotsil in Chiapas. As Gloría Elizabeth Chacón reminds us, postcolonial Mexico, and to a certain degree most postcolonial Latin American states, were founded on a capitalist liberal model rooted in a colonial doctrine that intended to absorb and assimilate Indigenous nations. The eradication of Indigenous languages and cultures for the sake of a linguistically homogenous Spanish-speaking nation was at the core of this doctrine. This is the reason why, Chacón argues, "Maya and Zapotec alphabetic writing decreased dramatically after the consolidation of the nation-state,"[15] a trend that marks a shift from earlier Spanish colonial periods that witnessed a revival of Indigenous cultures and knowledge through the writings of Indigenous scribes who used the Latin alphabet alongside Maya and algebraic numbers to record and preserve Mayan knowledge as well as important historical events. In a related vein, Dennis Tedlock observes that Mayans began using the alphabet to write in their own languages in the same period as the Spanish missionaries' public burning of books. Refuting claims of an absolute triumph of the roman alphabet and a "sudden and definitive end" to the Mayan writing system, Tedlock notes that the Mayan script continued to be in use for a long time after Landa's flames had died down.[16]

Alongside the erasure of ancestral Mayan knowledge, muffling the voices of Tsotsil speakers is another common practice in postcolonial Mexico. It traces back to the *indigenista* literary movement that emerged in conjunction with *indigenismo*, a public policy developed in the early years following the Mexican Revolution of 1910. Motivated by an aspiration to build a modernizing postrevolutionary Mexican nation that contends with its pre-Columbian origins, *indigenismo* sought to integrate Indigenous Peoples into a utopian antiracist vision of Mexico by claiming the unique racial and cultural mixture of the country, or *mestizaje*, as the common unifying factor.

While there is a wealth of scholarship commenting on the contradictory outcomes of this social engineering project and its unilateral one-directional linguistic and cultural assimilation of the "Indian" into the postcolonial imagined nation-state,[17] it is important to point out here two key critiques that speak to its problematic racist logic. For Aníbal Quijano, on the one hand, *indigenismo* in Mexico—and its reiteration in other Latin American countries—was a political and epistemic reproduction of a Spanish legacy of colonial modernity. Adopting a Eurocentric view of modernity, *indigenismo* was constructed on binary thinking, a dualist perspective on knowledge, and the exclusion of the Indian.[18] On the other hand, for Guillermo Bonfil Batalla, it is the symbolic exaltation of the Indian as an official icon of nationalism that fueled the racist discourse underpinning *indigenismo*. In postrevolutionary Mexico, the presence of the Indian in the public sphere was subjected to state control, through systematic symbolic erasure in murals, sculptures, archeological sites, and museums where the Indian was positioned as a dead artifact from a glorious mythological past. In anthropological museums, for example, the figure of the Indian was spatially relegated to the second floors and was depicted as a relic from the past belonging to a "dead world that [was] the seed of origins that gave rise to today's Mexico."[19] The visual abstraction and museumification practices inherent in this representation, which overlooked the living Indian, were woven into the social fabric of modern Mexico, where *de-Indianizing* that which is Indian became the political norm.

In the late 1940s, Chiapas became a central geography for *indigenismo* and a national hub for *indigenista* literature: texts written in Spanish by non-Indigenous authors (*ladinos/as* and mestizos/as) about Indigenous People and their seemingly unknown world. Shortly after the inauguration in 1948 of the *Centro Coordinador Indigenista* (Indigenist Coordination Center, CCI), a pilot program operating under the *Instituto Nacional Indigenista* (Indigenous National Institute, INI) in San Cristóbal / Jobel, El ciclo de Chiapas (The Chiapas Cycle) was formed.[20] While the INI attracted generations of Mexican and US anthropologists who relocated to Chiapas with the intention of developing culturally sensitive policy regarding the Indigenous Peoples of Mexico, members of the Chiapas Cycle embraced the emancipation ideal and the agrarian reform promoted by the Mexican Revolution in order to write in solidarity with the Indigenous *campesinos*. What distinguished the works of this group is the attempt to recreate Indigenous reality and tell the stories from an insider perspective based on personal and imagined encounters with impoverished Mayan characters from Chiapas, mainly Tsotsil and Tseltal speakers.

Nonetheless, the symbolic inclusion of Tsotsil and Tseltal voices, primarily oral, in ethnographic accounts and fictionalized stories inadvertently marginalized Mayan languages further. The unilateral mediation, translation, and editorial decisions that the *indigenista* authors made concerning these languages created skewed discursive and representational frameworks. In addition to establishing an Orientalist representation of the Indian as the "noble savage," *indigenista* authors wrote texts that generated "a discourse by non-Indians about Indians; a discourse that maintains a hierarchical social relationship between those who speak and those who are spoken about."[21] The ethnographic novels of the anthropologist Ricardo Pozas (1912–1994) and the historical fiction of the Chiapas-raised novelist Rosario Castellanos (1925–1974), both members of the Chiapas Cycle, are two key examples. Pozas's *Juan Pérez Jolote* (1948) is based on a series of interviews and observations that the author conducted during his anthropological fieldwork in the Tsotsil-speaking Mayan village of Chamula. The outcome is a Spanish reproduction of Pérez Jolote's autobiography, from his violent upbringing in Chamula to his child labor years on various *ladino*-owned fincas, incarceration due to false charges of murder, fighting as a mercenary in opposing fronts of the Mexican Revolution, and final return to Chamula as an outsider who struggles to speak Tsotsil. Castellanos's historical epic and classic of Mexican literature, *Oficio de tinieblas* (Book of Lamentations) (1962), on the other hand, retells the history of the Maya uprisings of 1712 and 1868, which are transposed in time to the 1930s, through the tragic encounter between a rich *ladino* landlord who exploits Mayan labor and a Mayan woman whom he rapes. From 1956 to 1957, Castellanos also wrote and directed plays for the puppet theater troupe Teatro Guignol, a CCI development project that involved a group of bilingual Mayan cultural promoters who most likely spoke Spanish and Tsotsil or Tseltal and performed in Mayan rural communities plays that focused on public health, education, and issues of alcoholism. However, these plays were not always well received by their intended audience. As Cynthia Steele points out, during the performance of a dramatized story about an encounter between Mayans and foreign visitors titled *Petul y el diablo extranjero* (Petul and the foreign devil), for example, the residents of San Juan Chamula interrupted the show by throwing rocks at Castellanos and her Mayan assistants and shouting "We are not like the people from Mukum" to express the great offense[22] they took at their misrepresentation as Indians who hold superstitious beliefs about strangers. Here, we observe not only an explicit rejection of Castellanos's prejudiced view of Mayan cultural practices, but also a symbolic assertion of the Mayan right to tell Mayan stories and how they are told, or per Paul M. Worley's apt summary of this incident, a refusal to recognize Castellanos's authority as cultural broker.[23]

Although the works by Pozas and Castellanos did not fully redeem Tsotsil and Tseltal from their devalued linguistic position, they did solidify colonial and racial binaries by situating their Mayan protagonists on the threshold between the primitive and the modern, extension and survival, assimilation, and Otherness.[24] Moreover, these works, regardless of their genre, conveyed the protagonists' entrapment in this threshold through a Spanish editing of their dialogue with the authors in Chiapanecan Castilla, the way Mayans speak Spanish in Chiapas. Influenced by the polyphony of the diverse Mayan languages in Chiapas, this form of speech is marked by a distinctive set of intonations and grammatical errors, including disagreements in gender and number.

Beyond merely critiquing the subalternization of Mayan language and culture and their presence as shadows in *indigenista* literature, the emerging generation of Mayan writers and critics have challenged its racial gaze. The Tsotsil-speaking poet and critic Ruperta Bautista Vázquez (1975–), for example, refers to the work of *indigenista* authors like Carlo Antonio Castro and Rosario Castellanos as literature of "*jkaxlan*" and "*xinula*" (Tsotsil for mestizo or a male Spaniard and mestiza or a female Spaniard, respectively).[25] In doing so, she reverses the racialized gaze of the non-Mayan outsider. Pointing to the significant political distinction between the literature of "*jkaxlan*" and "*xinula*" and the literary Mayan movement that flourished during the 1980s, Bautista Vázquez asserts that the latter was inspired by the empowerment it received from Mayan communities, or the Originative Peoples, as she identifies them. For the burgeoning Mayan literature, what became the main concern, she concludes, was the political role that art plays. How is art imagined and understood from an insider point of view? What political Mayan visions inspired the writing of Mayan narratives in originative languages? These questions were the driving force for the emerging Mayan writers who reclaimed Mayan languages and aesthetics to articulate an autonomous Mayan worldview.

Bilingual education is another domain where the structural marginalization of Tsotsil was prevalent. Although Indigenous students in Mexico gained their right to literacy and bilingual education only after the First Interamerican Indigenous Congress in 1940, in Chiapas it was not until the 1960s that this gain translated into actual institutional changes that aimed at offering classes in Mayan languages and providing access to secondary education.[26] The Mexican federal government notably sought help from Protestant missionaries from the US to develop bilingual curricula. It relied on two major Protestant-linked missionary groups from the US, the Summer Institute of Linguistics (SIL) and Wycliffe Bible Translators. Both groups arrived in Chiapas in the 1940s on a mission to apply their linguistic expertise and language preservation to translate the Bible into Tsotsil. In 1951, the *Instituto Nacional Indigenista* (Indigenous National Institute, INI) utilized the material that was developed by these missionary translators for bilingual education of Tsotsil speakers. Although this collaboration between Mayan languages and Anglo-Christian missionaries in twentieth-century Mexico did not entail the same degree of settler violence that characterized the imperial expansion of Spanish Christian missionaries in sixteenth-century Mexico, its underlying cultural coloniality continues to punctuate the subordination of contemporary Mayan language and culture. Nevertheless, critics observe the undeniable impact that this collaboration between the INI and the Protestant missionaries had on the evolution of Indigenous literatures throughout Mexico. Zapotec writer Javier Castellanos Martínez from Oaxaca, for example, remarks that the oldest members in the contemporary generation of Indigenous writers are fifty or sixty years old. A large number of them, he adds, are most likely the children of rural teachers who were formed in the bilingual education system of the 1940s and thus had access to both Spanish and the alphabetical culture of Indigenous languages.[27] Along these lines, Jan Rus states that "no known documents were written in Tsotsil from the 1524 Spanish invasion to the 1940s."[28] Here, it is worth noting that a possible explanation for the historical marginalization of Tsotsil can be attributed to the fact that it was not considered of great political, demographic, religious, or cultural importance, in contrast to other Indigenous languages like Nahuatl, Peninsular Maya, and Zapotec, which were transferred to the Latin script in earlier periods for these reasons.[29] However, the discovery of oil in Chiapas in the early 1970s and the dramatic transformation of the poor state from the margins of national life into a strategic site for Mexican and multinational capitalist corporations galvanized a renewed colonial attention to Tsotsil and other Mayan languages.

Over the last two decades, the national and international attention paid to Indigenous languages and literatures in Mexico grew rapidly. A pivotal moment was the establishment of the Instituto Nacional de Lenguas Indígenas (National Indigenous Languages Institute, INALI), a federal public agency created in 2003 after two consecutive legislative acts pertinent to Indigenous cultures. Another significant development was the amendment in the Mexican constitution in 2002 that reinforced the nation's pluricultural nature alongside the introduction of El Ley General de Derechos Lingüísticos de los Pueblos Indígenas (The General Law on Indigenous People's Linguistic Rights, LGDLPI), in 2003, which declared the sixty-eight Indigenous languages as joint official languages of the country. On the international level, it is important to observe two transformative events that took place in the second decade of the twenty-first century. When Pope Francis visited Chiapas in 2016, he authorized the liturgy in Tsotsil and said some biblical words in Tsotsil. In 2019, INALI organized an international literary festival to commemorate the International Year of Indigenous Languages (IY2019) in Chiapas. In this two-day meeting, titled "Writing the Future of Indigenous Languages," which was held in San Cristóbal / Jobel in collaboration with UNESCO, PEN International's Translation and Linguistic Rights Committee (TLRC), Universidad de Ciencias y Artes de Chiapas (University of Science and Arts of Chiapas [UNICACH]), Tsotsil writers, literary scholars, activists, and translators, together with peers from other Mayan languages, met with delegates representing at least thirty of the world's languages, including other Indigenous languages in the Americas, the Philippines, and India. They engaged in literary exchanges by reading from their work and participating in debates that promoted linguistic rights as human rights. At the meeting's inaugural event, the president of PEN International,

Jennifer Clement, emphasized that Indigenous literatures are integral to world literature: "Over the course of a century, we have never recognized the boundaries that *separate indigenous* literatures from *other* literatures."[30] Bearing in mind the very recent swell of attention given to Indigenous literatures in PEN's publications and festivals, one cannot but identify in Clement's celebratory speech a tone of multiculturalism and a rather symbolic gesture towards a post-border, yet homogenous, view of world literature that in fact foregrounds the boundaries between "Indigenous" literatures and "Other" literatures.

In sum, these initiatives and the concurrent rise of academic research and critical attention given to Mayan literature in translation, mostly in Spanish and English, in both Mexican and Anglophone literary culture outlets, contributed to an accelerated visibilization of Mayan literature beyond Chiapas. Notable platforms that had a great influence on bolstering the visibility of individual and collaborative works by Mayan authors through regular publications, translations, and mass circulations are *Ojarasca*, the literary supplement of the major Mexican daily newspaper, *La Jornada; Xochitlajtoli* (Flowery word in Nahuatl), a designated space for literatures in various Indigenous languages curated by the Nahuatl-speaking poet Martín Tonalmeyotl in the poetry journal *Círculo de Poesía; Siwar Mayu* (A river of hummingbirds in Quechua), an open access trans-Indigenous multilingual project that seeks to bridge Indigenous and non-Indigenous cultures through collaborative translations, creative exchanges, and anthologies featuring artists and writers from various native nations of Abya Yala, Turtle Island, and the Pacific; *Asymptote; Literary Hub; Words Without Borders; Latin American Literature Today;* and *PEN International.*

In consideration of the crucial role that the Zapatista rebellion played in making demands for Indigenous cultural autonomy and human rights for Indigenous Peoples, the legal and cultural recognition of Indigenous languages mentioned above—at the nation's cultural level, the state's institutional level, and on the international literary scene—are illustrative of some of the political gains that the Indigenous insurgency in Chiapas scored.

However, the neoliberal motives lurking behind some strands of the rapid hypervisibility that Mayan literature has received since the early 2020s may not be the type of recognition that the Zapatistas originally fought for. After all, as Hannah Burdette reminds us, the cultural and literary project of the Zapatistas was not making demands to be seen simply for the sake of visibility. Quite the opposite. As a decolonial social movement, the Zapatistas revealed the insufficiency of visibilization in transforming Indigenous realities. The insurgent poetics that informed their writing conveyed the significance of literature as a key weapon in the struggle for political and intellectual sovereignty by serving as "a means to render subjected knowledge visible *(visiblizar)* and to envision alternatives to modernity/coloniality *(visualizer)*."[31] To paraphrase Burdette, for the Zapatistas, the visibility of Indigenous literatures was inextricably entwined with the affirmation of possible alternatives to hegemonic power structures.

From Writing Against Extinction to Imagining Emancipation: The Political Redemption of Literary Tsotsil

Reading contemporary Mayan narratives against the backdrop of this historical arc that reveals the co-occurrence of a systematic process of minoritization, subalternization, and racialization of Mayan languages, on the one hand, and an enduring potency of Mayan *ṣumūd*, on the other hand, impels us to reckon with the significance of using Indigenous languages to write Indigenous literatures. In our case, this means interrogating the ways in which Tsotsil was envisaged in writing Mayan narratives. How is Tsotsil employed in literary works through specific literary practices, linguistic strategies, and aesthetic choices? In what ways does the revitalization of written Tsotsil manifest in literature, and how does this process articulate or embody indigeneity within contemporary Mayan narrative traditions? To address these questions, I will conduct a close reading in a selection of poems dedicated to Tsotsil. Given the centrality of poetry in contemporary Mayan narratives and its revival of a pre-Columbian notion of writing, examining the diverse ways in which Tsotsil has been conjured up is highly relevant. As Ámbar Past remarks in her introduction to *Incantations: Songs, Spells and Images by Mayan Women* (2005), the contemporary oral poetry of ritual speech in Indigenous languages in Chiapas holds ancient memories of Mayan libraries. Poetry is also called *"nichimal k'op"*—"the word in flower."[32] Thus, it is no coincidence that in the late twentieth century Mayan writers in Chiapas evoke the Spanish word *florecimiento* (flowering) to describe their literary renaissance.

Before delving into the analysis of Tsotsil poetics, it is important to recognize that its revindication extends well beyond the literary realm, manifesting also in political, spiritual, and other cultural spheres. Although the Zapatista uprising itself did not inaugurate Mayan literature in Chiapas, the subsequent national and global political mobilization that it ignited and its call for the recognition of Indigenous cultural rights as human rights paved the way for the insurgency of Mayan languages. In this respect, Bautista Vázquez reminds us that poetry in Tsotsil and other Indigenous languages in Chiapas emerged largely within a movement of struggle and resistance that sought to dismantle the subjugation infrastructure that the Mexican state had built for minoritized populations who were, as Originative Peoples, reclaiming their position as a majority.[33] An exemplary articulation of this tendency is the seamless integration of Tsotsil and Tseltal in the political and cultural programming that the Zapatistas have organized from the early stages of their formation as a decolonial social movement until the present.

Without a doubt, the autonomous Zapatista communities contributed to furthering Mayan cultural production in Tsotsil and Tseltal. Both languages were regularly used in the extensive written and audiovisual documentation of the daily struggle of the communities toward building a Mayan political and cultural autonomy. Enacting a symbolic decolonial move, these productions intentionally subvert the linguistic colonial domination by prioritizing Tsotsil and Tseltal over Spanish. Public gatherings in Zapatista communities, for instance, often begin with reading speeches written in Tsotsil before proceeding to the translation in Spanish. This is also true for the mural "To Exist Is to Resist" (discussed in Chapter 1). The motto of "To exist is to resist" appears in a hierarchical order according to which the Tsotsil version, *"Ts'ik vokol ja' kuxlej,"* is on the top, while its respective Spanish, English, and Italian equivalents follow below or to the side.

In late 2020 a group of Tsotsil writers convened at UNEMAZ for an intergenerational dialogue on the significance of the alphabetization of Tsotsil and the future trajectory of Mayan narratives written in Tsotsil. Organized under the title *Kojtikinbrtik xch'ulel li jk'optike* (Recognizing the Essence of Our Language),[34] the participants reflected on their personal experience of teaching and learning in Tsotsil and what this process has offered them in terms of their relationship to the language. What emerged from this gathering was a consensus concerning the fundamental role that writing in alphabetical Tsotsil has played in recuperating not only Mayan visions that are specific to the Tsotsil People, but also the mathematical-logical aspects of Mayan thought. The concluding remarks underscored that writing in Tsotsil was imperative for building and empowering Tsotsil language and culture. According to Bautista Vázquez, these conversations about using the alphabet to write in Tsotsil brought to the fore the very definition of writing. The revival of *ts'iib*, a Tsotsil notion of writing, or alternative literacy that includes other forms of recorded knowledge, such as painted codices, textiles, embodied performances, and other artistic creations,[35] gained momentum throughout the 1990s alongside the resurgence of *nichimal amtel* (flowery work, or art in Tsotsil). In other words, to write in Tsotsil is not merely a textual visualization of spoken language, but rather a reclamation of a Mayan philosophy of writing that honors that multivocality of Mayan speakers and the different expressive registers they use to say "We are here."[36]

The poem *"Bats'i k'op"* ("Tsotsil")[37] (2005) by Mariano Reynaldo Vázquez López (1974–) is a pristine example of how Tsotsil writers have revindicated Indigenous languages. In this ode to his native language, Vázquez López, a translator, instructor of creative writing, and cultural promoter of Tsotsil who was among the first to receive a diploma in creative writing in Mayan languages from Centro Estatal de Lenguas, Art y Literatura Indígena (CELALI),[38] places Tsotsil ontology at the heart of a living Mayan cosmovision. Through imagery that creates symbiosis between the creative power of speakers of Tsotsil and the natural landscape of Chiapas, particularly volcanos and Quetzal, a sacred bird representing freedom in Mayan mythology, the poem asserts the ecocultural power of Tsotsil. It also conveys a Mayan cosmovision where harmony between human and nonhuman is the natural state of being.

Bats'i k'op	Tsotsil
Ye sti' mutetik	Idioma de pájaros,
Sk'euj ch'ul ik',	canto del viento,
Unen jkil xojobal k'ak'al	rayo del sol,
Jp'ej tubtub vits ta Chiapas.	volcán de las montañas de Chiapas.
Ti yu'un k'alal chat'ome, chik'opoj	Cuando estallas, hablo
ti yu'un k'alal chak'opoje, chit'sibaj.	cuando hablas, escribo.
Chi-ok' chajit'in,	Lloro pronunciándote,
chiste'in chakalot.	río enunciándote.
Jt'omel vits chavokan yilel:	Cráter que bulle:
k'op, ti', lo'il jol o'onal,	voz, idea,
sbonol snopbenal,	color del pensamiento,
snopbenal yu'un vinik iximetik,	pensamiento de hombres de maíz,
ants jal vayichiletik.	de mujeres tejedoras de sueños.
Yu'un vo'ot chkav o li balamile,	Por ti labro la tierra,
yu'un vo'ot ta jk'el o li vinajele.	por ti contemplo el cielo.
K'uku'mut ta yosilal svinajelal Maya	Quetzal del mundo Maya
sk'euj kuxlejal,	murmullo del tiempo,
teot ta sbelel jch'iel	estás en las travesías de la vida
nakalot li'ta vo'one,	vives en mí,
nakalot ta ye sti' bolom	vives en la boca del jaguar,
ch'ail, sakilal, yets'anil jteklum.	humo, luz, eco del pueblo.

Tsotsil / Language of birds, / song of the wind, / sunbeam, / volcano of the Chiapas mountains. / When you erupt, I speak / when you speak, I write. / I cry pronouncing you, / I laugh enunciating you. // Crater that seethes / voice, idea, / color of a thought, / thought of men of maize, / of women who weave dreams. / Because of you, I work the land, / because of you, I contemplate the sky. // Quetzal of the Maya world / whisper of time, / you are in the crossings of life, / you live in me, / you live in the mouth of the jaguar, / smoke, light, echo of the people.[39]

The poem is also saturated with metaphors that evoke Mayan artistic traditions and sacred texts. This is illustrated in the reference to women weavers in the line *"ants jal vayichiletik"* / *"mujeres tejedoras de sueños"* and the allusion to the Mayan story of creation in the sacred book of the *Popol Vuh* through the image of men of maize in the line *"snopbenal yu'un vinik iximetik"* / *"pensamiento de hombres de maíz."* A poignant redemption of Tsotsil as a language that can express complex ideas—in contrast to its depiction in colonialist discourse as culturally primitive and limited only to *"usos y costumbres"* (so-called customs and traditions)—is evident in the repetition of the word *snopbenal/ pensamiento*. In this clear subversion of colonial logic, the poet reclaims Tsotsil as a language of thought belonging to a rich philosophical tradition.

Playful use of Tsotsil poetics and self-translation[40] is another literary strategy mobilized in the poem to expose colonial dispossession and to assert Mayan *ṣumūd*: the linguistic significance of Tsotsil as a native language is established in the metaphysical correlation that the poem establishes between land and language in the lines *"Yu'un vo'ot chkav o li balamile"* / *"Por ti labro la tierra"* / "Because of you, I work the land." The word choice *balamile*, a homonym in Tsotsil for land, earth, world, and place, is especially intriguing. It cements the connection between a multidimensional philosophical notion of land in Mayan cosmogony and the cultivation of the land as an act of anticolonial resistance to the ongoing dispossession of Mayan farming lands in Chiapas. That strong bond between Tsotsil speakers and the territory where it is spoken is summed up in the last stanza where the poet draws a clear distinction between the spiritual and political location of Tsotsil. This distinction becomes particularly sharp in the Spanish version of the poem when Tsotsil, a language that lives in the body of its speaker, the mouth of the jaguar, and the echo of the people, is contrasted with its peripheral geopolitical location as a minoritized language. This contrast is sustained in the line *"estás en las travesías de la vida,"* and more specifically in *las travesías*. Although the word denotes trails, distance traveled, and side streets, especially roads that pass through a village, its metaphoric deployment here as crossings accentuates its border position.

The poems *"Jme'tik ta bats'i k'op"* / *"La madre luna Tsotsil"* / "The Tsotsil Mother Moon" (2018)[41] and "Flowers for the Heart" (2020)[42] by the Tsotsil poet Xun Betan offer another vivid illustration of how Mayan writers revindicated Tsotsil. For Betan, a prolific writer and translator and an avid defender of saving Tsotsil from "the danger of extinction," Tsotsil is not only a sacred language, but a political one too.

Jme'tik ta bats'i k'op[43]

Ta ch'ul ak'ubal xi sk' eojinta
ta ch'ul ak'ubal xi sk'opon.
Stuk xi slo'ilatabe xk'uxul yo' on
Xk'uxul ko' on jchikintabe.

Ta yut ch'ul chobtik xitajinkutik
Ta j nak' j ba stuke xi sa'
Ta xojobtasun ta sat
Tsobol xitseinkutik.

Ta sti' uk'umaltik
Ta k' eojimol ta jtus stsatsal jolkutik.
Ta jluch jtsekkutik
Chilil ta j alkutik.

Stuke mu xlubtsaj
Julem ta sba skotol osilaltik
Xcha'bi ololetik ta osilaltik
Xcha'bi ololetik ta teklumetik.

J a' vixil yu'un ch'ul k'analetik:
J a' srevos olol tsebetik ta be
Xk'ech olol tsebetik oyik ta chamel
J a' bats'i jch'ul me'tik.

La madre luna Tsotsil

Por las noches me canta
por las noches me platica.
Ella me cuenta sus secretos
y yo le cuento los míos.

Entre los maizales jugamos
me escondo y ella me busca
me alumbra con sus ojos
y juntas nos reímos.

A la orilla de los ríos
nos peinamos cantando.
Bordamos nuestras nahuas
tejemos nuestro huipil.

Ella nunca se cansa
siempre despierta esta
cuidando a los niños del campo
a los niños de la ciudad.

Es la hermana de las estrellas
rebozo para las niñas de la calle
abraza a las niñas de hospital
es nuestra madre luna Tsotsil.

The Tsotsil Mother Moon / At night she sings to me / at night she talks to me. / She tells me her secrets / and I tell her mine. // In the cornfields we play / I hide and she seeks me / She brightens me with her eyes / and together we laugh. // On the riversides / we comb our hair singing. / We embroider our *nahuas* / we weave our *huipil*. // She never gets tired / She is always awake / taking care of countryside children / taking care of city children. // She is the sister of the stars / a *rebozo* for street girls / She hugs the girls at the hospital / She is our Tsotsil moon mother.

In *"Jme'tik ta bats'i k'op / La madre luna Tsotsil /* The Tsotsil Mother Moon," the holiness of Tsotsil is established first in the title, where the language is metaphorized as the Virgin Mary. In Mayan Catholicism, which has been deeply influenced by Mayan cosmology, the Virgin Mary is associated with the moon, whereas the image of God the Father, or Jesus Christ, is associated with the sun. This sacred image of Tsotsil as a mother tongue embodied in the holy guardian spirit of the Virgin Mary is repeated throughout the poem. The feared absence of Tsotsil is countered by the omnipresence of the Holy Mother figure. It is emphasized further in the allusion to her powerful presence in the sky at night and on earth during daylight. Glorified and femininized, Tsotsil, as a "she," is at once the protective mother, the cosmic sister, and the playful friend in the cornfield.

The strong bodily and spiritual bond between Tsotsil speakers and their mother tongue is a recurring motif throughout the poem. Imagined as an intimate relationship between an inseparable child and a mother, it exists in the realm of the sacred, the profane, and the mundane everyday life, from embroidering *nahuas* (spirit animals or spirit companions) to sharing secrets and singing together by the riverside. The convergence of the "I," the Tsotsil speaker, and "She," the Tsotsil mother tongue in the first and second stanzas into the "We" in the third stanza and the return to the "She" at the end is anything but a straightforward link between one entity and another. The relational connection is altogether fluid and intimate. This movement from the first person and the third person singular to ultimately the first person plural traces a trajectory that leads to union, inclusivity, and kinship. The fact that the poem ends with the image of Tsotsil embodying the duality of the sacred Virgin Mary and the moon, "our Tsotsil moon mother," recenters the primordial nature of mother tongue / native language. Tsotsil is evoked both as the protective mother who shields her Tsotsil-speaking children wherever they may dwell and as the spark of life and light that gathers the community under her brightness, forging an everlasting bond.

In "Flowers for the Heart," Betan pays tribute to the Mayan notion of poetry, *nichimal k'op,* "the word in flower," by celebrating the various ways in which the language flourishes. The speaker anchors Tsotsil in the duality of heart and land, a duality that is synchronized with the movement in time in the poem.

The reader witnesses the growth of Tsotsil as it unfolds like the change in season in five stanzas. Thus, the seeds of corn that the "language [that] speaks from the heart" plants in the first stanza blossom into fresh tortillas and woven memories in the last stanza. Throughout this cycle of life in which "[the] heart blossoms" and "[the] words bloom," Tsotsil is portrayed as an exceptionally emotive language that invokes a fecund land and fertile memories. The prominence of the heart in Tsotsil poetics and in Mayan subjectivity is the connecting thread that holds the poem together. In the last two stanzas, however, the heart and the land emerge in a more politicized form. In addition to elucidating the affective qualities and linguistic richness of Tsotsil by listing the different meanings of the heart, the speaker evokes the number 43 in reference to the case of Ayotzinapa in the state of Guerrero where 43 students were forcibly abducted, and disappeared, by the Mexican military in 2014. The dictionary-style form employed in these stanzas expresses the profoundness of Mayan solidarity with Ayotzinapa. The affirmative positive tone on which the poem ends, from "We remember the 43 students, from the heart," and the last words in Tsotsil, *"xnichimal ko'ontontik"* (words bloom) bring the poem full circle, but not without an implicit declaration of future victory of those united in the struggle against the militarized Mexican state. Because, as the poet reminds us, Tsotsil is "poetry on its own," not only does it express the ineffable, from sorrow and pain to peace in the heart, but by singing to time, counting the years, and weaving memories, it is also timeless, a language with history and a heritage, and, as the poem ends, a future.

Flores para el corazón	Flowers for the Heart[44]
En mi lengua se habla desde el corazón	Our language speaks from the heart
tenemos *ch'ulel* y volamos en los sueños	we have *ch'ulel* and we fly in dreams.
cantamos con el viento y reímos con las nubes	We sing with the wind and laugh with the clouds
sembramos el maíz y cosechamos las tortillas.	we plant the corn and harvest the tortillas.
Cuando estoy alegre mi corazón florece	When I am happy my heart blossoms
tristeza es tener el corazón partido en dos pedazos	sorrow is my heart torn in pieces.
cuando me enfermo el dolor surge desde mi corazón	When I am sick the pain surges from my heart
cuando luchamos es buscar la paz del corazón.	when we fight we seek peace in the heart.

El tsotsil es una lengua que se canta al hablar	Tsotsil is a language that sings to speak
como las otras lenguas, en sí sola es poesía	like the other languages, it is poetry on its own
como es poesía se le canta al maíz y al tiempo	poetry that sings to corn and to time
se cuentan los años y se bordan los recuerdos.	counts the years and weaves the memories.
Xmuk'ib ko'onton es tener esperanzas	*Xmuk'ib ko'onton* is to have hopes.
ta jk'anot ta skotol ko'onton es amar con el corazón	*Ta jk'anot ta skotol ko'onton* is to love with the heart.
jun o'ontonal es paz en el corazón y en la vida	*Jun o'ontonal* is peace in the heart and in life.
k'ux ta ko'onton es dolor en mi corazón por las injusticias.	*K'ux ta ko'onton* is pain in my heart for injustice.
Los años se viven y del maíz se hace tortillas	The years live and the corn becomes tortillas
se tejen las historias y se recuerdan los tiempos	stories are woven, times remembered
recordamos a los 43 estudiantes, desde el corazón	we remember the 43 students, from the heart.
y qué de las palabras broten *xnichimal ko'ontontik.*	And that the words bloom in *xnichimal ko'ontontik.*
	(Translated by Sean S. Sell)

Intriguingly, "Flowers for the Heart" is a truly vivid illustration of the concept of *'ulfa–kuxlej/kuxlejal.* Its reflection on the significance of the heart in Tsotsil resonates with the affective roots of affinity in Arabic as I discussed it in the previous chapter. Here, we can observe the depiction of *'ulfa* in Tsotsil as the language of the heart that is rooted in solidarity and unity. It may in this regard be instructive to consider the rich historical tradition of the poetics of the heart and its pre-Columbian origins. Indeed, historical records indicate that a 1590s dictionary of ten thousand Spanish words and their Tsotsil equivalents—composed by anonymous Dominican friars working in Chiapas—includes more than eighty metaphors[45] that refer to the heart. As the records show, this dictionary is "a testament to the Mayans' deep reverence for what they believe to be the locus of all that is human. Repentance, for example, is expressed in five different Tsotsil metaphors: 'my heart cries,' 'my heart grows small,' 'my heart hurts,' 'my heart withdraws,' and 'my heart becomes two.'"[46] Hence, the threads outlined in the poems noted above, which tie Tsotsil with a Mayan reverence for the heart and an Indigenous kinship to the land, render Mayan *ṣumūd* palpable. This is precisely the linguistic revindication that Betan achieves, because, *from* the omnipresent moon to "poetry [that] sings ... to time," Tsotsil is depicted in its timeless glory as the language that transcends and unites, above all else.

The Linguistic Erasure of Palestine: A Historical Overview

As a minoritized, subalternized, and racialized language, Arabic in Israel shares an affinity with Tsotsil in Chiapas. However, these different forms of structural inferiorization of Arabic have developed in a markedly different context of language vitality and colonial trajectory. Unlike the recent alphabetic revitalization of Tsotsil, Arabic did not necessitate inventing a writing system to promote literacy. As Yasir Suleiman reminds us, "Palestinians had no language project of their own because of their linguistic homogeneity, and this includes the indigenous Palestinian Jewry. Arabic in its multiple varieties was a living language in need of no revival."[47] Indeed, before 1948, Arabic in its standard form was used in schools, the press, and literary production. In this respect, a recent study on the history of Palestinian literature before 1948 by Ibrahim Mahfouz and Refqa Abu-Remaileh portrays the cultural loss that resulted from the events of the Nakba in terms of an "apocalyptic scale."[48] The decimation of the literary infrastructure, they remark, brought a premature end to a Palestinian literary *Nahda* (awakening or renaissance) that was taking place in the 1930s and 1940s with an upsurge in *adab maqālāt* (periodical literature).[49]

The material and symbolic devaluation of Arabic, which fits squarely within a longer history of the de-Arabization of Palestine, was and continues to be an ideological cornerstone of the Zionist settler colonial project and its vision of Israel as an exclusive ethno-religious state. Whereas the imposition of Spanish in postconquest Mesoamerica evolved in tandem with the conversion of the natives to Catholicism, the religious purity of the state as Jewish was upheld through the twin process of making Hebrew its official national language and the dissolution of Arabic as a native language.

Historian Nur Masalha traces the origins of the de-Arabization of Palestine to the late nineteenth-century Zionist ideology in Europe during the height of social-scientific racism and social Darwinism. The Zionist romantic resurrection of Hebrew as a secular language pertinent to modern nation-building entailed the incorporation of the colonialization of Palestine within the conquest tradition of the Hebrew Bible.[50] That is why, Masalha adds, early Zionists constructed a mythical narrative based on a common vernacular language and a shared past to bring together Jewish settlers from diverse ethnic, linguistic, and cultural backgrounds. In addition, they de-Arabized Palestine through a reconstruction of its heritage as uniquely centered in an ethnolinguistic understanding of Judaism.[51]

Already by the turn of the twentieth century, early signs of Zionist attempts to foreground the domination of Hebrew in the future Jewish state became facts on the ground in Historic Palestine. Such attempts were undertaken by pro-Hebrew Zionists in the 1910s and socialist Zionists during the British Mandate period in the 1920s. During what came to be known as the "Language War" in 1913, pro-Hebrew Zionists defeated a proposal of Jewish students from the German-run schools to use German to teach science and technology in a tertiary-level institute of technology in Haifa. According to Suleiman, the success of the pro-Hebrew activists speaks to the strength of their movement, especially after their wide recruitment of the Jewish students from the German-run schools to their demonstrations. This fact, Sulieman adds, "indicates the degree of mobilization which the pro-Hebrew Zionist movement had achieved among the Jews in Palestine then."[52] Oddly enough, and in contrast to the pro-Hebrew Zionists, socialist Zionists used Arabic to elicit Palestinian support of their politics. In 1925 the *Histadrut* (General Organization of Workers in Israel) launched a series of weekly publications in Arabic with a press run of five hundred copies distributed free to Arab railway workers. The content of these publications showed no interest in either the Arabic language or Arab culture. On the contrary, they aimed at assimilating Arab workers into socialist Zionism by countering the strongly anti-Zionist stance of most of the Arabic press and spreading propaganda through translation of works by socialist authors who endorsed the Jewish state, like Ferdinand Lassele, or European writers, such as Oscar Wilde.[53]

In a related vein, Lital Levy asserts that in the case of Hebrew, "it was not even the state that created the language, so much as the *language* that created the state."[54] In its pre-state stage, this tendency, she emphasizes, involved not only the reinvention of a traditional and liturgical biblical Hebrew as noted above, but also an Orientalist fascination of early European (Ashkenazi) Zionist settlers and literary figures with Arabic as a model of "authenticity." [55]In an attempt to proclaim indigeneity, both groups appropriated Arabic words and cultural symbols, thus self-fashioning a "Hebrew Bedouin" identity. Regardless of these contradictory ideological attitudes toward Arabic, the performative acts of "going native" lasted throughout the formative years of the Jewish state, thus foregrounding a Eurocentric narrative of Hebrew modernity that systematically diminished Arabic—both the Palestinian vernacular and the Arabic of Mizrahi Jews—casting it as a subordinate and a threatening counter-language to Modern Hebrew. In effect, Arabic came to signify not merely the language of the enemy, but a racialized marker of the dangerous Other.[56]

It is worth mentioning here that recently the figure of the "Hebrew Bedouin" has undergone a more blatant colonial revival. As the Israeli journalist Amira Hass reports, a nascent group of armed Zionist settlers living in the Occupied West Bank that identifies itself as the "Jewish Shepherd" organized in 2023 virtual classes for its volunteers to study spoken Arabic with the objective of expelling Palestinians more efficiently. After attending a class for journalistic-reporting purposes, Hass recounts the instructions given in the course by Shabtay Kushelevsky, one of the founders of a Jewish militia and an owner of an illegal farm in the Occupied West Bank: "Of course the shepherd will also know the language spoken in the field, the Arab shepherd who shouts something, or the clan you meet along the way. If we want to take hold of the land and own it, knowing the language is an important part of being the landlord."[57]

The imposition and institutionalization of modern Hebrew as a defining characteristic of the ethno-nationalist monolingual Jewish state was sustained in the early years of the Israeli state in the 1950s and was consolidated further to affirm its hegemonic position today as the only official language. Alongside the ethnic cleansing of Palestine and the destruction of its geography in the Nakba in 1948, Israel established its linguistic coloniality through a spatial and cultural erasure of Arabic. This de-Arabization, as Yasir Suleiman, Muhammad Amara, and Camelia Suleiman, among others, demonstrate,[58] began in the domain of education through the omission of Arabic and Palestinian literary works from the curriculum designed for Palestinian public schools. It expanded further, as Ismail Nashef highlights, in the state's institutionalization of a structural arena for Arabic based on a rewriting of the social history of the language, controlling its variation and expropriating its semiotic means of production and its products from the collective ownership of Palestinians in Israel.[59] It extended as well to the land itself by altering the maps of Historic Palestine through a Judaization of the names of places. The driving force behind this settler colonial move was to obliterate the deep linguistic ties between Palestinians and their land, and instead impose Hebrew to claim Jewish indigeneity and ownership of the land.

Moreover, the absence of Arabic from the linguistic landscape of the lived environment demarcated a border of racial segregation between Jews and non-Jews, and to a certain extent between Ashkenazim and Mizrahim within a Jewish-only space. After 1967, this de-Arabization became even more entrenched, as the Zionist settler colonial state annexed the West Bank including Gaza (until then under Egyptian administration), the part of Palestine not conquered in 1948, which became the West Bank of the Kingdom of Jordan, and the Syrian Golan Heights. The numerous wars that Israel has launched with these neighboring countries since then and its ongoing settler colonial expansion in all Historic Palestine created a conflict zone in which Arabic became racialized twice. First, it was Orientalized and demonized as the language of a dangerous enemy. Second, it was militarized due to its association with national security. As Yonatan Mendel shows, during the pre-state period, and especially during the years 1936–48, the seeds for using Arabic as a security tool for the Zionist project were already planted. The connection between Arabic studies and security was strengthened further in the following years when Arabic and Arab culture in the young state were permissible only as long as they operated within clearly defined Zionist boundaries and where they contributed to the state's pressing political and security needs. This orientation, Mendel emphasizes, was harnessed further in the Israeli education system, where Arabic "underwent an unofficial process of foreignisation and perhaps even Ashkenazisation and Europinisation [sic]."[60] This process, which was initiated by the leaders of the Zionist project (mainly its Ashkenazi elite, who were actively engaged in differentiating themselves culturally from the Arab world), culminated in the production of a new "type" of Arabic. As Mendel concludes, this unique "type" of Arabic "served as a barrier that separated Jews who studied Arabic from the object of their studies—Palestinians and other Arabic-speaking communities."[61]

One of the most recent developments in the ongoing structural erasure of Arabic took place in 2018 when the Israeli Knesset annulled a 1922 law from the period of the British Mandate that recognized Arabic as the official language. Promulgating the Basic Law: Israel as the Nation-State of the Jewish People,[62] according to which Israel is not the homeland of all its citizens but the "national home of the Jewish people," Hebrew was reinstated as the sole language of the state and Arabic was relegated to a "special status" whose use in state institutions or contacts with them "shall be prescribed by law."[63] This juridical subalternization of Palestinian citizens and Arabic speaks volumes to the exclusionary logic of the settler colonial Zionist state. Read in light of the legal recognition that Tsotsil was granted in 2002 under the LGDLPI, which declared that all Indigenous languages in Mexico and those coming from the peoples existing in the national territory before the establishment of the Mexican sate are an integral part of the national cultural and linguistic heritage, the depth of the structural racist systems set to enforce the minoritization of Palestinians and the denial of their national collectivity becomes abundantly clear. Comparatively speaking, this means that Arabic in Israel is even more minoritized than Tsotsil in Chiapas.

In his autobiography, *An Takuna 'Arabiyyan fī Isrā'īl* (To be an Arab in Israel, 1975), the writer, public intellectual, and cofounder of the Arab Writer's Union in 1958, Fouzi El-Asmar, provides testimony in respect to the first manifestation of the minoritization of Arabic in the post-state era, namely in the domain of education. Describing the transformation of the educational system in the early 1950s from the British system that existed during the Mandate Palestine period to the Israeli matriculation program, El-Asmar notes the general lack of textbooks in Arabic and the systematic elimination of works by Palestinian authors and poets. The material taught instead, he adds, featured a set of Hebrew texts by Zionist patriotic poets, such as by Bialik, Ahad ha-Am, Shim'oni, and Pertez, among others, along with the Bible and a scant collection of poems about nature, love, mediation, and similar carefully selected topics from Arabic literature that lacked any patriotic feeling and had no national tone. El-Asmar writes: "It seemed to us that we studied the Bible in order to learn that Palestine was not our land but that of the Jews, and that the Jewish people were the chosen people. Although we had to study numerous chapters of the Bible, the curriculum didn't provide at all for the study of the Koran."[64]

In respect to shedding Arabic from the identity of Arab Jews, the cultural theorist Ella Habiba Shohat, a daughter of Iraqi parents who migrated to Israel in the 1950s and one of the first thinkers to expose the de-Arabization of the Mizrahim, evokes the metaphors of taboo, dislocation, and schism to capture the cultural and linguistic displacement of the Arab Jew vis-à-vis the cultural and racial hegemony of Ashkenazim:

> In Israel, partly because my parents' culture was that of the enemy, my family felt out of place. My parents used to say: "In Iraq we were Jews, and in Israel we are Arabs." Our Arab culture was taboo. Yet, even if we tried, we could not easily escape the mark of otherness. It was written all over our bodies, looks, accents. . . . Being raised between Arabic and Hebrew was far from being a situation of happy bilingualism. It was a conflictual linguistic experience, where my school language was at war with my home language, which we were expected to forget and erase. This schism nourished my fantasies of an elsewhere. Israel may have been a land of many immigrants and displaced people, but it was never a multicultural democracy. It was a centralized nation-state dominated by the ideology of modernization that permitted only Eurocentric narratives of belonging.[65]

The link between the militarization of Arabic and the racialization of its speakers as a security threat was foregrounded during the Martial Law period between 1948 and 1966. The direct surveillance that prevailed during this period entailed sanctions, censorship, and indirect monitoring of the Palestinian education system. In addition to enforcing restrictions on movement, political organization, and access to means of livelihood,[66] the military government outlawed literary publications in Arabic that were deemed a security threat. For example, Mahmoud Darwish and Tawfiq Zayyad—two preeminent poets who led the resistance poetry front with their anticolonial traditionally rhymed poems and electrifying performance at the poetry festivals that bloomed in Palestinian villages in the Galilee in the 1950s and 1960s—were detained and harassed. In fact, Darwish was targeted by the continuous harassment of the General Security Service (*Shin Bet*), a special military unit established in 1949 to surveille Palestinians and crack down on their literary and political activities. After repeated investigations by the military ruler and imprisonments, Darwish tragically left the country in 1971 to spend the rest of his life in exile. In his memoir, *Yawmiyyāt al-Ḥuzn al-ʿĀdī* (*Journal of an Ordinary Grief*, 1973), a personal account that depicts his life in that period, he writes: "I threw a poem at the conqueror's car, and it blew them up. They arrested me and charged me with mass murder."[67] During his incarceration in 1955, Zayyad, on the other hand, was punished for singing Arab folk songs from the 1936–39 revolt against the British, the leftist anthem "The International," and an Arabic translated version, "Peoples of the East," of the following lines from the Soviet Russian "Partisan Song": "They dispersed us in exile / and filled that prison with us / but nights will come / whose lightning will herald your demise."[68] The guards who sent him to solitary confinement accused him of using Arab nationalist slogans. In line with these punitive and oppressive actions, the military government, aided by the *Shin Bet,* regularly arrested and expelled writers and teachers from their government jobs for speaking out against Zionism and the appearance of their texts in the Arabic-speaking communist press.[69] To prevent contact with Palestinian refugees and families across the boundaries of the so-called Green Line border and Arab culture more broadly, they also arrested poets and writers who smuggled in books from neighboring Arabic-speaking countries. The poet Rashid Hussein (1936–1977), for instance, was arrested and imprisoned "for the high crime of possessing six issues of an Egyptian newspaper and two copies of a Lebanese magazine."[70] This process of the militarization of Arabic went hand in hand with the militarization of the border.

Given this historical account of de-Arabization, it is thus hardly surprising that for the first post-Nakba generation of Palestinian writers, writing in Arabic was overwhelmingly conceived as an Indigenous struggle. The poet Hanna Abu-Hanna (1928–2022), who came to be known as *ḥāris al-lugha al-ʿarabiyya* (the guardian of Arabic), thanks to his great influence on the preservation of Arabic as a poet and a language teacher for generations of Arabic teachers, cultural activists, and poets—including members from the resistance poets movement of the 1960s—captures what is at stake in this struggle in the following words: "Land *(al-'arḍ)* and language *(al-lugha)* ... are the two essential bases for the preservation of our existence."⁷¹ Strikingly, by drawing a link between land and language in his framing of the plight against de-Arabization of Palestine, Abu-Hanna not only situates Palestinian literature as Indigenous literature, but also establishes *ṣumūd* as its foundational paradigm. But how did Palestinian writers handle this double struggle? How did they configure indigeneity in light of this connection between land and language? The answer to these questions, as I will detail in the next section, lies largely in what I call "the linguistic revindication of Palestine." This approach, which was wholeheartedly adopted by the first post-Nakba generation of Palestinian writers who were acutely aware of the precarious status of Arabic in the newly founded settler state, considered Arabic an endangered native language. In fact, this outlook on Arabic is entirely analogous to how Mayan writers viewed Tsotsil. However, in the Palestinian case, the plight to save Arabic did not involve revitalization, but rather a process of preservation that was based on consistent collective attempts to reconnect it with its long-standing pre-Nakba presence as the lingua franca of Historic Palestine. To repair the local, national, and civilizational links that Arabic had before 1948, Palestinian writers reappropriated Arabic with a distinct revolutionary vigor and a reassertion of the close affinity between the language and the land. By redeeming the temporal and geographical imaginary of Arabic, they created a literary landscape of *ṣumūd*, thus deepening the roots of contemporary Palestinian literature. In the process, they challenged the Zionist ideologies that racialized the language and the settler colonial boundaries that reduced it to a minorized space and a subalternized position.

It would be misleading to think that Palestinian writers from this generation and succeeding generations did not experiment with writing in other languages, including writing in Hebrew—and to a lesser extent English—while still taking part in the linguistic revindication of Palestine.⁷² The early Hebrew poems of Anton Shammas (1950–), alongside his much-celebrated novel *Arabesques* (1998), are prominent examples. According to Lital Levy, Shammas's poems in Hebrew and those of his contemporaries Salman Masalha (1953–) and Na'im 'Araidi (1950–) are seminal works because of their embedded intertextuality. By incorporating biblical allusions and Jewish textuality in their verses, an act that Levy terms as "Palestinian midrash," these poets trespassed the religious limits of Hebrew and "transformed[ed]" the association of the Hebrew language with Judaism.⁷³ Although this mode of resistance cannot be dismissed, it is important to note the limited scope of writings in Hebrew. Indeed, the current literary scene of Palestinian literature produced in Hebrew is largely kept alive by a handful of novelists and media figures, namely Sayed Kashua (1975–) and Ayman Sikseck (1984–). Nevertheless, recent years have seen a notable rise in Palestinian writers, particularly journalists and academics, producing nonfiction essays, op-eds, and political analysis in Hebrew, especially in left-leaning Israeli media outlets, such as *Haaretz* and *Sicha Mekomit*.

I believe that the ongoing Nakba and the exclusionary structure of Israel as a Jewish state based on racial, religious, and cultural segregation are the main reasons why the wave of composing Palestinian literature in Hebrew did not grow exponentially since the 1960s and 1970s. This also applies to writers and poets who engaged regularly with Hebrew through translations, intellectual debates, journalistic publications, and joint political work with their Jewish counterparts in communist and leftist-Zionist circles. Especially notable is the case of Darwish and Hussein, who became spokesmen for the Palestinian Liberation Organization (PLO), in Beirut and New York, respectively, in the 1960s and 1970s after being exiled. Both poets continued to publish works in Arabic despite their ability to write in Hebrew and their close familiarity with the inner workings of Israeli politics and society, which they circulated in the Arab world[74] in Arabic through the press of the PLO. The fact that both poets shared a preference for producing literary and cultural texts in Arabic before and after working at the center of the Palestinian revolution and participating in solidarity discourses that extend from celebrating the triumph of Pan-Arabism against Western hegemony to the decolonization of Algeria and Congo merits attention.[75] As Maha Nassar points out, Darwish, for example, was very interested in the decolonial aspect of francophone literature in Algeria. He admired how francophone Algerians writers who—like himself—had been cut off from their Arab heritage contested French rule using the language of colonial power. Despite that, he still favored writing in Arabic.

The Land Speaks Arabic:
Preserving Language in Landscapes of Erasure

For the first post-Nakba generation of Palestinian writers who witnessed firsthand the material destruction of Historic Palestine and its territorial erasure, the struggle to preserve Arabic from total loss was not merely a matter of political equity. On the contrary, it was an existential battle for human and cultural survival. The structural foundations for the settler colonial state were being erected across the geography of Historic Palestine, and the status of Arabic in this land was more precarious than ever. The imposition of Hebrew as the dominant language of the newly founded Jewish state alongside a military rule

(1949–66) not only entailed the institutionalization of minoritization, subalternization, and racialization, and thus second-class citizenship, but also reinforced systematic dispossession, exclusion, and discrimination. The subsequent annexation and Judaization of Palestinian land after the June 1967 War, together with the expropriation of thousands of donums of Palestinian land in 1976[76]—a settler colonial policy that Palestinians responded to with nationwide protests and strikes, which were countered by the Israeli police killing six citizens—endangered further the topography of Arabic. Figuratively speaking, Arabic was vanishing along with the forcefully disappeared landscape.

With this historical context in mind, the impetus to write Palestinian narratives in Arabic was less of a choice and more of an urgency. Yet, for foundational Palestinian writers from this generation, such as Emile Habibi (1922–1996), a novelist and a towering figure in rebuilding Palestinian literary culture in Arabic after the Nakba, as well as the poets Zayyad and Darwish, the question was not simply about writing in Arabic, but rather the type of Arabic to use and the way to disseminate texts written in Arabic to save both Palestine and Palestinians from the violence of settler colonial erasure. When it comes to this deployment of Arabic as an Indigenous language, it is no coincidence, then, that the work of these eminent writers—who are very different from each other in terms of style—displays a common assertion of the strong correlation between linguistic preservation, cultural resistance, and political mobilization to stay on the land.

Arabic is not a monolithic language. There are multiple versions of Arabic: Classical Arabic of the Quran and Islamic exegesis and practices, a language deeply rooted in the literary heritage of pre-Islamic Arabia; Modern Standard Arabic (MSA), a standardized literary Arabic that developed in the late nineteenth and early twentieth centuries in response to the rise of modernization and Arab nationalism; and colloquial Arabic, an everyday language with a wide range of local and regional variations. Where both Classical Arabic and MSA are commonly referred to as *fuṣḥa* by Arabic speakers, colloquial Arabic is broadly known as *'amiyya*. Since the mid-twentieth century, and due to European colonialism and globalization, there has been an increase in code-switching and border crossing across these varieties.

However, for Habibi and Zayyad, the construction of a post-Nakba Palestinian literary tradition had to be in *fuṣḥa*. Texts written in *fuṣḥa*, they insisted, were necessary for the preservation of a Palestinian and Arab national culture. As a tool of linguistic resistance, *fuṣḥa*, they contended, counters the double political and epistemological erasure of Arabic. As two communist writer-politicians, both Habibi and Zayyad did not consider *fuṣḥa* as an impediment to the emancipatory political project of the folk, in this case, the Palestinian masses who spoke ʿamiyya. In an interview with Habibi in 1996, the last before his death that year, he continued to defend his choice of *fuṣḥa*:

> More important than anything, I worship the Arabic language! I love it! I may not be different than others in this matter, but what separates me from other writers, is that I don't go to the printing house with my manuscript unless I make sure first that the language is correct. And because we live in a society that contaminates our language, I feel ready to write a literary work. I go back to read the classics, mainly the Quran.[77]

Habibi's use of the word "contamination" is an explicit reference to both the threat that Arabic faces as a minoritized language and its susceptibility to colonial distortion and appropriation. Zayyad deploys a similar language to explain his attempt to salvage Palestinian and oral tradition by documenting it in *fuṣḥa* instead of the Palestinian ʿamiyya vernacular, the language in which it was originally narrated and circulated. In ʿAn al-Adab wa-al-Adab al-Shaʿbī fī Filasṭīn (On literature and folk literature in Palestine, 1970) he urges his fellow Palestinians to document the rich historical and geographical diversity of Palestinian folk repertoire, which includes stories of struggles against the Turks and the British, lullabies, wedding songs, donkey drivers' cheers, fishermen's chants, and anecdotes of peasants in the rural villages of the Galilee and the Triangle. To preserve this "treasure of folklore," he insists, Palestinians should not resort to a "disfigured language," but rather 'translate' their folklore into *fuṣḥa*, "the proper correct language," as he describes it.[78] As a communist writer who took on himself the mission of documenting the oral tradition of his people to save it from colonial erasure, Zayyad privileges the use of *fuṣḥa* over the local vernacular. The shift in language register that he calls for here, in my view, does not deny the voices of the Palestinian peasants, the people whose rights he defended throughout his careers as a politician and a poet. On the contrary, what we observe is an attempt to elevate the status of Palestinian folklore as a national patrimony by collapsing the discursive registers of *fuṣḥa* with the national. Although Zayyad attributes his decision to abandon ʿamiyya to aesthetic considerations, his dedicated efforts to retrieve and revitalize the cultural heritage of Historic Palestine aligns seamlessly with his lifelong project of countering the de-Arabization of Palestine.

Along these lines, the keen interest in the linguistic revindication of Palestine extended to the realm of excavation in the *turāth* (tradition or heritage) of Arabic literature and its historical roots in Palestine. Abu-Hanna, who was an advocate for Arabic education, and a chief editor and cofounder of Palestinian literary magazines such as *al-Jadīd* (The New) in 1951 and *al-Ghad* (Tomorrow), observes that he and his peers compiled a list of prominent Arab poets, explorers, literati, and religious scholars who were born in Palestine a millennium ago and who were named after their villages and towns, such as Kashjem Al-Ramli (n.d.–971), who was born Al-Ramla; Ibn al-Qaysarani (1058–1153), who grew up in Caesarea; and Abu Ishaq al-Ghazi (1023–1130), who was born in Gaza, among others. Such efforts, he asserts, were driven by a deep commitment to recall the rich and deep history of Arab culture in Palestine and at the same time to counter the Zionist claim that Palestine was a land without a people.[79]

By cementing the linkage between Arabic and the land, those who participated in the linguistic revindication of Palestine were seeking to restore Palestinian subjectivity and territory. Precisely for this reason, we must consider the work of the first generation of Palestinian writers for the pivotal role that they have played in this regard. As Ghassan Kanafani reminds us, the resistance literature that this generation wrote between 1948 and 1966 galvanized a revolutionary vision that shaped the distinctive Palestinian nationalism that emerged after the June 1967 War,[80] which, alongside the Nakba, constitutes another key moment of historical and geographical rupture. In a related vein, Manar Makhoul's study of Palestinian fiction in Israel between 1948 and 1967 demonstrates that, despite the existence of paradoxical discourses concerning Palestinian identity and modernization in canonical novels from that period vis-à-vis Zionist-Israeli discourses of modernization, these fictional narratives grappled with Arabic and its capacity to address the shifting sociopolitical landscape and the domination of Hebrew that was imposed to formulate the idea that Israel was a modern nation-state. This tendency, Makhoul points out, was most salient in the early works of Tawfiq Muʿammar (1914–1988), particularly the novels that focused on the portrayal of the struggle for the memory of the 1948 war. The novelist's enhanced use of lexical structures in Arabic to articulate a Palestinian national discourse that centers "Palestinian Indigenous rights for self-determination and independent from any foreign power" is an illustrative example.[81] This trend suggests that the linguistic revindication of Palestine is inherently decolonial.

Some Palestinian critics, though, question the ability of Arabic in Israel to reclaim anything. Nashef, for example, insists that Arabic in Israel is still colonized because it exists outside a nation-state despite being a national language. He even goes as far as arguing that Arabic has no structure of resistance, because it is a byproduct of a compulsive literacy mode that emerged as a reaction to the excessive literacy mode of Zionism, which serves as a superstructure that reads/writes the Palestinians in Israel. In this structural area, Nashef contends, Palestinians remain trapped. The Nakba, he adds, "created a situation whereby they lost their ability to lose, denying them the possibility of constituting an independent collective."[82] This loss, he concludes, is part of their elimination as natives.[83]

To a certain extent, I tend to agree with Nashef's assessment that Arabic in Israel is entangled in the colonial infrastructure founded by the settler colonial state. The contemporary Palestinian cultural sphere, including Palestinian literary criticism, NGOs, activists, Arabic studies departments in Israeli universities, and Arab language academics and teachers, continues to operate within the sociologistic arena of "Israeli-Arabic." However, we must not overlook the parallel sphere in which Palestinians in Israel engaged with Arabic outside this infrastructure and beyond the hegemonic dominance of print culture as the sole model of literacy. My point here is not only about recognizing the structural dynamics of spoken Arabic that evade this colonial trap, but also about acknowledging the rich tradition of unwritten Arabic, or to borrow the Mayan term, *ts'íib*, the broader system of nontextual and nonverbal forms of expressions. Accordingly, we must consider the dense use of Palestinian Arabic in recording oral traditions, folktales, transmission of ancestral knowledge, and other embodied practices of salvaging the collective memory of the Palestinian subject and the stolen fractured land of Palestine from erasure. In this regard, Palestinians in Israel have a salient *'ulfa–kuxlej/kuxlejal* with Mayans in Chiapas and Indigenous Peoples in other settler colonial contexts where language, subjectivity, and land are deeply intertwined, if not inseparable.

In relating the incident when the Spanish conquistador Luis Marín invaded several towns in Chiapas to steal land and subjugate the native Mayans, Arturo Arías remarks how the Tsotsil-speaking people of Chamula revolted by forming an armed resistance front and calling themselves *batsil winik'otik*, or "true men,"[84] thus identifying themselves with Tsotsil, or *Bats'i k'op (La verdada lengua, the language of the true people)*. Parallel incidents occurred in Palestinian villages that gangs of Zionist settlers destroyed and depopulated in 1948. As Susan Slymovics points out in her study of memorial books from these villages, people from the village of Ruways, for instance, took the surname Ruwaysi—someone from Ruways—instead of the customary clan eponymic.[85] By replacing the name of their clan with that of their original village, the Ruwaysis, who became present-absentees as internal refugees in Historic Palestine after the Nakba, created a new structure of kinship based on their affiliation with their ancestral land and village solidarity. From a strictly linguistic point of view, both incidents reveal a similar pattern of resistance to erasure and the revindication of the Indigenous subject. This resistance is translated into the identification of language and land.

One of the central stages where the linguistic revindication of Palestine gained momentum was the poetry festivals that Zayyad co-organized together with other communist Palestinian writers and poets,[86] who later became known as *shu'arā' al-muqāwama* (Resistance Poets). Inspired by socialist realism, these festivals, which took place in Palestinian villages, like traditional Palestinian weddings, were political/populist/literary events, although often replete with danger for those who attended them in "violation" of military rule for traveling without permits and reciting anticolonial poetry. Abu-Hanna, who played a leading role in the organization of these festivals, which were affectively dramatic and subversive in their reclamation of a Palestinian public space, pointed out that the focus was on delivering the political message, because the poetry that was performed was meant to reach the people directly. If no venue was available, he added, the festival would take place under the sky, and that was "a violation of another law."[87]

The salient sense of urgency that underscored this poetry, coupled with the need to write for the "masses," propelled the poets to use the 'amūdi form of Arabic prosody.[88] This rhyme scheme, however, a traditional form of Arabic consisting of hemistiches of equal length or metrical pattern, was abandoned by their contemporary peer Arab poets, who experimented with modernizing Arabic poetry by means of al-shi'r al-ḥurr (free verse), which naturalizes the construction of lines to fit the natural flow of thought. Even more, "the traditional sound structures, the pre-modern rhythmical architecture of verse remained intact when the poetic product was initially erected on a modern ideology of socialist realism."[89] By turning to 'amūdi poetry, these Palestinian poets paid homage to the classics in Arabic poetry and at the same time affirmed their position as being both Indigenous and Marxist poets, leading the frontline of ṣumūd through a deepening of their linguistic attachment to the homeland, while also appealing to the Palestinian and Arab masses with a clear call for collective mobilization against oppression and colonialism. It is worth mentioning that many of the poems that were recited in these festivals became popular songs later, because of the rhyming schemes and regular rhythms of the 'amūdi form, which makes it easy to remember the verses and is also conducive to being set to music.

If we were to translate the motto "To exist is to resist" into poetry, then Zayyad's poem "Hunā bāqūn" (Here we shall remain, 1965)[90] would be its most accurate adaptation. Thanks to its spoken-word style and Zayyad's fierce performance, this iconic ṣumūd poem gained national popularity and became a symbolic anthem for Palestinians in Israel. The repetition of the lines "As if we were twenty impossibilities in Lydda, Ramla, and the Galilee" alludes to the stubborn existence of Palestinians who remained on their land despite the Judaization of the villages and towns in the Galilee, as well as Lydda and Ramla, towns depopulated and destroyed in 1948. The source for this stubbornness, as the speaker in the poem implies, resides in the spiritual attachment of Palestinians to the features of their land: the olive tree, the fig tree, rocks, dirt. Likewise, the imagery of remaining rooted in the land is conveyed in the motif of sacrifice across generations. The collective willingness to die for the land is emphasized in the "we" that speaks assertively about shedding blood to maintain the ancestral connection with the land across past, present, and future generations.

Here We Shall Remain[91]   هنا باقون

Like twenty impossibilities	كأننا عشرون مستحيل
In Lydda, Ramla, and the Galilee	في اللد ، والرملة ، والجليل
Here ... we shall remain like a wall on your chests,	هنا .. على صدوركم ، باقون كالجدار
In your throats,	وفي حلوقكم
Like a shard of glass, like a cactus thorn	كقطعة الزجاج ، كالصبار
And in your eyes,	وفي عيونكم
A whirlwind of fire	زوبعة من نار
Here ... we shall remain like a wall on your chests,	هنا .. على صدوركم ، باقون كالجدار
We wash the dishes in your bars,	ننظف الصحون في الحانات
And pour drinks for the masters,	ونملأ الكؤوس للسادات
We mop the floors in the black kitchens,	ونمسح البلاط في المطابخ السوداء
To snatch a piece of bread for our children	حتى نستل لقمة الصغار
From your blue fangs[92]	من بين أنيابكم الزرقاء

Here ... we shall remain like a wall on your chests	هنا غلى صدوركم باقون ، كالجدار
We may starve	نجوع .. نعرى .. نتحدى
We may go hungry	ننشد الأشعار
And go without clothes	ونملأ الشوارع الغضاب بالمظاهرات
Yet we chant poems	ونملأ السجون كبرياء
Fill the angry streets with demonstrations	ونصنع الأطفال .. جيلا ثائرا .. وراء جيل
And the prisons with pride	
And we produce children—one revolutionary generation	
After generation ...	

The defiant tone of the speaker who expresses in direct speech the insubordination of the colonized native vis-à-vis the oppression of the settler colonizer persists throughout the poem. A clear distinction between the settler and the native is made through the use of "we" versus "you." This distinction is emphasized further in the lines that describe the asymmetrical class and racial dynamics between the two. The racialization of Palestinians as exploited workers whose jobs constitute servitude is emphasized in the imagery of cleaners mopping "black kitchens" and pouring drinks for the "masters." The line "To snatch a piece of bread ... from your blue fangs" employs strong language together with a critique of the presumed racial superiority of the European Zionist settler. While "snatch" alludes to the exploitative labor conditions that Palestinians are subjugated to, "your blue fangs" emphasizes the savagery of the colonizer settler.

In the second part of the poem, specifically the last stanza, the speaker's voice strikes a more militant tone. The celebration of persistence and perseverance in the first part of the poem shifts into professing faith in a future victory that the speaker foresees for the colonized. This victory, as the imperative phrase "Read . . . the Book" in the last line suggests, will come from either the Divine justice promised in the Holy Books or the proletarian revolution delineated in Marx's *Capital*. Although "the Book" can refer to any book, the interpretation suggested here considers the political function of this poem and its public performance within the broader anticolonial and socialist context of the Resistance Poets movement. Moreover, the fierceness of Zayyad's *ṣumūd* poetry is unmistakably evident in both the assertive short title of this poem and the fact that he did not engage in verbal evasion throughout his political career as a representative of the Communist Party in the Israeli Knesset and as the mayor of Nazareth.

Like twenty impossibilities	كأننا عشرون مستحيل
In Lydda, Ramla, and the Galilee	في اللد ، والرملة ، والجليل
Here, we shall remain.	إنا هنا باقون
You may drink the sea;	فلتشربوا البحرا
We shall guard the shade of the fig and the olive tree	نحرس ظل التين والزيتون
Planting ideas	ونزرع الأفكار ، كالخمير في العجين
Like yeast in the dough	برودة الجليد في أعصابنا
The coldness of ice in our nerves	وفي قلوبنا جهنم حمرا
And a burning hell in our hearts	إذا عطشنا نعصر الصخرا
We squeeze rock to quench our thirst	ونأكل التراب إن جعنا .. ولا نرحل
And if we starve	وبالدم الزكي لا نبخل .. لا نبخل .. لا نبخل
We eat the dirt	هنا .. لنا ماض .. وحاضر .. ومستقبل
But we will not leave	
Our redolent blood we don't spare . . . we don't spare . . . We don't spare	
Here—we have a past . . . a present . . . and a future.	

Like twenty impossibilities	كأننا عشرون مستحيل
In Lydda, Ramla, and the Galilee	في اللد ، والرملة ، والجليل
Oh, our living roots, hold firmly!	يا جذرنا الحي تشبث
And let our origins strike deeply into the earth.	واضربي في القاع يا أصول
Let the oppressor review his accounts	أفضل أن يراجع المضطهد الحساب
Before the turn of the wheel.	من قبل أن ينفتل الدولاب
For every action: . . . Read	لكل فعل: ... إقرأوا
What's written in the Book	ما جاء في الكتاب

The early poetry of Darwish, namely, his seminal poem "Biṭāqatu huwiyya / بطاقة هوية" (ID card, 1964), which starts with the assertive statement "Write down, I am an Arab," is composed using a similarly vigorous and politically charged language. Certainly, the obstinacy with which these two poets and their comrades from the Resistance Poets movement expressed the spirit of *ṣumūd* galvanized a distinctive Palestinian vernacular of Arabic. However, for Darwish, who became a refugee in 1948 after Zionist forces destroyed his village El Birweh in the Galilee, and who was imprisoned later for writing in Arabic against the settler colonial violence that uprooted his people and destroyed his homeland, the intimate link between language and land is a distinctive element of how Palestinians perceive their indigeneity. Drawing on the connection between linguistic dislocation and territorial displacement, Darwish developed his own philosophical approach for conveying the correlation between being native and writing in a native tongue. The contrast between linguistic location and dislocation that undergirds his meditative poetics of indigeneity and exile, from which he wrote after he left Palestine in 1971, is an illustrative example of this correlation. While Darwish's lines "the land is inherited, like language" and "I am my language" are often quoted as a reflection of the metaphysical link between language, land, and identity, I opt for other examples from his earlier work, *Yawmiyyāt al-Ḥuzn al-ʿĀdī* (*Journal of an Ordinary Grief*, 1973), where he initially establishes this link.

In this memoir, a primary example of the earliest conceptualization of indigeneity is evident. Here, he fashions Indigenous subjectivity by stitching together an intimate and reciprocal relationship between language and land. In this relationship, language emanates not from the vocabulary of nationalism, but rather from a deep spiritual sense of belonging to the land, with all its geographical, topographical, and historical memory. This subjectivity is not rooted in either ancestry or the question of who was here first. It originates, conversely, in the language that articulates the very idea of homeland. To this end, he makes a clear distinction between the poetics of (be)longing of settlers versus natives. He draws a contrast between "longing that comes from afar" (settlers) and "a longing that rises from nearby"[93] (natives). The following exchange between Darwish and an imagined interlocutor summarizes the philosophical underpinnings of this definition.

> So, what is a homeland? You are part of a whole, and the whole is absent and subject to annihilation. And why are you now afraid of saying "homeland is where my ancestors lived"? You reject the pretext of your enemies, for that is what they say.
>
> —What did you learn in school?
> —*Salute the bird returning from the distant land to my window in exile. O bird, tell me, how are my ancestors and my people?*

—And the song that came before that?
—They erased it.
—What are the words of the song they erased?
Salaam to you
Land of my ancestors
In you it's good to dwell
And for you it's good to sing.[94]

There is not a significant difference between the two songs, except for the contrast between "a longing that comes from afar" and a longing that "rises from nearby." Both songs express love for the same land, and both define homeland in terms of ancestry. The first was written by a poet living in Russia (the settler); the second by a poet born in Palestine (the native), who never experienced exile nor heard of it. Yet, within a short period, the first song overshadowed the second, and the second poet began to sing his longing for the distant homeland.[95]

The difference between a song composed to the homeland by a poet who lives in Palestine versus a song composed by a poet who lives in Russia is reflected in the contrast between using *salute* to greet the land in a European language, versus the act of blessing the land with peace by using the greeting of "Salaam" in Arabic. Formally speaking, this distinction is accentuated further in the visual representation of the settler's poem versus the native poem in the text, hence a line versus a stanza. It is also allegorized in the reversed juxtaposition of exile in the image of the Jewish poet in exile erasing the song of the Indigenous Palestinian poet before displacing the latter and forcing him into exile.

This clear distinction is reiterated in later works by Darwish in which he disavows the conflation of the figure of the Zionist settler with that of the Jew vis-à-vis language identity and belonging to the land of Palestine. In response to a question by the Israeli journalist Helith Yeshurun about how exile contributed to transforming his idea of the homeland from a physical place to imagined idea in a fashion similar to exilic Jewish thought, Darwish states:

> The Jew won't be ashamed to find the Arab element within him, and the Arab won't be ashamed to acknowledge that he is also composed of Jewish elements. Especially when speaking about "Eretz Israel" in Hebrew and "Palestine" in Arabic. I am a son of all the cultures that have passed through the land—the Greek, the Roman, the Persian, the Jewish, the Ottoman. A presence that exists at the very core of my language. Every powerful culture passed through and left something. I am the son of all these fathers, but I belong to one mother. Does that

mean that my mother is a prostitute? My mother is this land; she received all of them. She was both a witness and a victim. I am also the son of the Jewish culture that was in Palestine.[96]

While Darwish does not essentialize or conflate Palestinianness with Arabic, he asserts that Zionist settler colonialism cannot Hebrewize the land: "For the Palestinian this is not Eretz Israel. This is Palestine. A foreign body is a foreign body."[97]

Recognizing the threat of effacement embedded in minoritization, subalternization, and racialization, Zayyad and Darwish, and fellow writers from their generation too, reclaimed Arabic as an Indigenous language that prefigures and epitomizes the bond between Palestinians and their land. As precursors in the struggle for a linguistic and a cultural Palestinian continuance in a militarized settler colonial state pursuing an expansionist Zionist vision, they deployed an intentionally heightened affect in the use of Arabic to write ṣumūd. Fifty years later, and after crossing many ḥudūd (borders), this ṣumūd has metamorphosed into a cornerstone of a collective Palestinian spirit of resistance in the homeland and in the global shatāt (diaspora). Moreover, it undergirds contemporary Palestinian narratives in Israel, the great majority of which continues to be written in Arabic.

Conclusion

This chapter began with an ethnographic reflection on the affinity between the fragmented bilingualism and the racialized borders that characterize the minoritization of Tsotsil in Chiapas and Arabic in Israel. The subsequent comparative reading in the divergent processes of the revitalization of Tsotsil versus the preservation of Arabic—both of which were undertaken to counter analogous patterns of inferiorization—showcased a parallel persistence of ṣumūd, despite the different historical trajectories of these processes. Indeed, the significant commonalities between how Mayan and Palestinian poets deployed a heightened affect of Tsotsil and Arabic to resist colonial erasure and to affirm their rootedness in the land illuminates the resemblance between the configurations of indigeneity in Mayan and Palestinian poetics. This 'ulfa-kuxlej/ kuxlejal reveals the comparability of different aspects of the linguistic battles that remain at the heart of the Indigenous struggles in Chiapas and Palestine. More important, it sheds light on the reasons why writing in Tsotsil and Arabic continues to form a mode of cultural resistance to the respective structures of settler colonialism in Chiapas and Palestine in the present.

Indeed, the exploitation of lands and resources in Chiapas and the erasure of indigeneity in Chiapas are still ongoing. In this respect, 2019 was an eventful year. On the one hand, Chiapas was back on the global scene as a critical cultural geography that offers significant insights into the revitalization of Indigenous languages and cultures. Following the United Nations' declaration of the International Year of Indigenous Languages (IY2019), literary festivals and gatherings were held around the world to celebrate Indigenous languages and to advocate for their survival and revitalization. As noted earlier in the chapter, Chiapas celebrated this occasion by hosting an international two-day reunion supported by the Mexican government, titled "Writing the Future of Indigenous Languages," in San Cristóbal / Jobel. On the other hand, Zapatistas regained their global visibility as a decolonial Indigenous social movement. Commemorating the twenty-fifth anniversary of the Zapatista uprising, the Zapatistas resurged with two politically powerful statements.

First, there was a celebration of the enduring quest for Mayan autonomy by declaring major expansions of the Zapatista autonomous territories through the establishment of new *caracoles* (autonomous municipalities) and an almost doubling of the number of *las juntas del buen gobierno* (governing bases). Second, the Zapatistas renewed commitment to the legal battle and cultural war against *el mal gobierno* (the bad government), that is, the Mexican state. To draw attention to the fact that the Indigenous struggle is still ongoing, the Zapatistas organized protests and community gatherings to reaffirm their rejection of the Mayan Train project, one of the most ambitious proposals of President Andrés López Obrador. For the Zapatistas, the construction of the train is a settler colonial encroachment on their autonomous territories, a destruction of Indigenous farmlands, and an endangerment of sacred forests, wildlife, and natural habitat throughout the Yucatán peninsula and Chiapas.[98] To commemorate the ongoing cultural battle against erasure, the Zapatistas organized an international festival titled "Celebration of Life: A December of Resistance and Rebellion." The program of the festival included screenings of films in Mayan languages; dance sessions; political forums that focused on land defense, environmental resistance, and Mother Earth; and a second international meeting for Women Who Struggle; in addition to other encounters that celebrated cultural resistance and the anniversary of the uprising, also known as the "War Against Oblivion." In contrast with the international festival for Indigenous languages that was held in collaboration with the Mexican federal government, the Zapatistas' international festival of resistance and rebellion took place in their autonomous Zapatista communities with no funding from the state, thus aligning with their quest for cultural autonomy. Despite this contrast and the conflict of interest behind it, one thing remains clear: Mayan languages and lands are in a precarious condition because of the settler colonial Mexican state that is deepening its soft power and militarized presence in Chiapas.

While Tsotsil writers and Zapatista rebels—sometimes the same group of people—were engaged in a dual struggle for reappropriation of Mayan languages and lands beyond the coloniality of borders demarcated initially by the Spanish conquest and reinforced later by the Mexican state, Palestinian writers were marking the seventh anniversary of the World Arabic Language Day. This international event was announced by UNESCO on December 28, 2012, in commemoration of the same day in 1973 when the General Assembly of the UN adopted Arabic as the sixth official language of the organization. In honor of World Arabic Language Day, Palestinians in Israel, mainly Arabic language teachers, writers, cultural activists, and religious clerks, organized a series of special educational games, extracurricular programs alongside literary gatherings, poetry readings, folklore and heritage festivals, and other cultural activities. The celebratory events took place in schools, academies, mosques, churches, literary cafes, and social media outlets, and also extended to a handful of bilingual Arabic-Hebrew schools located mostly in mixed Arab-Jewish cities, and even to major Israeli academic institutions where Arabic literature and culture are taught. Interestingly enough, the Israeli military spokesperson and other departments in the security apparatus have created a tradition of "celebrating" this day for propaganda purposes. For example, in 2022 a government organization called Israel Speaks Arabic published a tweet titled "Surprising facts about Arabic in Israel" together with an iconograph with data about the number of Arabic speakers; blanket statements about the supposedly visible presence of Arabic in the media, street signs, and Jewish schools; and a visualization of the similarity between the scripts of Arabic and Hebrew to illustrate the affinity between the two as "twin languages."[99] The exclusion of Arab-Jews, not unexpectedly, from the list of Arabic speakers, which includes Muslims, Druze, and Christians, is a clear indication of how the Jewish Hebrew-speaking state upholds the subordination of Arabic as the language of the racial Other. Similarly, the total lack of statistics about the number of Jews who study Arabic or an acknowledgment of the fact that the study of Arabic is optional, unlike Hebrew, which is mandatory in all schools, speaks to the structural minoritization of Arabic.

Since the celebration in 2019 came a year after the declaration of the Basic Law, the commemoration of World Arabic Language Day was intensified. Alongside a dramatic increase in creative initiatives for the promotion of Arabic in schools, a plethora of catchy slogans that reclaimed Arabic as the language of Palestinian and Arab national belonging popped up organically. In addition to popular rhyming slogans like "Lughatī hawiyyatī / لغتي هويتي" (My language is my identity), there were several slogans with an affirmative tone of cultural resistance, such as "'Arabī wa-bi-lughati aftaḫiru / عربي وبلغتي أفتخرُ" (I'm an Arab and I take pride in my language), "Lisān al-ḍād yajmma'unā / لسان الضّاد يِجمَعنا" (The language of Ḍād[100] brings us together) and "'Arabiyyu al-qawmiyya, al-lugha wa-al-huwiyya / عربيُّ القوميّة، اللغة والهُويّة" (An Arab by nation, language, and identity). Other slogans mobilized more sophisticated literary techniques, adaptation above all, and revised the universalist poetry of Darwish to showcase their message of ṣumūd and hope. For example, Darwish's famous line "'Alā qadr ḥulmik tatas'u al-'arḍ / على قدر حلمك تتسع الأرض" (In accordance with your dreams, the land expands) was transformed to "'Alā qadr lughatikum tatas'u al-'arḍ / على قدر لغتكم تتسع الأرض" (The land is as large as your language). Taken together, these slogans reject the colonialist and racist characteristics of the Nationality Bill while responding to its alarming consequences: the ongoing structural erasure and minoritization of Arabic since the Nakba in 1948.[101]

Given the *'ulfa–kuxlej/kuxlejal* in these recent developments in Chiapas and Palestine, and the ongoing settler colonial projects of the Mexican and Israeli states, and the parallel structural erasure of Maya and Palestinian cultures embedded in the dispossession of Mayan and Palestinian lands, we cannot but observe the similarity between the precarity of Tsotsil and Arabic as two Indigenous languages undergoing the same struggle: preserving an existence through linguistic defiance and imagining a decolonial future beyond colonial and racialized borders. In the next chapter, I will examine how this struggle is depicted in other literary genres, particularly in narrative forms that challenge colonial assumptions about the geographical boundaries of Tsotsil and Arabic. By delving into a comparative reading of Mayan and Palestinian novels and short stories written in Tsotsil and Arabic, I analyze fictional accounts and vignettes that tell us stories about rural-urban divides, linguistic confinement, cultural segregation, and moving through settler spaces.

3
Border Crossers and City Dwellers: Narratives of Indigenous Urban Culture

As Indigenous literatures, contemporary Mayan literature in Chiapas and Palestinian literature in Israel are inherently border literatures.[1] Having been stripped of their land and living in fragmented geographies demarcated by the concurrently ongoing legacy of the Spanish conquest in Chiapas and the expansionist project of Zionist settler colonialism in Palestine, Mayan writers and their Palestinian counterparts exist in parallel colonized spatial structures. In addition to being characterized by systematic territorial and demographic dispersion, these structures are foregrounded in internal racial borders that enforce regimes of racial segregation and socioeconomic apartheid that keep apart Mayans and non-Mayans (*ladinos*), on the one hand, and Jews and non-Jews (i.e., Arab Palestinians), on the other. Apart from demarcating a clear line of partition, these borders either construct new rural-urban divisions or ossify precolonial ones. Departing from this analogous colonial spatiality that undergirds the lived experience of Mayan and Palestinian writers, this chapter explores the representation of interior borders and the rural-urban divide in contemporary Mayan and Palestinian narratives, namely in texts composed by writers who themselves are border crossers. Indeed, since the late 1990s the literary and cultural landscapes in Chiapas and Palestine have witnessed a comparable surge in narratives that center the overlapping themes of racialized borders and the rural-urban divide. Considering this, it comes as no surprise, then, that border crossing and the city are salient motifs in a plethora of contemporary novelistic, dramatic, poetic, and performative texts authored by Mayan and Palestinian writers/artists who draw on their own individual experience as border crossers. Examples of such works in Chiapas include the play *Las risas de Pascuala* (Pascuala's laughter, 2005) by the Mayan feminist theater collective La FOMMA, Mikel Ruiz's debut novella *Cha'yemal nich'nabiletick / Los hijos errantes* (*The Errant Children*, 2014), and Manu Pukuj's poem *"Vovijel"* (2018). A parallel representative set of examples from Palestine features two novellas and a short story—or what I label "the diaries of crossing in/into Haifa"—including Ibtisam Azem's *Sāriq al-Nawm: Gharib Ḥayfāwī* (*The sleep thief*, 2011), Majd Kayyal's *Al-Mawt fī Ḥayfā* (*Death in Haifa*, 2019), and Sheikha Helawy's *"Al-Jadīla"* ("The Braid," 2018), respectively. In addition to centering the colonial spatial aspect of interior borders and Indigenous urbanity as key thematic concerns, these texts, originally written in Tsotsil, Tsotsil and Spanish, and Arabic, share a common preoccupation with the liminal world of Mayan and Palestinian border crossers and city dwellers. At the core of these texts, some of which are semiautobiographical, are stories that recount the intricacies of crossing versus passing and the contradiction of belonging versus alienation among labor migrants, urbanized students, dispossessed villagers, displaced refugees from destroyed cities, peripheralized characters, and other marginalized figures as well. At the backdrop of this affinity, *'ulfa–kuxlej/kuxlejal*, between the centrality of internal borders in Mayan and Palestinian narratives, I set out to address the following questions: How do Mayan writers *claim* the colonial city of San Cristóbal as Jobel ("place in the cloud" in Tsotsil) as a future Indigenous landscape? How do Palestinian writers *reclaim* the indigeneity of Palestinian cities from the colonial domination of Jewish cities constructed on their ruins? And more significantly, how does the common thread of border crossing in Mayan and Palestinian literatures convey the divergent patterns of spatial resistance to racist segregation, geographical fragmentation, and linguistic and cultural erasure? By answering these questions, I seek to demonstrate the similarity in the way Mayan and Palestinian writers and artists decolonize their own geographies by redrawing the lines on the map and reimagining their territories. This act of remapping the land, as Leanne Betasamosake Simpson reminds us, is, by definition, a rebellious form of Indigenous resurgence, because it derives from the reconnection of Indigenous Peoples to their ancestral land and the social relations, languages, and knowledge systems that arise from it, thus disrupting settler colonial commodification and ownership of it.[2]

Before delving into my analysis, though, I must first point out the common, yet divergent, histories of forced displacement and local migration in Chiapas and Palestine vis-à-vis the city as a place that inhabits the incommensurability of coloniality and indigeneity, thus affirming what Eve Tuck and K. Wayne Yang have underscored in their contention that decolonization is not a metaphor.[3] Whereas the expulsion of Mayans from their villages in the 1970s was triggered by a combination of the legacy of Spanish colonialism and the neoliberal expansion of the Mexican settler state, thus leading to the collapse of rural economy, interethnic conflicts, and the militarization of the countryside,[4] the uprooting of Palestinians from their cities, namely the coastal cities of Haifa, Jaffa, Askalan (Ashkelon), and Akka (Acre), among others, during the Nakba was a direct outcome of Zionist settler colonialism. Perhaps the clearest way to explain this would be the following: Whereas Mayan villagers were expelled into the periphery of San Cristóbal, a colonial city that was built on the exclusion of Indigenous Peoples in the first place, Palestinians were dispossessed from their urbanity and expelled either into other Palestinian villages or pushed into the periphery of their own cities that continue to undergo a systemic process of Judaization, thus becoming ghettoized in mixed Arab-Jewish cities.[5] In respect to local migration, the movement of Mayan and Palestinian writers in the late 1980s and 1990s to urban centers to seek higher education and other professional opportunities led to a multilayered encounter with the city and the emergence of individual and collective initiatives to develop an Indigenous urban landscape.

Jobel, Chiapas: Settling in the Clouds and Reimagining the City

The roots of the rural-urban divide in Chiapas are entrenched in the long history of the Spanish colonial legacy in Mexico and the construction of exclusive cities for the Spanish elite. In a way, as Jan Rus and Gaspar Morquecho Escamilla observe, San Cristóbal remained a racially exclusive city until the early 1970s, even though when the Spanish-speaking *ladinos* were the minority in the area, they were outnumbered at least four to one by the Tsotsil- and Tseltal-speaking Mayans. Describing it as a city that "maintained a strict ethnic exclusion of Indigenous Peoples, almost a kind of apartheid," Rus and Morquecho Escamilla emphasize the fact that this system continued throughout the 1990s when *ladinos* rejected the migration of Mayans into the city, perceiving it as an Indigenous "invasion."[6] Ironically, the Zapatistas' takeover of the city during the uprising in 1994 was carried out like a true invasion. Reading the border and rural-urban divide in contemporary Mayan texts against this historical backdrop, it becomes clear that both border crossing and the self-fashioning of urban identities are embodied forms of spatial transgression and resistance to structural racism. The work of La FOMMA, Mikel Ruiz, and Manu Pukuj illustrates this trend.[7]

La FOMMA (*La Fortaleza de la Mujer Maya*/The Empowerment of the Mayan Woman) is a feminist theater collective that was established in 1994 by two playwrights from the first generation of contemporary Mayan writers: Petrona de la Cruz Cruz (1965–), a Tsotsil-speaking Mayan playwright and actress from the village of Zinacantán, and Isabel Juárez Espinosa (1958–2023), a Tseltal-speaking Mayan playwright and actress from Aguacatenango. In addition to writing and performing in Spanish and Mayan languages, and sometimes in both, FOMMA's activities include classes in cooking, sewing, accounting, and drama writing. In 2008, FOMMA's repertoire took a transnational turn when the Hemispheric Institute for Performance and Politics in the Americas, based at New York University (NYU), established its first regional research and cultural center in FOMMA's theater. The new joint project, Centro Hemisférico / FOMMA, received support from NYU and the Ford Foundation. Based on off-the-record conversations that I had in person with several Mayan cultural activists in 2019, FOMMA's center still operates as a cultural space though the group no longer exists as a theater collective. Some attributed the group's dissolution to rumors of financial mismanagement, which reportedly led to the withholding of external funding and to internal conflicts. With the recent death of Juárez Espinosa, one of the co-founders of the collective and its internationally recognized powerhouse, it remains unclear how her passing will affect the future of the group. At present, it is also uncertain whether FOMMA is still active.

What distinguishes the work of FOMMA is not only the feminist agenda of the collective, but also the intersection between the personal histories of its founders, Cruz Cruz and Juárez Espinosa, who crossed the borders of their communities and challenged the status of women there. In fact, the troupe staged several plays based on the life stories of Cruz Cruz and Juárez Espinosa. These plays depict the plight of Mayan women who suffered rape, domestic violence, and sexism at the hands of Mayan men in communities already enduring rampant alcoholism and exploitive *ladino* landlords. In this chapter, I focus on the play *Las risas de Pascuala* (Pascuala's laughter, 2005), which was a major theatrical production. The racism that Cruz Cruz and Espinosa experienced firsthand after they moved to San Cristóbal / Jobel is interwoven with the racism that other Mayan labor migrants, peasants, and street vendors encounter daily in the city. The result was a dramatic performance about the everyday struggle of subalternized Mayan characters redefining their identity while reclaiming the city despite its exclusion, racism, economic exploitation, and sexism.

The play describes the daily lives of Mayan women and children street vendors. The main characters are two young single mothers, Pascuala and Lorenza. Together with Lorenza's kids, Ciro and Abel, the two mothers commute daily from their hamlets early in the morning to San Cristóbal / Jobel to sell ceramics, embroidered clothes, and other *artesanias*. The play depicts the hardships of making a living from selling Mayan folk art in the street. It highlights the resilience of Pascuala as a Mayan woman who can both negotiate with the *ladina* and mestiza dealers and stand up for her rights against state police brutality and discrimination. The play ends on a note of triumph: Pascuala is celebrated as a heroine for her relentless efforts to receive a police permit that would ultimately allow her to remain in her vending spot, and hence officially enter the local urban economy.

Unlike other plays by FOMMA, *Las risas de Pascuala* was written in Spanish.[8] However, the show begins with an editorial footnote that alerts the reader that the dialogues intentionally include several grammatical errors in gender and number. These errors are kept in the script as well as in the performance to convey a realistic representation of a Mayan in the city who speaks "broken Spanish."[9] The second scene opens with an internal monologue by Lorenza, capturing the hardship of making a living from selling Mayan *artesania* in the street. The uncertainty of making a living from a marginal space in a street economy, the lack of appreciation on the part of shoppers, implicitly *ladinos* and tourists, for the true financial and emotional value of her handmade ceramics, as well as their lack of understanding of her abject poverty, are the highlights of Lorenza's monologue. Exhausted and mournful, she confesses from her vending corner:

> *Parece que hoy no es mi día, nadie quiere comprar mi mercancía, ya estoy cansada de estar ofreciendo de un lado para otro: en las tiendas, con las personas . . . y nada, todos quieren pagar barato, como ellos no sufren para conseguir la leña para cocer, ni el barro. Y todavía venir a ofrecer en sus casas, ni así quieren. Lo malo es que no voy a tener para comprar las tortillas y polvito de chicharrón para que coman un poco mis hijos. ¿Será que me dicen algo aquí si tiendo mi venta? (Mira por todos lados) No creo que me regañen, voy a tender las cosas más pequeñas, ojalá que compren alguna.* (It seems that today is not my day. Nobody wants to buy my goods; I'm tired of offering them from one place to another: in stores, to people . . . and nothing, everyone wants to pay less, since they don't suffer to get firewood for cooking or to get mud. And even when I go offering them house to house, they don't want to buy them either. The problem is that I won't have enough money to buy tortillas and pork rinds for my kids, so they can eat a little. Will they say something to me if I lay out my wares here? (She looks all around.) I don't think that they will scold me. I'll spread out my smallest things. I hope people will buy some.)[10]

One of the most dramatic moments in the play occurs when Pascuala confronts Germán, a policeman who wants to evict her from the street market for selling without a city permit. This confrontation reveals Pascuala's feminist resistance to a male representative of corrupt state power. It also unmasks the double racist treatment she receives because she is Indigenous and poor. However, in a moment of "talking back to" Germán, Pascuala demonstrates self-assertiveness and agency:

> Mire señor, no nos hagamos tarugos. Aunque me ve vestida toda traposa, pero no soy tonta para no darme cuenta de cómo es que trabaja. Y si quiere conservar su trabajo, déjenos en paz con nuestra venta porque yo no le voy a darle mordidas en dinero para que me deje vender mi mercancía. (Look, Mister, let's not play the fool. Although you see me dressed in ragged clothes, I'm not so stupid that I don't realize how you work. And if you want to keep your job, leave us alone and let us sell, because I'm not going to bribe you with money so you will let me sell my goods.)[11]

A striking feature of this play is its invocation of the hierarchical and structural oppression of Mayan women through its focus on Indigenous migrant labor. It vividly illustrates how Lorenza and Pascuala struggle as women at the intersection of Indigenous poverty, the exploitation of Indigenous labor, and the racism against Indigenous communities. Both characters fight on several fronts. They exist outside the national economy, yet must negotiate for a space within the margins, while relying on an "imperfect" use of the national language. They also exist outside the legal framework of the federal and state-level governments, which require them to show proof for their economic presence in the city. While none of the characters appear desperate, their attitude oscillates between resilience and resistance to the oppressive hierarchies. The play ends on a positive note as Pascuala declares triumph by asserting the right for a Mayan presence in the city. Curiously enough, this "happy ending" invites the viewers to reflect on the discrimination that Mayan vendors face at the margins of the booming ethnic tourism market that has exploded recently in the colonial cultural capital.

Indeed, since the beginning of the early 1980s, the city has witnessed a dramatic surge in the number of foreign tourists, mostly Europeans. This trend witnessed a sharp increase after the Zapatista uprising in 1994, as San Cristóbal/Jobel gained more international visibility, attracting more solidarity activists and visitors from the US, Canada, and many other countries. Throughout these years, however, Mayan villages and bodies have become a must-see sight. Pierre van den Berghe argues: "Ethnic tourism is interested in the 'Indianness,' not in the 'peasantness,' of Indians. Indians are interesting precisely because they are not like the garden-variety, 'acculturated' Mexican *campesino*."[12] He further writes that, although Mayans have been an important resource for ethnic tourism, it was the local *ladino* bourgeoisie who "seize[d] this new opportunity for small and medium scale entrepreneurship. They became the middlemen by developing the infrastructure necessary to make the ethnic tourist feel physically and psychologically comfortable."[13] These dynamics evolved in the past decade as more Mayan writers created their own independent artistic spaces in the city away from the tourist industry, thus challenging the *ladino*-built infrastructure and its exploitative racialized gaze.

In this regard, Galería Muy is a notable example. Established in 2014—exactly twenty years after the foundation of FOMMA—Galería Muy, unlike FOMMA, operates as an independent nonprofit initiative. It is a gallery, workshop, and shop that exhibits the work of more than twenty Mayan- and Zoque-speaking artists working in glass, sculpture, fabric, painting, and new media. Tucked in a residential street away from San Cristóbal / Jobel's *zócalo* (main plaza), the gallery welcomes its visitors with these words in Tsotsil: "*Chimuyubajotik li li'oyotike*" (We are very happy that we are here), followed by a statement in Spanish: "*La galería orgullosmente reúne el mejor arte maya/ zoque contemporáneo y colabramos con artistas del mundo para residir creativamente li'e (aquí). Bienvenidas y bienvenidos a un centro de arte felizemente marginal-universal*" (The gallery proudly brings together the best contemporary Mayan/Zoque art and we collaborate with artists from around the world to creatively reside *li'e* ["here" in Tsotsil]. Welcome to a happily marginal-universal art center).[14] The insertion of the word *li'e* in the statement noted above merits attention. In addition to interrupting the visual monotony of the Spanish text, *li'e* (here) anchors the visitor in the original map of the land on which the gallery is founded. This symbolic act of reclaiming the indigeneity of the space is accomplished in a single word in Tsotsil. By using *li'e* Mayan artists underscore their firm belonging to the entire territory of the gallery and acknowledge the visible presence of Mayan languages, art, and culture in the city.

Along similar lines to the plays of FOMMA, Mikel Ruiz's fiction explores the rural-urban divide through a critique of violence within Mayan villages. Born in Chicumtantic, Ruiz (1985–) is a Tsotsil-speaking novelist, translator, and literary critic. He completed his BA at the Chiapas National Autonomous University. His short stories have been translated into several languages and his novella, *Cha'yemal nich'nabiletick / Los hijos errantes / The Errant Children*—regarded as the first novel in Tsotsil—came out in a trilingual edition in 2023 with English translation by Sean S. Sell. In contrast to the work of FOMMA, which attributes the domestic and gendered violence to the ailments of patriarchy, the novella depicts the escalating violence that targets women, men, and children alike in previously peaceful Mayan communities in rural areas as a destructive consequence of capitalist and hypermodernist invasion led by the *ladino*/mestizo/Mexican agenda of forced urbanization.

The novella begins with the story of the protagonist Ignacio, a young Mayan villager with fantasies about living in the city. Refusing to work in his family's *milpa*, he spends his time locked in his room watching porn and playing video games before a dormant evil beast within him is triggered to go on a violent rampage of rape and murder. The rest of the novella focuses on the village's reaction to this banal violence and the collective attempts to trace the culprit, to solve the mysterious killing, and to restore harmony in the village. Written in a style part thriller, part social realism, the narrative combines intergenerational dialogue between Ignacio and his mother about the evils of the city, internal monologues of the alienated Ignacio, and depictions of blood, tears, and the horror of a dismembered body that haunts the community and its pastoral landscape. In his afterword to the novella, Arturo Arias argues that Ruiz's critique of modernity aims at pointing out its coloniality and hegemonic cultural power in Mexico. While the Mexican state may think that modernizing rural communities is a good development project, the locals view it with mistrust, if not as a true danger to the cohesive social fabric: "Gone are the idealized Arcadian collectives where everyone lived happily, members of the idyllic community were not differentiated among themselves, or even constructed as subjects, heterosexism was toned down, and all sources of evil trying to harm these communities inevitably were of external and/or foreign origin."[15]

While Ignacio is depicted as a lost soul, the title of the novella, *The Errant Children*, suggests that the entire community is in a similar state of confusion and loss. The image of the wandering tribe is evoked in the narrative as well. Characters are depicted as delirious figures devoid of their *ch'ulel*, their sacred spirit, which provides them with supernatural powers.[16] When they lose this connection to the supernatural, they lose themselves. The narrator portrays this existential loss by evoking the disoriented steps of the people in the community who cannot follow their familiar routes in the woods, or even trace the path that could potentially lead them to the body of the man Ignacio murdered and later hanged on a tree in a spectacular scene that replicates a narco-violence style of theatrically displaying mutilated bodies. The violence of this image taints the romanticized view of the rural landscape, shattering the notion of an idyllic community.

The seemingly unresolved division between the rural and the urban is reiterated throughout the novella. Whereas the imposed top-down rapid modernization of rural Chiapas is depicted as a spiritual illness, the move to the city is portrayed as an injury to the soul. For example, the bleak end of Manuel, a young man from the village who had to move to Jobel to get a better job to pay back money he had borrowed to buy presents for his in-laws—a traditional Mayan custom followed before asking for someone's hand for marriage—allegorizes the fatal danger of the city. Describing Manuel's condition upon return from Jobel, his distressed mother, Pascuala, says:

> We couldn't stand his putrid smell, his bones like an old man's, it was a miracle that he kept on living. We called an *ilol* [shaman/ healer] to cure him of his horror, of the evil airs and evil words of the *kaxlanetik* [the white devil in Tsotsil, or *ladinos*], because his thoughts were no longer the same, his breathing was agitated, and he wanted more than air.[17]

The racial exclusion of Mayans from the city is presented as another inevitable outcome for those who cross the border. Even Ignacio, who yearns to make the big move, is aware that his future in the city will keep him out of place, dwelling at the margins of the *ladino* urban world as the displaced Other:

> What Ignacio's eyes long to see is cars, large buildings, and girls. His hands yearn to touch them, be close to them. He wishes this life that is passing by in the little village were not his. Yesterday, he saw on television free young couples. He lay awake into the night, the world of dreams eluding him; he imagined himself in that environment, among the multitudes, but *different*.[18]

In contrast with FOMMA's and Ruiz's representations of the multifaceted dimensions of the rural-urban divide and the various ways Mayans reconfigure their relationship to Jobel as an imagined city and a place where they wish to affirm their belonging, Manu Pukuj writes a fierce poem with explicit imagery of rural resistance that pokes at the racist structure upholding the rural-urban divide. Pukuj, a native of Yibel Osil in Chenalhó, is an environmentalist who has conducted research on the *milpa* as organized by the Tsotsil agricultural calendar. In his poetry, Pukuj draws on his work as a coordinator of ecological projects in rural communities and organizer of events on Mayan spiritual and cultural development. His bilingual poem *"Vovijel"* offers an overt critique of both internal and external borders that restrict the movement of Mayan people to the rural areas. Interestingly, the poem appears in the anthology *Snichimal vaychil/ Sueño florido* (Flowered dream) and is printed on hand-drawn illustrations and textured, grainy paper that resembles *amatl*, or tree bark paper.[19] In fact, the entire production process of the anthology encapsulates the poem's critique of the borders and rural-urban divisions. Assembled by the Tsotsil-speaking poet and translator Xun Betan and the collective *Sna Jk'optik* in San Cristóbal/ Jobel in 2017, the anthology was part of a larger underground project that works at the margins of the literary market and government institutions by publishing DIY chapbooks and purposely issuing a limited number of editions of works by Tsotsil writers who write only in Tsotsil or both Tsotsil and Spanish. By identifying Tsotsil speakers as their primary audience and controlling the means of production of Tsotsil literature and art from their location as "migrant" poets in San Cristóbal / Jobel, the collective reshapes the racialized boundaries that were imposed on them.

Although *"Vovijel"* is a bilingual Tsotsil-Spanish poem, its title and its opening and ending stanzas are left intentionally untranslated, even in the translated English version. Sandwiched in the middle between the stanzas in Tsotsil, the body of the poem offers a bold rejection of *ladino* racism and colonial boundaries that confine the existence of the Mayan subject to the rural world:

Vovijel
Oy k'usi k'ux ta ko'on
xk'unim ko'on
chi ok'
li' jch'ulele la svol sba
la sch'ay sba batel
mu xa xka'i bu oy
yu'un li chibesat
la jnuptan vokol ta be
ja' yu'un la jch'ay jba batel ta ko'on.

Xi jk'oplal:

You dirty Indian with your bare feet. Get out of here.
Fucking stupid Indians.
No Tonto talk, speak right.

Yes, I go everywhere
with my bare, calloused feet
because the earth has no limits
because I believe the world is infinite,
without borders in the valleys, mountains, and seas
I'll keep feeling the heart
and the embrace of Mother Earth

Yes, I'll humbly accept my ignorance.
But Indians are from India. The Tsotsil are a millenarian
Maya people.

Mexico, a political division.
Yes, I'll use proper grammar to tell you that saying this feels good.
Xi, ilo'ilaj ko'on
xi lok' ta alel ku'un.[20]

The speaker in the poem rejects the ingrained racist views and prejudices that *ladinos* in the city perpetuate to keep the Mayan villagers away from the city: the bare feet, the lack of proficiency in Spanish, and the naïveté of the peasant. Reclaiming his voice through the millenarian history of Mayan civilization, the speaker rejects the racist views and boundaries that limit his movement and asserts his freedom as a citizen of the world. The repetition of the affirmation lines, "Yes, I go everywhere," "Yes, I will humbly accept," and "Yes, I will use" amplifies the speaker's steadfastness and resistance to settler colonial boundaries too.

It is important to note here that I have chosen not to translate the Tsotsil stanzas of the poem as an intentional act of cultural and political respect, preserving both the integrity of the original text and the poet's approach to bilingual writing, which prioritizes autonomy over legibility. Several Mayan authors in Chiapas similarly employ bilingual or partially translated texts, navigating the space between accessibility and self-determination. Their work often leaves key terms or passages untranslated, asserting linguistic sovereignty and drawing attention to the limits of comprehension. This approach is not exclusive to Chiapas; Mayan poets in Guatemala, such as Humberto Ak'abal (K'iche'), and Indigenous writers on Turtle Island, such as Leanne Betasamosake Simpson (Nishnaabeg), have also adopted similar strategies. Following this tradition, the decision to preserve the Tsotsil stanzas intact honors the intended opacity of the poem, aligns with Indigenous literary practices, and foregrounds the ongoing struggle over language, visibility, and epistemic authority.

Moreover, this decision resonates with the cautionary stance advocated by Doris Sommer regarding the translation of Indigenous languages into colonial ones. Urging scholars and translators to resist the compulsion to make all texts accessible to majority-language readers, Sommer reminds us that some cultural expressions "resist translation not because they are incomprehensible, but because they are already complete."[21] To translate the Tsotsil stanzas against the poet's original decision would risk reenacting symbolic violence and reinscribing a hegemonic structure onto his voice, thereby undermining both the text's sovereignty and the poet's intent.

In the previous chapter, I noted the inextricable connection between the critical revitalization of Mayan languages, namely Tsotsil, and the flourishing of a vibrant Mayan literature and art scene in San Cristóbal/Jobel. In this regard, one cannot dismiss the pivotal role that Mayan writers and artists have played since the 1980s in transforming the cultural landscape of the city by carving a space for independent and semi-independent Mayan cultural productions in Mayan languages that challenge the racist history of the city and the political and cultural hegemony of its *ladino* colonialist elite. While FOMMA, Ruiz, and Pukuj should be recognized for presenting and amplifying the marginalized voices of Mayans from the rural area and in the city and at the same time redrawing the entrenched boundaries between Mayans and *ladinos,* claiming Jobel as an Indigenous city that has a deeply seated colonial past and a bright decolonial Mayan future is what they ultimately seek to achieve. As their assorted body of works demonstrate, the power of this form of Indigenous resurgence is embedded in spatial resistance and constant transgression of the rural-urban divide.

Haifa, Palestine: Borders, Wounds, and the Names We Carry

In *Atlas of Palestine, 1917–1966*, Salman Abu Sitta records the depopulation and disappearance of more than five hundred villages during the Nakba, alongside the destruction of thirty towns and cities.[22] In this pivotal geographic archive of Historic Palestine, Abu Sitta presents maps that show the large scale of rural landscape in Palestine before the Nakba. While emphasizing the fact that Palestinian society before 1948 was primarily that of landowning peasants, *fallāḥīn* (*fellaheen*), he pinpoints a cluster of Mediterranean coastal cities that had extensive regional connections, such as Haifa, Jaffa, Askalan (Ashkelon), and Akka (Acre), and several inland cities that played a major role in Palestinian urbanity as intercultural crossroads attracting multifaith religious pilgrims and international trade. In addition to Jerusalem, he lists Nablus and Hebron alongside his native city of Beersheba, which served as an administrative, military, and commercial capital of southern Palestine during the Ottoman rule of Palestine.[23] My reading of internal borders and the rural-urban divide in the assemblage of texts by Azem, Helawy, and Kayyal that comprise "the diaries of crossing in/into Haifa" is set against the backdrop of this geographical mapping of Palestine.

The growing urbanization of third-generation Nakba Palestinians marks the emergence of an intellectual and creative class, members of which have experienced both social and geographical mobility after relocating from their villages and towns in the Galilee in the north and the Triangle in the center to major cities such as Tel Aviv, Jaffa, Haifa, and Jerusalem. The outcome of this process of urbanization is particularly evident in Haifa, where the growth in the number of Palestinian civic organizations and university graduates and professionals has led to the city's accelerated cultural revival. Palestinian-owned cafés and bars, world-class music clubs, independent theaters, and publishing houses are some of the cultural institutions that have shaped the resurgence of Haifa as "the 'Palestinian cultural capital' in Israel."[24] That said, Naama Blatman and Areej Sabbagh-Khoury, who consider the recursion of pre-1948 life in Haifa as a manifestation of a presence of the absence, caution us about reading contemporary Palestinian urbanism solely in relation to the post-1948 settler structures and processes. Instead, they urge us to look at Palestinian urban life through a lens of indigeneity, arguing that the de-urbanization of Palestine has become a core element around which Palestinian urbanism is organized.[25]

Mindful of this incommensurability between settler colonialism and indigeneity, my close reading of trespassing and *re*-Palestinization of urban spaces in "the diaries of crossing in/into Haifa" considers the topography of the border not only as a material barrier, but also as a psychic wound, to borrow Gloria Anzaldúa's words.[26] In this context, however, the wound is not simply a mental and emotional scar caused by the clash between the first and the third world. The borderland, also, is not a place for multiplicities, but rather a wound caused by the colonial fragmentation of the land. This fragmentation, I contend, not only upholds the existing pre-1948 rural-urban divide, but also imposes a new racialized one.

Azem (1974–) went to Jerusalem from her hometown of Taybeh (in the Triangle) in the early 1990s to study at the Hebrew University. Later, she moved to Germany, where she completed a master's in Islamic studies, as well as in German and English literature, and worked as a journalist, producer, and correspondent for Deutsche Welle TV's Arabic service. She moved to New York in 2012 and became a correspondent for *al-ʿArabī al-Jadīd (The New Arab)* while being a coeditor of *Jadaliyya* and editor of the e-zine's Arabic page. These peripatetic trajectories and Azem's own personal history as a granddaughter of a displaced Palestinian from Jaffa inform her two novels, *Sāriq al-Nawm: Gharīb Ḥayfāwī (The sleep thief: Gharib from Haifa*, 2011) and *Sifr al-Ikhtifāʾ (The Book of Disappearance*, 2014; translated to English by Sinan Antoon in 2019). At the center of both novels, the male protagonists cross several temporal and geographic borders while navigating a complex relationship with the cities of Haifa and Jaffa, respectively. To align with the focus on narratives about Haifa in this chapter, I will address only the first novel.

Narrated in nonlinear fragments, the novel tells the story of Gharib, a young Palestinian student from Haifa attending the Hebrew University in Jerusalem in the 1990s. Gharib, which means both "strange" and "stranger," was born in Haifa. His nickname, Ḥayfāwī (of Haifa, or the Haifan), alludes to the widespread Palestinian view of Haifa as a city that welcomes strangers. Each vignette is a snapshot of Gharib's political evolution and the events that shaped his consciousness as a native Palestinian in Israel. His introspective and soul-searching reflections unfold like a photo album, with each tableau capturing his maturation during a period of profound political and social transformations in the Palestinian landscape of the early post-Oslo years. As he moves between Haifa, Jerusalem, and Tel Aviv, Gharib has recurring flashbacks to major milestones in his life: his childhood in Haifa in a working-class family, his coming of age as a political activist during the First Intifada (1987–93), his subsequent imprisonment by the Israeli secret police, and his passionate relationship with Hamsa, a young woman from Haifa whom he meets in Jerusalem.

As he moves between the three cities, Gharib crosses temporal borders to make sense of the perpetual alienation he feels in each of them. This manifests in flashbacks from the collective memory of Palestinians, which transport him back to pre- and post-Nakba times, and include both oral and literary elements. He looks to the past for clues to connect and cope with the alienating present. The first flashback occurs when Gharib becomes aware of the story behind his name. As he delves into the etymological significance of the name Gharib the Haifan, he realizes that his *ghurba*, or exile, is a collective national experience of uprooting that began in 1948 with the Nakba and the destruction of his city then and was repeated again in 1967 with the Israeli occupation of the West Bank and Gaza, which fragmented Palestinian geography even more. From his mother's point of view, Gharib is estranged because he came into the world during the aberrant times of the 1967 war. "As if the pessoptimism once used by that writer with the raspy voice and penetrating look to describe his people did not wish to part company with them until today," his mother tells him. "This should not be surprising because their circumstances have not changed," she adds.[27]

Gharib's reflection on his name evokes both the defeat of 1967 and the resulting additional loss of Palestinian territory. Gharib's flashback to Emile Habibi's canonical novel *Al-Mutashā'il: al-Waqā'i' al-Gharība fī Ikhtifā' Saʿīd abī al-Naḥs* (1974, translated into English by Salma Khadra Jayyusi and Trevor Le Gassick in 1982 as *The Secret Life of Saeed, the Ill-Fated Pessoptimist*) creates an intertextuality between the two works that establishes a memory within Palestinian literature. Gharib's birth during the 1967 war embodies the generation of the Naksa, or setback, just as Habibi's ill-fated pessoptimist represented the Nakba generation.[28] Saeed and Gharib are thus parallel and interconnected figures despite the historical gap between them and the fact that their alienation is triggered by a different set of borders. Gharib, who became "alien" from the day of his birth in 1967, resembles Saeed, whose "pessoptimism" derives from his precarious identity as the native who becomes the archetypal stranger in his own homeland after 1948. This persisting alienation over time and space signals the collective emotional stagnation of '48 Palestinians.

In Jerusalem, Gharib has two encounters that underline the ways in which the chronic spatial and temporal alienation he experiences is aggravated by being in a Jewish-Israeli space such as the western part of the city. The first encounter occurs in Mahane Yehuda Market, where Gharib meets Shaheen, a young boy from Hebron who sells pencils for a living. The "border" between Palestinians in Israel and Palestinians in the West Bank dissolves as Gharib recognizes that he and Shaheen share a history of racialized and class oppression. As a Palestinian from the West Bank working in a Jewish market, Shaheen is subjected to racism and hostility by both customers and shop owners. Observing Shaheen, Gharib realizes that West Jerusalem is not welcoming to him either. As he watches Shaheen being humiliated selling pencils in Jerusalem to help support his family, Gharib is visited by traumatic flashbacks to his own childhood in poverty in Haifa when he used to walk the streets selling avocados, feeling overcome by shame. "Shaheen was no longer the poor young man whom store owners chased off to keep their customers from being annoyed," says Gharib. "What I saw was Shaheen, the poor Palestinian. The two images merged and left me confused. Did they despise Shaheen because he was an Arab? Because he was poor? Both?"[29]

The second alienating and dislocating encounter takes place when Gharib attends a party at a house that had been owned by Palestinians before 1948. As soon as he steps into the house, now inhabited by Danny, his friend from the Hebrew University, he is overwhelmed by the surreal "Arabness" of the atmosphere: the familiar tabbouleh on the table, Umm Kulthum songs playing in the background, the lemon tree in the garden, and haunting images he conjures of the Palestinian family that used to inhabit the house. His sense of utter dislocation propels Gharib to question why the party is taking place and what brings the guests there. Danny, a self-proclaimed liberal Jewish Israeli who can even recite Umm Kulthum lyrics by heart, picks up on Gharib's discomfort and distress. He launches into a defensive monologue describing the history of the house and the new owners' attempts to preserve its Arab feel. But Gharib flees the scene, unmoved by Danny's argument and repulsed by the Orientalist Zionist gaze it betrays. Gharib says, "To alleviate my pain, [Danny] said, 'This house is built in an Arab style like all the houses around here. The owner did not want to change, alter, or affect the aesthetic feel of the city. He also cherishes Arab civilization and appreciates it. This house is not like the others in the area . . . it's a house whose people were not displaced. Gharib, do you understand?'"[30]

Danny's assertion that the house does not belong to a displaced Palestinian family only aggravates Gharib's distress, which eventually evolves into a tragic realization that Danny is complicit in the cultural appropriation and erasure of Palestinian memory that are characteristic of the Zionist project. His friend's proclaimed liberalism becomes fully unmasked when Gharib's dramatic exit from the party provokes one of Danny's friends to dismiss Gharib as "a Palestinian who drank a bit too much."[31]

Gharib's sense of alienation in this encounter with his presumed friend involves another literary flashback. While Gharib can be viewed as another iteration of Habibi's Saeed, the figure of Danny can be likened to Dov/Khaldun in Ghassan Kanafani's 'Ā'id ilā Ḥayfā (1969, published in English in 2000 as *Returning to Haifa*). Dov/Khaldun remains estranged from the memory of his parents when they return to Haifa to reclaim both him, their son, and their former home. Similarly, Danny is estranged from the memory of the Palestinian house he occupies. Spatial absurdity is manifested in the lurking presence of "absent" Palestinians in Jerusalem and Haifa houses. The inability of both Danny and Dov/Khaldun to inhabit the real memory of the houses in which they live conveys both the acute feelings of alienation and the ongoing Nakba that Palestinians witness and experience, living amid the remains of destroyed and depopulated Palestinian cities.

In the vignette titled "Hamsa," Gharib reflects on his relationship with the eponymous character during their time together as students in Jerusalem. Here, the reader learns that after he witnesses Israeli municipal workers cutting down a particular oak tree in Jerusalem, Gharib decides to move away to live in Tel Aviv. Watching the tree being severed from its roots, Gharib is confronted with the physical erasure of his own memories of that tree, against which he and Hamsa had made love one rainy night. Shortly after experiencing this emotional severance, Gharib moves to Tel Aviv, despite his reservations about the city. "I don't like Tel Aviv much either," Gharib says, "although I didn't give the city a chance. To me, it has always seemed fake and over-the-top, appearing to live on the ruins of Jaffa. In fact, it swallowed up Jaffa and left it to die."[32] Here, the delineation between Jaffa and Tel Aviv encapsulates the polarities of authenticity and fakeness, of life and death. Tel Aviv, a city that "swallowed up" Jaffa, functions as a metaphor for the conquest of Palestine beginning with the Nakba. And the Nakba persists to this day with Tel Aviv's continued expansion as Israel's hegemonic and economic center and the systematic gentrification that uproots Jaffa's Palestinian inhabitants.[33]

Going and coming between Haifa, Jerusalem, and Tel Aviv exacerbates Gharib's alienation. Each city reveals a colonial reality that negates his existence, memories, and roots as a Palestinian. This continues until the last vignette, when Gharib undergoes an ultimate existential crisis. As the accumulated sense of estrangement and nonbelonging turns into mental stagnation, Gharib feels he has reached a dead end and renounces his name altogether. Like the first vignette, the last one, titled "Ḥāja" (Need), features one of Gharib's recurring dreams: He is being held at an Israeli police station for interrogation, but this time his interrogator asks him about his nationality. Gharib rejects all the options suggested: Arab, Israeli Arab, Palestinian. With much irony, he responds: "Believe me! I am Nada. My name is Nada ["dew" in Arabic and "nothing" in Spanish]."[34] The metaphorical lightness of dew embedded in this chosen female name and the renunciation of his male identity foreshadow Gharib's dramatic resolution to give up his ID card, thereby renouncing the offered identities, because none of them encapsulate who he is: He is nothing.

Like Azem, Sheikha Helawy's (1968–) professional and fictional peregrinations entailed border crossing and the cultural alienation of a student protagonist's experiences in Haifa. Born in Dhayl 'Araj, an unrecognized Bedouin village near Haifa, Helawy went to high school in the city before moving to Jaffa to pursue her undergraduate and master's studies in Arabic and Hebrew literature at Tel Aviv University. In addition to authoring four collections of short stories, she has published a collection of poems, worked in the field of educational counseling and curriculum development in East Jerusalem, and taught Arab feminism at Ben-Gurion University of the Negev (Naqab) in the south. Her short stories were translated into several languages, including Hebrew. In 2019, she won the Al-Multaqa Prize for the Arabic Short Story for *"Al-Talabiyya C345"* ("Order no. 345," 2018). In the semiautobiographical story *"Al-Jaddīla"* ("The Braid," 2018; translated by Aicha Yassin) a young nameless student leaves her Bedouin community to study in a private Catholic high school in Haifa. To fit in, she pleads with her single mother to take her to the hair salon to get rid of her braid, an act that her conservative uncle condemns as an imitation of city girls. The cultural gap between the traditional world of rural society and the modernized urban setting is dramatized in the equation between the loss of the braid and the character's own sense of self:

> The pupils in the Convent of Nazareth were a mix of city dwellers and nearby village commuters; each with her own dream and her own motivations. Upon arriving at the school gates, the doors of heaven and hell opened. I temporarily erased my memory of my brother, my mom, and myself. I denied my eternal "Bedouinness." My tongue complied, forgetting its shameful Bedouin dialect. Only my name and my braid exposed what I tried to hide. I failed to convince them that I was a descendant of desert kings and that I had the privilege of bearing my name.[35]

Throughout the story, Haifa is called upon repeatedly to save the protagonist from her profound sense of alienation. Initially, Haifa is imagined as a dream city. Later, it is personified as a seductive yet "treacherous friend."[36] In the end, it appears once again as an allegory for a lost city that cannot protect its own children, as the last line in the story, "only to be stung by its absence," showcases. It is relevant to mention here that Helawy writes in *fusḥa*, but mixes in Palestinian vernacular, namely the Bedouin dialect of the north. In a recent interview, she emphasizes that writing in this mixture not only is important for preserving the oral heritage of the colonized land, but also contributes to the linguistic revindication of Bedouin dialect, which, according to her, remains invisible in Palestinian literature. Helawy states:

> When I wrote the characters' dialogues or ideas, I liberated them from the injustice that Bedouins in Palestine endure. I returned to my dialect, which was at this point influenced by the musicality of the urban dialect and began practicing on my tongue all the guttural letters to give it back its well-deserved position among the dialects of Palestine. It was not merely a question of conveying a rural reality, but rather making a statement. I also felt an obligation toward my tribe and family.[37]

A distinctive aspect of Helawy's story, and her oeuvre more broadly, is the self-reflexive yet assertive juxtaposition of Palestinian Bedouinness vis-à-vis Palestinian urban settings through linguistic playfulness that teases the national reproduction of a precolonial rural-urban divide.

Though born in Haifa, unlike Azem and Helawy, Majd Kayyal (1990–) inhabits a similar position of a border dweller. Born into a family displaced from the village of Birwa, destroyed and depopulated in 1948, Kayyal studied philosophy and political science in Jerusalem. Apart from being a novelist, he is a political activist. As a journalist, he contributes regularly to the Palestinian press and the Beirut-based newspaper *As-Safir* (Arab Ambassador) before it stopped publishing in 2016. In addition to writing his novel, *Ma'sāt al-Sayyid Maṭar* (*The Tragedy of Mr. Matar,* 2016), for which he won the Qattan Young Writer Prize, he published a collection of short stories, *al-Mawt fī Ḥayfā* (*Death in Haifa,* 2019), and wrote songs for adults and children alike. His songs in the album *Aḥla min Berlin* (Better than Berlin, 2020), performed by Faraj Suleiman, became a popular hit and are considered a lyrical protest against the gentrification of Haifa.[38]

Kayyal's story "N" (translated by Thoraya El-Rayyes) from the collection *Death in Haifa*, is featured in the anthology *Palestine + 100: Stories from a Century After the Nakba* (edited by Basma Ghalayini) as an exemplary text of Palestinian futurism. Since its publication in English, the story—alongside

Azem's second novel, *The Book of Disappearance*—has gained wide recognition within Anglophone literary circles as an original work of Palestinian science fiction. In this respect, critics have focused on how technology encapsulates many facets of the story, from characters escaping the present through virtual reality machines to explicit use of codes, as evident in the title of the story and the name of a main character, the eponymous N. These future technologies, as Layla AlAmmar argues, serve as media that simultaneously store cached memories and severe inter- and trans-generational transmission of trauma, thus speaking to the "tension between the duty to remember and the desire to forget" that keeps characters in "a state of postmemorial absence."[39]

Divided into three sections, "Departure," "Encounter," and "Return," the story recasts the racial segregation of Haifa as a spatiotemporal journey between two parallel universes: the Palestinian Haifa and the Israeli Haifa. While it is not entirely clear which Haifa is real and which is the imagined one, the movement between the two cities is portrayed as a supernatural skill mastered only by Palestinians in Israel because they either inhabit the two dimensions of the land of Palestine before and after the Nakba or have inherited the ancestral knowledge of navigating their movement across it from the first generation of the Nakba who have lived throughout the original rupture of the homeland in 1948. This geographical configuration of the position of Haifa is evident in the vivid imagery of Palestinians moving vertically across layers of colonized territories as well as in the surreal futuristic image of a special tunnel through which Palestinians move horizontally across colonized temporalities. Intriguingly, the tunnel functions more as a black hole than as a third space that could potentially bridge the abyss between the two Haifas.

The unbridgeable gap between the two cities is mirrored in the intimate sphere, the relationship between the nameless narrator who lives in the Palestinian Haifa and his son N who studies in the Israeli Haifa. Despite their close bond as father and son, the narrator and N dwell in separate urban spaces governed by different maps of the same geography. Rather than being described as merely a matter of a generational gap, the divided Haifa is conjured up through the father's embodied palimpsest of a memory of the city before partition. His acute visceral awareness of the Haifa that existed before 1948 is alluded to in his reaction to the tunnel as well as in his heightened perception of the temporal and spatial map of the city.

For the father, the tunnel, which is located at a "PhotonTransit station," is a "beam chamber" that "swallows [Palestinian][40] children to over there, to the other over there."[41] Therefore, he accompanies N for his departure, as if the latter were embarking on a dangerous journey with no return. Intriguingly,

Kayyal inserts Hebrew into the exchange between the father and the son in this scene, thus foreshadowing the linguistic transition embedded in the movement between the two Haifas:

> As he walked into the station with his bag, I called out to him to make sure he has not forgotten his ID. So he wouldn't think I was clinging to a last chance to keep him here longer, I joked, in Hebrew: 'Do you have your ID?' He turned around, laughing and gave the reply he'd memorized by heart from all the time he'd heard me say it, even though he didn't really know where it came from: 'Where are the fish?' and walked away. Remember how much you used to love that film? Elia Suleiman ... *The Time that Remains*. Father and son fishing at night under military surveillance. I grew to love that dialogue.[42]

Interestingly, in the original texts in Arabic, the questions "Do you have your ID?" and "Where are the fish?" are written in vernacular Hebrew in what could be translated as "Got ID?" and "Got fish?" While the two questions are seemingly unrelated, they underscore the common awareness that the father and the son share in respect to the settler colonial present in Haifa, primarily the racialization of Palestinians and the ongoing dispossessions of their land and water. Indeed, "Do you have your ID?" or "Got ID?" is an explicit reference to the generic question that Israeli soldiers regularly pose at militarized checkpoints in the Occupied West Bank and Gaza. Likewise, Israeli police and security guards use it in Jewish spaces for racial profiling of anyone who might look like a Palestinian. The question about the fish, however, is an implicit allusion to the fish that disappeared with the familiar waterscape of the sea at Haifa after 1948. It is repeated throughout the story in the father's quest to find a grouper fish to cook for a meal to share with his son. He looks for it in the city's local market and among Palestinian fishermen, who lament its absence by reminding him that it "disappeared from what's left of the sea."[43]

For the father, to go back and forth between the two Haifas is to move between a native map and a settler colonial one. Despite the fact that both cities are located in the same place, the movement between them entails temporal and spatial border crossing akin to transcontinental traveling: "Moving from Palestinian Haifa to Israeli Haifa, from Jaffa to Tel Aviv, from Palestinian Hebron to Israeli Hebron, from Nablus to Shakhim, it's no different from travelling to Berlin or London or Boston."[44] Moreover, this movement necessitates a decolonial remapping of the city and a restoration of its urban features, from *re*claiming its Palestinian street names to imagining its future urban identity despite of and beyond the limitation of the settler colonial present:

We always used to dream about bringing back the real names of the streets, the names that Zionists changed for those 76 years, names like al-Muluk, Iraq, Ma'moun, Saladin, al-Jabal Street. And al-Karmel Boulevard that those losers, the Cultural Liberation Movement, renamed after Abu Nawwas[45] Street. Fuck cultural liberation. But after the victory of the revolution . . . we found that the Nakba would have been enough for all the names of the martyrs even if the Agreement had let us use those names, so we had to use much older, traditional ones instead.[46]

Manar Makhoul identifies alienation as a hallmark of fictional works written by the third generation of the Nakba. In these works, which belong to a category that he describes as "perplexity novels," alienation is problematized. These novels seek to capture the experience of being "present-absentified," as Makhoul describes it, and as they do so, the uncertainty of Palestinians in Israel about the direction in which they need to head becomes evident.[47] This perplexity manifests in disjointed narratives or storylines, the disclosure of protagonists' thoughts and recollections in a progression that isn't necessarily linear, but with temporal and spatial fluidity. Despite their distinct styles, all three writers engage in a "*re*-Palestinization" of space (and time) through a critical examination of contemporary life in a real and fragmented Palestine. That reclamation of a national space is also a characteristic of third-Nakba-generation writers and artists whose work is an embodied articulation of powerful Palestinian presence. Nadera Shalhoub-Kevorkian and Himmat Zoabi observe that, while living amid the destruction of Palestinian cities, including Jaffa—the city they examined in their study—Palestinians in Israel have come to realize that they are not only an Indigenous national minority, but also exiles in their own land. As Palestinians develop strategies of psychological, social, and political resistance to their ongoing dispossession, racism, and exclusion, Jaffa has become the locus of their challenge to colonial history and a place to "put down their roots," despite their internal exile.[48] Thus, to cross into Haifa, Jerusalem, Jaffa, and Ramallah, the growing de facto cultural capital in the Occupied West Bank, is to resist the erasure of the Palestinian landscape and space.

In "the diaries of crossing in/into Haifa" Azem, Helawy, and Kayyal capture the prevalence of quotidian encounters with internal borders and spatial erasure in the everyday life of Palestinians in Haifa. By *re*-centering these lived experiences among border crossers and city dwellers alike, these writers enact a decolonial move that aspires to *re*store the Palestinian social landscape of the city to its pre-Nakba era. However, this move does not idealize Haifa or re-imagine it as a paradise that was lost. On the contrary, the link between the two Haifas that these fictional works explore is mediated through a critical, if not ironic, intertextuality with canonical novels by canonical Palestinian authors like Habibi and Kanafani and a hyper-observant reflective narration devoid of nostalgia. Moreover, apart from the repetition of internal monologues that oscillate between sarcasm and playfulness, all three authors poke at internal strifes within Palestinian society by alluding to how the border crossers stumble upon mundane parochial linguistic and social quarrels that arise from clashes between different classes across rural and urban areas alike. Grief, longing, alienation, and confusion are represented as integral elements of this emotional landscape of the border crossers. All in all, by mirroring this wide range of emotions and perspectives of the border crossers in and to the contemporary Haifa, Azem, Helawy, and Kayyal *re*claim the old Haifa as a polyphonic living place that had its own contradictions, its beauty, its ugliness, and above all, its own Palestinian character.

Conclusion

As I elucidated in this chapter, several parallels can be drawn between the similar representation of internal borders in Mayan and Palestinian narratives. On the physical and material level, this representation epitomizes Anzaldúa's border theory, namely the image of the border as a "wound" and a "barbwire." Considering the different histories and cartographies of colonial and settler colonial spatiality in Chiapas and Palestine, we can observe that despite the permeability of internal borders—which in itself is an embodied expression of indigenous spatial resistance—Mayan and Palestinian writers depict internal borders as violent material structures of territorial dispossession and racial segregation built to deepen the settler colonial foundations of the Mexican and Israeli states, respectively.

For Anzaldúa, the US-Mexico border lines that were drawn in 1848 in Aztlán, the Chicano/a homeland, "*es una herida abierta* [an open wound] where the Third World grates against the first and bleeds."[49] In this evocative metaphor, Anzaldúa succinctly encapsulates the violence of the border and the asymmetrical power dynamics between the imperial/settler colonial US and colonized Mexico. In the following passage she elaborates further on this metaphor by providing a painful description of the enduring psychic wounds that scar her as a Chicana because of her geographical and cultural inhabitance of the colonial border in her ancestral homeland:

> 1,950 mile-long open wound
>   dividing *a pueblo*, a culture,
>   running down the length of my body

>   staking fence rods in my flesh,
>   splits me   splits me
>   *me raja   me raja*
>
>   This is my home
>   this thin edge of
>   barbwire.
>   But the skin of the earth is seamless.
>   The sea cannot be fenced,
>   el *mar* does not stop at borders.
>   To show the white man what she thought of his
>   arrogance,
>   *Yemayá* blew that wire fence down.
>
>   This land was Mexican once,
>   was Indian always
>   and is.
>   / And   will be again.⁵⁰

As noted above, all these violent elements of the border as "barbwire," a "fence," and a "wire fence" are entwined by geographical rupture, land theft, and psychic wounds. Anzaldúa's allusion to the double fragmentation of the Chicano/a ancestral homeland, which "was Mexican once / was Indian always," by these different forms of the border is sharply contrasted with the assertion that the Chicano/a homeland "is" and "will be again" both Indian and Mexican. This affirmation of Indigenous *ṣumūd* against the colonial violence of internal borders and their ensuing outcome of territorial and human erasure resonates with the perception of the border in the Mayan and Palestinian narratives discussed in this chapter.

Further, there is a triangulation of *'ulfa–kuxlej/kuxlejal* here between the Mayan, Palestinian, and Chicano/a understanding of the materiality of the border. This triadic space of affinity reveals yet another dimension of the resemblance between Palestine and Mexico in relation to borders, thus inviting us to think more broadly about the various latitudes of connections that can be drawn between the two contexts. Although it is beyond the scope of this chapter to fully explore these connections, it is important to highlight here that affinity, as a lens through which we can discern the shared contours of these connections, does not imply equivalence.

First, the internal borders in Chiapas, in Palestine '48, and in Aztlán emerged in different contexts of settler colonialism. The intricacies of border crossing, therefore, are not the same. Second, the articulation of the fundamental tension between indigeneity and border crossing is highly specific in each case. Border crossing in Atzlán, for example, is primarily situated within the US political economy of migration. As Audra Simpson points out, the dynamics of border crossing for Chicano/as in Atzlán along the US-Mexico border is markedly different from that of Native Americans and First Nations across Turtle Island. In the case of the Iroquois, for example, Simpson observes that crossing the US-Canada border is not simply an act of transgression but rather "an activation of their *rights* as members of reservations, or Haudenosaunee, or Iroquois Confederacy peoples."[51] In contrast, she argues that when Chicano/as cross the US-Mexico border, they undergo a shift in juridical and cultural identity—from Mexican, Mayans, or otherwise—into a Chicano/a designation within the United States. Emphasizing this contrast, Simpson explains: "Iroquois people crossing borders are reserve members or Iroquois before they cross, they are especially Iroquois *as* they cross, and they are Iroquois when they arrive at the place where they want to be."[52] This explanation underlines a critical difference between exercising Indigenous rights and passing through the juridical authority of the settler colonial state. By making this distinction, Simpson asserts the incommensurability of indigeneity across analogous, yet asymmetrical, settler colonial contexts.

The comparative analysis of Mayan and Palestinian narratives of border crossing in this chapter illustrates a common depiction of the border that echoes Anzaldúa's metaphor of the open wound. This image of the border, however, does not contradict Simpson's framework concerning the particularity of border crossing in different settler colonial experiences, nor align with Anzaldúa's approach to border crossing as a fertile ground for hybridity. Indeed, when it comes to border crossing, both Mayans and Palestinians, as border crossers, demonstrate greater affinity with Iroquois people than with the Chicanos/as. Perhaps to a large degree, this is due to the nature of territorial and racial segregation between Mayans and *ladinos* in Chiapas, on the one hand, and Jews and Arab Palestinians, on the other. Contrary to Anzaldúa's celebration of the borderlands of the Southwest as a site of racial and cultural mixing, or *mestizaje*, the borderlands in Chiapas and Palestine function as rigid territorial lines of partition, enforcing ethno-racial and religious separation. While Mayans and Palestinians do not live in formal reservations like the Iroquois, they are nonetheless confined to segregated villages and small towns, kept apart from neighboring *ladino/as* and Jewish towns and cities. These internal borders, established by the Mexican and Israeli states, are spatial structures designed to confine Mayan and Palestinian life to separate enclosed territories, thereby reinforcing their subaltern status as minoritized, racialized second-class citizens and cultural Other.

Given this, it becomes clear that Mayan and Palestinian narratives of and about border crossers and city dwellers are first and foremost literary modes of spatial resistance. In terms of indigeneity, these narratives reaffirm an Indigenous ontological relation to land. By *redrawing* internal borders, *reconfiguring* the landscapes of Jobel and Haifa, and *resignifying* what constitutes urbanity in these cities, Mayan and Palestinian narratives anchor their own definition of the land. Doing so, they symbolically revoke the state's ownership of the land, or to use Aileen Moreton-Robinson's concept, the "possessive logics" of the state. According to Moreton-Robinson, settler states, namely white settler states in the first world like the US, Canada, Australia, and New Zealand, disavow indigenous sovereignty by enacting "an excessive desire to invest in reproducing and reaffirming the nation-state's ownership, control, and domination."[53] Seen through this lens, we can observe that in envisioning San Cristóbal as Jobel, Mayan writers expropriate the Mexican state's vision of the city as an urban space designated for *ladinos* only. Instead, they envision Jobel not as an imagined Indigenous city mirroring mythological Mayan cities, but rather as a living contemporary urban space where Mayan languages and cultures are neither excluded nor marginal. To exist as a Mayan in Jobel, therefore, is to be central to the contemporary and future production of the spatial, social, and economic identity of the city. We can also notice how Palestinian narratives, whether through stories that seek to reintegrate the divided self of alienated border crossers or through the reassembly of the fragmented topography of the city, redeem Haifa from its constitutive presence-absence, thus making it possible to *re*claim not only its destroyed past, but also its future as a liberated Palestinian city.

Overall, the parallels between Mayan and Palestinian narratives of border crossers and city dwellers reveal yet another layer of *ṣumūd* that Mayans and Palestinians have in common in their corresponding Indigenous struggles. This *ulfa–kuxlej/kuxlejal* extends to the rural geographies as well, where internal borders are explicitly demarcated and controlled by the state's sanctioned violence and military oppression. Key evidence of this enduring affinity and the persistence of *ṣumūd* can be gleaned in the following chapter, where I shed light on comparable murals that document massacres committed by the Mexican paramilitary and the Israeli military police, respectively, against Mayan and Palestinian citizens in the villages of Acteal in 1997 and Kafr Qasem in 1956. As the visual stories in these murals show us, the message of "To exist is to resist" encapsulates more than the motto of a traveling mural of Indigenous solidarity.

4
Murals, Marches, and Metaphors: Performative Commemoration in Rural Chiapas and Palestine

Acteal is a small village in the municipality of Chenalhó in Los Altos (the Highlands) in Chiapas, about thirty-three miles north of San Cristóbal / Jobel. Although navigation applications give an estimate of about an hour and fifty minutes' drive from this cultural capital, the way to Acteal is significantly longer. First, one must secure a private mode of transport because of the general lack of regular public transportation between the *ladino* urban centers of Chiapas and the rural Mayan villages. Second, one must drive slowly to safely climb the winding mountainous bumpy road that passes through nebulous curves, small Maya villages and their adjunct green *milpas*, and signs that demarcate the borders of autonomous Zapatista territories of San Pedro Polhó. Third, with no cell phone service available, one must rely on an offline map or ask Mayan villagers encountered walking alongside the road for directions. Alternatively, one can simply keep an eye on the road until one reaches a sculpture of a mass grave composed of bodies stacked on top of each other on the side of the street. Underneath this concrete statue, a large white billboard peeking from the green bushes will announce: "*Acteal: Raíz, Memoria, Esperanza*" (Acteal: Roots, Memory, Hope). The word "Acteal" is printed in black curvy letters, whereas the words *Raíz, Memoria*, and *Esperanza* are printed in shades of cocoa and coffee brown, thus accentuating the brownness of the surrounding cocoa and coffee shrub. An image of bees roaming over the blossom of a truncated tree trunk with sprouting roots adorns the billboard, suggesting vibrancy, flourishing, and rebirth, and at the same time alluding to members of the Christian pacifist group *Sociedad Civil Las Abejas* (The Civil Society of Bees) for whom the commemorative statue was set up in the first place.

Kafr Qasem is a Palestinian town in *al-Muthullath al-Janūbī* (The Southern Triangle) situated on the furthest southern tip of the 1949 Armistice Line, or the so-called Green Line border. It is almost midway between Majdal Yaba, a Palestinian village that was destroyed and ethnically cleansed during the Nakba in 1948, and Ariel, the fourth-largest illegal Jewish settlement in the Occupied West Bank. The latter was built in 1978 about twelve miles east of the border.[1] Geographically speaking, Kafr Qasem is a quintessential border town situated between the coastal plains northeast of Tel-Aviv/Jaffa and the western foothills of the West Bank. Spatially speaking, however, it inhabits the colonial border demarcated by the ongoing expansion of Zionist settler colonialism. While its main western entrance is congested by the sprawling expansion of Afek Industrial Park, a major Jewish Israeli industrial and high-tech hub, its southeastern neighborhood is parallel to the Jewish town of Rosh Ha-'Ayin and Migdal Afek National Park, both of which were built on the ruins of Majdal Yaba. Although Kafr Qasem is in the center of the country, accessing it from Ariel involves passing through military checkpoints and separate roads designated for illegal settlements. Approaching it from Majdal Yaba, however, entails navigating through a maze of *mis*transliteration of its name across the English and Hebrew street signs as well as the sporadically installed bilingual ones in Arabic and Hebrew. A vivid example of this state-sanctioned policy of de-Arabization is evident in a trilingual street sign posted on a major junction on Highway 6 that runs along the Green Line in front of Kafr Qasem. The omission of the very word *Kafr* from the sign and the replacement of the letter *Q* with *K*, along with the reduction of the long vowel "*ā*" into a short vowel "*i*," thus transforms Kafr Qasem into *Kesem*. After passing this linguistic mutation, which demonstrates the ongoing erasure of Palestine, one can find an Arabic-only sign reclined against a black midsize billboard with an image of two lit candles standing like pillars of mourning. Between the two pillars, the town's official welcome is written: "Kufur Qāsim balad yaṭību al-'aysh fīh /كفر قاسم بلد يطيب العيش فيه" (Kafr Qasem, a pleasant place to live).[2]

While the way to Acteal and Kafr Qasem reveals two different histories of borders mapped across two disconnected and distant continents, the story behind the signs at their entrances tells a similar narrative of colonial violence and the ongoing Indigenous resistance to it by affirming existence and the right to live. As landmarks of mourning, these signs bear witness to the collective memory of the people in Acteal and Kafr Qasem and anchor their grief in the landscape of two brutal massacres that marked their history: the Acteal massacre in 1997 and the Kafr Qasem massacre in 1956.

Despite the transcontinental distance and a temporal gap of four decades, both massacres illustrate an analogous history of colonial violence committed by the Mexican and the Israeli military, respectively, against Indigenous peasants in border villages. Whereas both massacres were committed within a comparable context of what has been described as "low-intensity war," the ultimate motive was the displacement and uprooting of Indigenous peasant communities. In addition, each of the two massacres took place in a period when the states of Mexico and Israel mobilized their military to demarcate the borders of the state as a sovereign body, and thus killed unarmed Indigenous rural peasants in Acteal and Kafr Qasem in cold blood on these borders.

Departing from this analogy, this chapter examines how the survivors of the massacres, relatives of the victims, and their extended communities in both Acteal and Kafr Qasem engage in similar forms of commemorative practices to narrate the stories of the massacres while affirming an ongoing quest for justice. Apart from designing commemorative banners and writing poems and songs, the people of Acteal and Kafr Qasem employ intergenerational transmission of oral testimonies, visual storytelling, and communal embodied performance, most notably religious rituals and marches, to immortalize the massacres. On a broader level, these practices are associated with new commemorative forms that characterize a particular type of experiential museums, or what art historian Amy Sodardo calls the memorial museums, where memory is linked to democracy[3] and where the stories that are told, and the experiential mode of telling them, are more important than the object contained and displayed.[4] However, this chapter is less concerned with examining these commemorative forms merely for their aesthetic value or the question of institutionalizing memory. There is a robust literature on the built structures of memorialization and the recent global surge in memorials dedicated to atrocities and genocide.[5] Instead, my interest, first and foremost, is in elucidating the *'ulfa–kuxlej/kuxlejal* between Kafr Qasem and Acteal by demonstrating how the aesthetics in both memorial sites, which were established through local grassroot initiatives and are situated in proximity to the sites of the massacres, reflect similar artistic, philosophical, spiritual, and affective expressions of land-based relationality and *ṣumūd* vis-à-vis the ongoing struggle against settler colonial and state terror.

Given the fact that I am the first scholar to observe this affinity between the commemorations of the massacres in Acteal and Kafr Qasem and the aesthetic and politics that contribute to shaping the affinity between the two sites, I am compelled to prioritize unveiling it by focusing on what I consider to be important in this story: the invisible thread that connects these two villages, which have no previous contact with each other, by showing how the bereaved communities in Acteal and Kafr Qasem tell a similar story of Indigenous resistance, the quest for justice, and the immortalization of peaceful Indigenous peasant citizens killed in cold blood by a militarized settler colonial state.

The commemorative practices and the built structures that host them in both Acteal and Kafr Qasem draw upon a rich material culture. This abundance deserves further research to examine the multivocal artistic dimension of the artifacts displayed, the role of local activists and outsiders in curating and archiving, and the institutional aspect of museum-making in peasant communities. Although I present here a preliminary annotation and close reading of selected material objects in both sites, namely murals, the comparative framework that I am pursuing precludes me from delving into a deeper critical analysis of how these questions address other important aspects of the commemoration, such as the intimacy involved in the collective mourning in the villages versus the iconographic representation of the massacres in the national imaginary. Thus, I invite future scholars to expand on these issues and thus contribute to writing the history of the memorialization structures in both sites—which, apart from receiving some attention in anthropological studies that investigated the politics of memory,[6] remain largely undocumented.

As a Palestinian scholar seeing the *'ulfa–kuxlej/kuxlejal* through the double lens of an insider-outsider, I am keenly aware of how this position informed my comparative reading of the murals. Therefore, in addition to providing an extensive historical background in the following pages to illustrate this relational comparison between Acteal and Kafr Qasem, I offer personal reflections throughout the chapter to contextualize my analysis of the murals and the dynamics of my close engagement with the communities in Acteal and Kafr Qasem during my literary ethnography fieldwork. By doing so, I shed light on how issues of access, intrusion, language barriers, translation, and mediation facilitated the way I link the Indigenous struggle, and, at the same time, informed my position as the narrator-igniter of the conversation between Acteal and Kafr Qasem.

We must acknowledge here the inevitable limits of conducting a comparative analysis across different historical periods in different areas from a contemporary viewpoint. In this case, one of the key limitations is the use of the terms "village" and "rural" to describe both Acteal and Kafr Qasem. Without question, the impoverished village that Kafr Qasem was in 1956, with its small population of approximaitly1,500 people, predominantly peasants and laborers, is not the current town of 25,000 people living in an urbanized landscape characterized by a developing economy on the one hand and the siege of settler colonial neoliberal encroachment on the other. However, given the ongoing legal battle against state impunity and the active collective remembering of the massacre as an act of a state assault against a peaceful small village, the imaginary of the rural landscape of Kafr Qasem in 1956 still resonates poignantly. In addition, the sharp contrast between the town's underdeveloped infrastructure in comparison to the neighboring Jewish towns and settlements makes visible its rural landscape. Finally, the close familial networks that underpin the social structure among Kafr Qasemites and the use of the word *balad* (a place in the countryside, or town) at the entrance underscore its rurality.

In parallel, given the political structure of Acteal, to identify this site simply as a village would be misleading. Although Acteal is located in the heart of the rural highlands and is surrounded by several Mayan hamlets, it was not built as a village, but rather as a camp for displaced Mayan peasants fleeing interethnic land conflict caused by the militarization of the highlands following the Zapatista uprising in 1994, when the Mexican state deployed a third of its military to counter the Mayan insurgency led by the *Ejército Zapatista de Liberación Nacional* (Zapatista Army of National Liberation, EZLN). The fluctuating number of displaced Mayans living in Acteal from 1997 to the present, from almost 250 at the time of the massacre to 420 in the early 2000s, to 240 to date, reflects the political shifts that occurred during the aftermath of the massacre and the subsequent waves of displacement and forced removal from the community triggered by the deepening internal political factions and the violence of the Mexican paramilitary. With this history in mind, the geopolitical formation of Acteal as a village has been in flux, though in everyday language in Acteal itself it is evoked as the *pueblo* (people, village) or *comunidad* (community). Precisely for these reasons, my use of the term *village* to refer to both Acteal and Kafr Qasem is more figurative than definitive.

Since the main objective of this chapter is the illumination of the *'ulfa–kuxlej/kuxlejal* that links these two villages, I will examine their commemorative practices side by side despite the geographical and historical gap charted above. To this end, the next section delineates the historical context of the massacres vis-à-vis the geopolitical position of Acteal and Kafr Qasem to ultimately contextualize my comparative juxtaposition of them as border villages. To set up, I begin by outlining the history of Kafr Qasem to align with a more linear timeline. Although my use of the lens of affinity is rooted in examining relations with all their nonlinear points of connection, I will start the historical section with Kafr Qasem because a more linear timeline from Kafr Qasem to Acteal enables the reader to follow the invisible and fine thread that connects them. In the following sections, however, I will switch the order according to the itinerary of my travels between the two sites from 2016 through 2022 to capture more accurately how this affinity unfolded.

On Becoming Border Villages

Kafr Qasem *became* a border village due to the demarcation of an artificial border, or the so-called Green Line in 1949. It is situated on the southern edge of the Triangle, a flat terrain of about 50 km / 30 miles long and 5 km / 3 miles wide squeezed between the lines of the Israel-Jordan Armistice Agreement and the Mediterranean Sea. Kafr Qasem is part of the twenty-seven large and small villages and a number of small associate villages known as *al-kherab* الخِرَب (the ruins), or hamlets, that constitute the Triangle. Since its annexation after the 1949 Rhodes Ceasefire Agreement, Israel has considered the Triangle a strategic border area essential for securing the geopolitical, military, and economic colonial control of the nascent Jewish state. The Northern Triangle, particularly the area of Wadi ʿAra, became a strategic corridor, because of its location as the main transportation route connecting the coast and the northern and eastern parts of the Galilee.[7] The Southern Triangle, in contrast, shrank into a bottleneck area, allowing only a narrow pass, about one mile wide, between the Nablus mountains and the Maritime Plain. To dominate the country, it has been essential to dominate the pass.[8]

The strategic reconfiguration of the Triangle as a border area involved an overlapping process of militarization, partition, and dispossession. Alongside the imposition of a military rule between 1948 and 1966, the incipient state established a special Border Police unit in 1949 to patrol rural areas along the so-called Green Line. The policing and military surveillance of the border villages in the Triangle during this first decade of the state was part of a larger regional history of border warfare that Israel was declaring along its self-demarcated territorial lines with Jordan, Egypt, Lebanon, and Syria. During this period, particularly between 1949 and 1956, Israel implemented a policy of "shoot to kill"[9] against infiltrators, the majority of whom were unarmed Palestinian refugees returning to their homes and villages or gathering crops at night. In the border village al-Marjeh in the Northern Triangle, for example, there were three types of infiltrators: economic infiltrators who smuggled basic goods from Jordan into the Palestinian villages in Israel, political infiltrators who broadcasted news of the Israelis to the Jordanian side, and domestic infiltrators who crossed the borders weekly to visit their families on the other side.[10] It must be noted that Israel labeled those who crossed "infiltrators" to criminalize their actions as "illegal,"[11] a policy that legitimized killing between 2,700 and 5,000 infiltrators.[12] While none of the soldiers, police, and border guards were brought to trial for committing these killings, the bodies of the murdered infiltrators were systematically disappeared.[13]

The testimony of Mustapha Azem (1933–2019), a former vice-president of the Al-Taybeh Municipality in the Central Triangle and a long-standing member of *ha-Miflaga ha-Komunistit ha-Yisra'elit*, the Communist Party (MAKI), who was imprisoned in the early 1950s for punching the military ruler in his area after participating in a protest organized by MAKI against the killing of an infiltrator from his hometown, offers a vivid account of a disappearance story that was received by the peaceful Palestinian villagers as the first signs of state terror:

> Until 1949, there was no Border Police. Because of the scarcity of resources and produce, people used to go to the West Bank to buy products and sell them to the Jews, who were ecstatic to see even an onion. The police killed the people when they returned and disappeared their bodies. Before 1948, the Jews organized as Zionist gangs and killed Palestinians, but after 1948 they organized as a military because it was inappropriate for a state to act like a gang. After capturing the Palestinians who crossed the border, the Border Police would kill them and throw them into the quarries in the valleys between the hills and cover the bodies with stones and rocks. In our hometown, Abu El-Nabtiti lost his mind after his two sons, Ali and Ahmad, were killed and their bodies were never recovered.[14]

The militarized surveillance of the Armistice Line went hand in hand with the destruction of Palestinian houses and the confiscation of Palestinian lands that formed the borderline.[15] The establishment of new Jewish settlements under the pretext of blocking infiltration was also adopted as a primary strategic measure. Indeed, between mid-1948 and mid-1953, Israel built some 350 Jewish colonies modeled as rural villages, *moshavim*, along or near the borders.[16] This land theft occurred within a militarized dispossession of the areas alongside the Armistice Line and the vigorous settler colonial control of these territories solidified the reality of a geographical partition and the creation of a physical border within Historic Palestine. This actual deterritorialization, which resulted as well in disconnecting the villages in the Triangle from their surrounding Palestinian urban centers in Tulkarm, Qalqilya, and Jenin both socially and economically, set the stage for a future spatial confinement of the Triangle, which remains ongoing until the present. One outcome of this process was an economic transformation of the Triangle from a major farmland into a hub of unskilled labor. Due to its proximity to the Tel-Aviv metropolis, Kafr Qasem, for example, became one of the main providers of unskilled labor in the 1960s and the 1970s. And while it continues to be economically worse off than

Tel-Aviv and its surrounding *moshavim*, the confined village is dense and overpopulated due to Israel's spatial policy that prevents the geographical expansion of Palestinian villages.[17] A 2020 special Human Rights Watch Report on Israeli discriminatory land policies confirms that Palestinian towns continue to be squeezed while Jewish towns grow in the 93 percent of the land of Historic Palestine that the Israeli state controls, including occupied East Jerusalem. The report further highlights that land policies in more recent years have not only failed to reverse the earlier and largest land confiscation that took place during the military rule between 1949 and 1966, but in many cases further restricted the land available for Palestinian residential growth.

Like Kafr Qasem, Acteal faces systemic settler colonial dispossession of Indigenous land and state-sanctioned surveillance of militarized constructed borders. However, the history behind how Acteal became a border village is less straightforward. Indeed, Acteal emerged as a border site against the backdrop of a complex demarcation of territorial, ethnic, racial, and religious lines that were drawn in the sixteenth century and have been consistently redrawn since the late nineteenth century according to national, regional, and local interests. Ethnically speaking, Acteal is one of the 120 Tsotsil, Tseltal, and *ladino* localities that constitute the municipality of San Pedro Chenalhó, named after a saint and the Tsotsil word for cave water. It is adjacent to San Pedro Polhó, which became the autonomous Zapatista center of the township of Chenalhó in 1996, and Majomut, the major site for coffee production in Los Altos and headquarters for the *Unión de Ejidos y Comunidades de Majomut* (The Union of the Ejidos and Communities of Majomut). Before the Zapatista uprising, this region witnessed a series of local land struggles that originated in late nineteenth century because of Mexico's reconfiguration of its capitalist economy. The latter process entailed a combination of aggressive agrarian provisions that opened the territories of Los Altos for North American and European investments and, thus, turned large sections of land into plantations for export crops, namely coffee, and freed up more Indigenous labor for the global market.[18] At the same time, an elite of *ladino* landlords from San Cristóbal / Jobel fortified its power in Los Altos by privatizing land and invading the region with new *haciendas*.[19]

These transformations did not proceed without Mayan resistance. In 1938, Tsotsil-speaking *campesinos* (peasant farmers) in San Pedro Chenalhó and their Tseltal-speaking peers in the neighboring municipality of Cancuc led a regional agrarian struggle against the *ladino* landlords. This rebellion led to the expulsion of *ladinos*, or as some Mexican state officials describe it, "*desladinización o reindianización*" (De-ladinization or Re-Indianization) of Los Altos.[20] Despite this ethnic transformation in the demographic makeup of Los Altos, the economic and local power remained in the hands of *ladino* landlords who concentrated their takeover in the spaces that they occupied in mixed ethnic municipalities, such as Los Chorros, throughout the 1970s and 1980s.[21]

Following these reconfigurations of intracommunity dynamics, additional shifts in the local power structure took place when several political and religious organizations emerged to challenge the hegemony of old authorities in Los Altos. First, supreme councils were formed. They served as elected authorized representatives of the communities, and developed local rescue programs based on the language, customs, and resources in the communities, aimed at solving the problems of marginalized *campesinos*. Second, new parties, such as El Partido Socialista de los Trabajadores de México (PST), surfaced and gained influence, thus challenging the hegemony of the postrevolutionary party that ruled Mexico from the late 1920s, El Partido Revolucionario Institucional (PRI).[22] Ultimately, these nascent power bases forged new divergent paths for locally crafted models of self-government, which in effect became precursors for Indigenous autonomy. Third, the traditional hegemony of the Catholic Church was rivaled by the rise of liberation theology, which was led by Bishop Samuel Ruíz, who was often compared to Bishop Bartolomé de las Casas, the first resident Bishop of Chiapas, who became renowned as the "Protector of the Indians" because of his advocacy for justice and equal human rights for Indigenous communities.[23] The expansion of Pentecostal churches, which had doubled the number of Protestant converts in Chiapas by the 1990s, was another rival to reckon with. With the rise of Protestantism, there was an increase in the number of secular organizations that expanded the regional power of Indigenous civil society by encouraging dialogue across ethnic divides and enabling them to confront the power of enriched Indigenous leaders, *caciques*, in rural areas and elites in urban settings. Undoubtedly, this process was not free of new interethnic conflicts and a renewal of old land struggles that culminated in a series of intercommunal violence and a mass wave of expulsions of non-Catholic Indigenous communities from Los Altos into San Cristóbal/Jobel.

Flashing forward to 1992, we note that the Christian pacifist group *Sociedad Civil Las Abejas* moved into Acteal, after being harassed by the PRI mayor in their original hamlet in Tzajalchen. Formed by twenty-two communities, *Las Abejas* (The Bees) emerged as a collective response to land conflict and political injustice under the shelter of the society of coffee producers. The collective's choice to identify as bees is an embodiment of Mayan cosmology, Catholic beliefs, and Zapatista politics. Drawing on the Mayan belief in the existence of a spiritual bond between animals and humans,[24] *Las Abejas* embrace the bees as their *nahual* (animal companion spirit). In coming together under this name, the communities associated themselves with the industrious and collective work of the bees. This form of self-fashioning is also evident in other autonomous Zapatista communities, such as the group *Xi'Nich*, Tsotsil for ants. In interviews with Marco Tavanti,[25] members of *Las Abejas* remark that the bees symbolize their collective mobilization toward the double goal of defending rights and equal sharing of the fruit of their work. In a Catholic sense, *Las Abejas* conceive of the image of the bees as emblematic of their collective work for the Kingdom of God. That said, this Catholic iconography is domesticated in the parallels drawn between the figure of the queen bee and *Nuestra Señora de Cancuc*, a local Indigenous adaptation of the face of the Virgin Mary, and the popular Mexican version of it, La Virgen de Guadalupe. Others identify their iconographic image of the bees with their political intent and active resistance against the government and emphasized that the non-violent resistance of *Las Abejas* is akin to the power of the small insect, which can move even a sleeping cow when it pricks. Along with the use of animal identities and the role of the quest for autonomy in resistance movements, *Las Abejas*, like several Zapatista autonomous communities, adopted other nonviolent protest tactics, such as peace belts (the linking of arms by participants in a large circle along the perimeter of a displaced person camp or community in a gesture of nonviolent resistance), marches, fasting, the nonpayment of utility bills, and aid rejection,[26] all of which played a vital role in the protest against the Mexican state.

As the new home of a Christian Base Community adhering to liberation theology, Acteal *became* a border village located in the middle between Los Churros and Pantelhó. Whereas Los Churros was a stronghold for the PRI, which collaborated with the Mexican state in the militarization of civil society in Los Altos to suppress the power of the Zapatistas, Pantelhó was an official site of Zapatista autonomy and the locus of an expanding Indigenous civil society made up of a growing number of municipalities that gained autonomy and territory following the Zapatista uprising in 1994. Eventually, Acteal became a border village inhabiting a liminal position between state counterinsurgency and Indigenous resistance. Following the massacre in Acteal, the materiality of this border amplified. As Maria H. Hart points out, the Acteal massacre drew a line: "If before it had been possible to state that *Las Abejas* were EZLN sympathizers yet somewhere outside of the fray, now it was impossible to do so—they had been drawn into the center of it, irretrievably."[27] In the past few years, this in-between position intensified further due to the increasing presence of narco-violence in Chiapas caused by the infiltration of the Sinaloa and Jaslico cartels into the state.[28] The escalating militarization of the highlands in response to this development has transformed Acteal from a border village to a true *zona fronterista*, a borderland area.

Considering this comparative historical outline, one can observe that Kafr Qasem and Acteal became border villages in completely distinctive circumstances. Nonetheless, the parallel militarized encounter of Indigenous peasant citizens with a settler colonial state in both villages, which took place in an analogous context of low-intensity wars declared *on the border*,[29] is a compelling reason to examine their commonalities and to think about them together through a framework of relationality. We could ask, therefore, what do the visual commemoration of these seemingly unrelated massacres that are separated in time and space reveal to us about the similar Indigenous struggle of Mayan and Palestinian peasants for existence in the face of state-sanctioned violence? And more important, are these massacres truly unrelated? The answer is: No.

Although it is largely invisible, there is a connection that crystallizes the affinity between Kafr Qasem and Acteal beyond the border village analogy. This affinity is embedded in the increasing direct involvement of the Israeli military in the training and militarization of the Mexican counterinsurgency programs, whose presence in Chiapas increased dramatically after the Zapatista uprising. As Jimmy Johnson and Linda Quiquivix point out, Mexico began receiving Israeli weaponry in 1973 with the purchase of five Arava planes from Israel Aerospace Industries. They write: "Throughout the 1970s and '80s, infrequent exports continued to the country in the form of small arms, mortars, and electronic fences. Sales escalated in the early 2000s, according to research that we have undertaken."[30] Along similar lines, a recent study of unclassified documents from the Pentagon about the armed struggle in Chiapas reveals that Israel provides Mexico with training and weapons in its counterinsurgency against the Zapatistas in Chiapas. These documents confirm that, in addition to this military collaboration, which intensified after 1994 to counter the emergence of the Zapatista Army of National Liberation (EZLN), "Israel has intervened in training the military, as well as local and federal police forces [while] the Mexican army used modified Israeli Arava aircraft for intervention in Chiapas."[31] In a related vein, in his analysis of the documentary films that were made about the Acteal massacre, José Rabasa highlights a scene from the film *Acteal: Estrategia de muerte* (Acteal, Death Strategy [1998], by the Mexican filmmaker Carlos Mendoza), where explicit reference is made to the involvement of Israeli experts in the counterinsurgency efforts of the Mexican state and their participation in the training of the Mexican army on Mexican soil.[32] Given this less-known history of collaboration, and despite the distinct unfolding events of the massacres in Acteal and Kafr Qasem, it is not implausible to view what happened in Acteal in 1997 as a continuation of the story of colonial violence and state terror against Indigenous peasants that began in

Kafr Qasem in 1957. That said, it is crucial to allude here to an important paradox in the military cooperation between the states of Mexico and Israel. While Israel provides arms and counterinsurgency training to the Mexican army, it actively participates in the militarization of the US-Mexico border by selling the US federal government surveillance machinery and other cybersecurity technologies that ultimately block the entry of immigrants from Mexico and Latin America into the US.[33]

The Harvest of Blood and Honey: The Tale of Two Kindred Massacres

When the Tripartite Aggression against Egypt began in 1956, Kafr Qasem, along with all the seven Palestinian villages in the southern Triangle along the Armistice Line with Jordan, was placed under a nightly curfew. Colonel Yishhar Shadmi, a military brigade commander of Israel's Central Command, was instructed to take all precautionary measures to maintain quiet on the colonial Armistice Line, which marked the border with Jordan.[34] After receiving permission from the higher military command, he rescheduled the curfew to begin at 5:00 p.m., instead of 10:00 p.m. Shadmi further instructed Major Shmuel Malinki, who oversaw the Border Police tasked with enforcing the curfew, to shoot on sight any villagers violating the curfew. When the time gap was brought to Shadmi's attention and questions were asked about how to handle Kafr Qasemites who were returning from the fields or their work after 5:00 p.m., he responded in Arabic: "Allāh yarḥamhu" (May God have mercy on him).[35]

The news about the altered hours of the curfew arrived in Kafr Qasem at 4:30 p.m., when a young sergeant visited the home of the village's chief, *mukhtār* Wadi' Muhammad Sarsur. When the latter pleaded that there was not enough time to spread the word to the four hundred day laborers in the factories, quarries, olive groves, and fields located as far away as the depopulated Palestinian cities of Lydda/Lydd and Jaffa, as well as Pitah Tikva and Ramat Gan, two early Zionist colonies that were built on the ruins of the Palestinian villages of Mulabbis and Salame, depopulated before 1948, the sergeant responded: "We will take care of them!"[36] Little did the *mukhtār* know that the sergeant's promise was a vow to kill in cold blood and at close range forty-nine members of his community and wound thirteen more at the western entrance of the village over the course of two hours. In one of the earliest Palestinian literary documentations of the massacre, "Kufur Qāsim: Al-Majzara—al-Siyāsa" / "Kafr Qasem: The Massacre—Politics" (1976), the novelist Emile Habibi metaphorized the chronicle of the two hours as "The Nine Waves of Killing."[37] The first wave began after a Border Police officer issued a command of two words in Hebrew: "Tiqṣtor 'otām!" (Harvest them, or Mow them down!).[38] By the end of the ninth wave, the Border Patrol executed nineteen men, six women, including a pregnant one, ten teenage boys (ages 14–17), six girls (ages 12–15), and seven young boys (ages 8–13).

The curfew set prior to the massacre was extended as men from the neighboring village of Jaljoulia were called in and ordered to dig wells or small holes, allegedly for military use, throughout the silent night under the pointing guns of the Border Police. Only three days later were families of the victims allowed to visit the ad hoc graves, and their immediate response was to reopen them to reclaim the bodies of their loved ones and give them a proper burial in the local cemetery. A special trilingual pamphlet (in Arabic, Hebrew, and English) that was published on the sixtieth anniversary of the massacre by the local Public Committee for the Memorialization of the Massacre details the collective terror and grief that engulfed the village on that day: "The village broke down in tears, visiting the cemetery a lot of women fainted . . . 49 new graves all of a sudden."[39] In a personal phone interview that I conducted in 2021 with Helwa Saleem Taha, the sister of one of the victims of the massacre, Jamal Saleem Taha (eleven years old), she recounted: "We were a small village of 1,000 or 1,500 people when the massacre happened. Forty-nine persons is a significant size of the population." Taha emphasized the magnitude of loss by using the Palestinian peasant expression "*Biswū swayyithum* / بِسْووا سْوَيتهُم" (They carry a significant weight / They are a substantial number).[40] During this mass reburial, which was described by the Kafr Qasemites as a collective act of resistance, meant to assuage wounds and reclaim normal funerary rites,[41] headstones with the word "Martyr" were installed on individual tombs. Intriguingly, in his depiction of the massacre based on the personal accounts and testimonies of its survivors that were gathered by Palestinian lawyers, political figures, and the military court's archive, the poet Mahmoud Darwish recognizes the Kafr Qasemites who were killed in the massacre as "victims, not martyrs,"[42] thus emphasizing not only their innocence, but also the gravity of the criminality of the Israeli state.

Despite closure and media blackout, the news about the massacre leaked out almost immediately. The first outsiders to enter the village and later publicize the atrocity were Knesset members Tawfiq Tubi and Meir Vilner from MAKI and Latif Dori, a member of the leftist-Zionist MAPAM Party (*Miflaga ha-Po'alim ha-Me'uhedet*). They managed to bypass the police roadblocks at the entrance of the village and collected the testimonies of the survivors and the traumatized and isolated people of Kafr Qasem. In the following two years, the grief- and hunger-stricken village would endure further insults added to their injuries because of two spectacles: a forced reconciliation and a staged military trial of the perpetrators.

In November 1957, a group of government officials accompanied by Knesset members and notable figures from neighboring Palestinian villages arrived for a state-organized ceremony of reconciliation. Appropriating the Arabic term and ritual of *ṣulḥa*, a Bedouin clan-based conflict resolution custom, state officials and the military generals entered the village with the aim of terminating the "Kafr Qasem affair."[43] Staged as a performance of appeasement and multiculturalism, the ceremony was nothing but a "charade" or, as Shira Robinson puts it, a "spectacle of sovereignty"[44] that reflected the dramatic effort of the state to impose its own memory and to subordinate the Palestinian citizens for the sake of Jewish privilege. While the Hebrew press gave a favorable account of the ceremony, newspapers in Arabic denounced it by relying on reports and testimonies of Kafr Qasemites who confessed that members of the mourning villagers were pressured to participate in the ceremony out of fear and the absence of a viable alternative.[45] Their participation, however, did not go without resistance. When the *mukhtar*'s son announced in his speech that the government would pave roads and connect the village with a water grid as compensation for the blood that was spilled and asked Kafr Qasemites to forget the massacre, the villagers protested by making loud grumbling noises to denounce his insult to the memory of the victims and by walking away from the ceremony toward the cemetery, thus subverting the instructions of the event's organizers. In fact, they went even as far as chasing away a government official who tried to follow them at the cemetery, where they gathered to cry and weep over the graves of their loved ones.[46] In 2000, the mayor of Kafr Qasem summed up the events of this day by saying that the martyrs were slaughtered twice, once on the day of the massacre and again on the "Day of Reconciliation."[47]

After public pressure, then–Prime Minister Ben-Gurion called for a closed military trial. The trial began its proceeding on January 15, 1957. Palestinians throughout the country organized a general strike in solidarity with Kafr Qasem. The strike was also a symbolic rejection of the legality of the military court. During the two years of the trial, the injured and the families of the victims faced a series of legal manipulations that involved visits from state-sponsored officials and collaborators who tried to coerce the families into accepting a privately arranged damage settlement on the condition that they cancel their claims against the state.[48] The trial ended in 1958 with a verdict of long terms of imprisonment for the Border Police and a fine of one penny for Colonel Shadmi. But within three years, all the perpetrators were released and promoted to senior positions in the government. Malinki, for example, became a security officer at the Dimona nuclear plant, while Lieutenant Gabriel

Dahan was appointed as a director for the department of Arab Affairs in the municipality of Ramla.

From a political perspective, the trial focused on the doctrine of a "manifestly unlawful order" in Israeli military law, which granted the military legal impunity. It also relegated the civic status of the Arabs to the level of a noncentral issue for the court.[49] Over the last two decades, the legal battle against the immunity of the state and its military archives developed in contradictory forms. In 2018, Adam Raz, an Israeli historian and author of the first book in Hebrew about the massacre,[50] submitted a petition to the Military Court of Appeals with a request to open the still-closed files. Transcripts of the trial were revealed only in 2022. They confirmed what Israeli and Palestinian historians, such as Ilan Pappé, Ruvik Rosenthal, and Nur Masalha, had already established in previous studies: the Kafr Qasem massacre was part of the hidden *Operation Hafarferet* (mole), a mass expulsion of Palestinians during a possible war.[51] In 2022, on the sixty-fifth anniversary of the atrocity, more precisely, the Israeli Knesset dropped a bill that was proposed by *al-Qa'ima al-Mushtaraka*, the Arab-majority Joint List party, to recognize the Kafr Qasem massacre. If accepted, the bill would have seen the state formally accept responsibility for the massacre.

In a parallel land, on the morning of December 22, 1997, there were some 325 displaced members of *Las Abejas* in Acteal. They had been fleeing the violence that was perpetrated by paramilitary groups in their communities since mid-1997. Entering their third day of fasting, they gathered in a makeshift wooden chapel that was constructed on a dirt floor about 500 feet below the road level. In addition to reciting prayers and discussing liturgies, the aim of the gathering of *Las Abejas* at the chapel was to coordinate a solution for the recent escalating violence of the paramilitaries, which involved personal threats, robbing, burning the houses of the displaced communities, and night shootings in the neighboring community of Pechiquil the night before.

According to eyewitnesses and investigative reports of the massacre,[52] a group of thirty to forty paramilitaries wearing police-like uniforms arrived in Acteal at 8:00 a.m. in *Policia de Seguridad* (Public Security Police) pickup trucks. With red bandanas wrapped on their heads and AK-47 rifles in hands, the paramilitaries, who would be later identified as Mayan men from several Chenalhó communities who belong to *Máscara Roja* (Red Mask), one of the 250 anti-Zapatista PRI militants groups in Chiapas, started shooting in the air before proceeding to the center of Acteal and later into the chapel to slaughter the unarmed members of *Las Abejas* with their high-caliber weapons and machetes. The shooting continued undisturbed for over six hours. At 4:30 p.m., the paramilitaries shot the last bullet in the air and drove away in their pickup trucks. The assault resulted in forty-five people dead and about twenty-five wounded, some of them seriously. Among the slain were twenty-two women, including five pregnant ones, fifteen children, and nine men. Those who were able to flee the "frightening rain of bullets [that] were coming like water drops,"[53] as some survivors describe it, found refuge under the big leaves of banana trees and in nearby ravines and caves.

Whereas the violent methods of execution used by the paramilitaries underscored similar jungle warfare tactics used by Guatemalan Kaibiles against Mayan communities in counterinsurgency operations across the border in Guatemala, the uninterrupted sequence of the killing confirmed the complicity of both the Mexican military and the local government of the State of Chiapas. As several reports and human rights observers reveal,[54] the gunmen of *Máscara Roja* not only had access to new semiautomatic rifles that were purchased from the military spoils of the Guatemalan Civil War (1960–96),[55] but also were highly trained in the Guatemalan Kaibiles violent style of killing by relying on a combination of point-blank shooting and machetes to mutilate the bodies of their victims. In the early hours of the massacre, public security forces were present on the road of Acteal less than a mile away. The retired Brigadier General Julio César Díaz was also positioned at the entrance. None of them intervened to stop the atrocity. Local government officials responded in a similar way despite the urgent alerts and calls for intervention in messages they received from the San Cristóbal/Jobel Dioceses in the Human Rights Center, Centro de Derechos Humanos Fray Bartolomé de las Casas (CDHFBC), and the National Mediation Commission (CONAI). They dismissed these messages by arguing that everything was under control in Acteal and that only a "few shots in the air" had been heard. In his analysis of the documentaries that were made about Acteal and the response of the Mexican state and federal governments, particularly their denial of the responsibility of the paramilitary, dismissal of the violence as a battle between two equals, and later attempts to hide the bodies, José Rabasa recalls the Sabra and Shatila massacre that took place in the Palestinian camp in Lebanon in 1982 when Israeli-backed Lebanese Phalange militia slaughtered between 2,000 and 3,500 Palestinian refugees and Lebanese civilians in two days.[56] In one of the first Tsotsil accounts of the Zapatista uprising, Marián Peres Tsu points a similar accusing finger at the state government:

> On January 8, the governorship of Ruiz Ferro was cut short, supposedly because he was to blame for the *J'atejal* [Acteal massacre]. He is the one who gave the weapons for the assassination, they say. They were good new rifles. According to the *ladinos* in the marketplace, they're worth around five or six thousand pesos each and he handed

them out over a hundred of them. And the bullets cost something like eight pesos each. It's absolutely certain that the Priístas of Chenalhó didn't buy them; the governor handed them out. Of course! We thought. The government won't help us because it says it has no money. It can't provide houses, or galvanized metal sheets of laminated cardboard or seeds; it won't help us get our own tortilla bakery.... The money ran out because it was secretly used to buy guns! We asked for the wrong kind of help![57]

It was not until 5:00 p.m. when the Public Security Police entered Acteal and began evacuating the bodies under the supervision of government officials. Reports and testimonies describe a rushed process of disturbing the massacre scene and piling up bodies in trucks to transport them to Tuxtla Gutiérrez for autopsy[58] and orders to "pick them up before the journalists get [there]"[59] despite the strong objection of the survivors of *Las Abejas* and their families. María Vázquez Gómez, a lay preacher who lost eight members of her family, recalls:

The village was full of soldiers and nobody could enter, so I had to stay where I was. Then they told me that the dead were to be buried in Tuxtla. Nobody came and asked me if that was what I wanted. It was the governor official that said the bodies had to stay in Tuxtla, but I could not accept that. The bodies had to come back now. They said that they would bring the bodies, but only as far as Polho and so once again I said no. I didn't want them to be there. I wanted them brought here back to the place where it happened ... to Acteal.[60]

On Christmas Day, December 25, the bodies were returned to Acteal for a collective funeral and burial ceremony that was presided over by Bishop Samuel Ruiz. In the days and months following the massacre, a series of military, political, and legal developments transformed Acteal and the social fabric of the Zapatista Mayan communities nearby. The commemoration of the massacre and the ongoing quest for justice for *Las Abejas* should be understood within this context.

Several days after the massacre, the Mexican state deployed an additional five thousand troops to Chiapas. The army set up military bases on parts of Acteal's territory near the camps for displaced persons. This dramatic increase was part of a massive militarization and culminated in the fact that, by 2000, one-third of the Mexican army was stationed in Chiapas. In live footage from the first commemoration events of the massacre, we observe a military helicopter roaming the sky to surveille the event. In numerous documentaries about the massacre, we also witness many scenes of Mayan peasants confronting the military. The dialogues in these scenes, as I will elaborate later in this chapter, epitomize the colonial encounter between the militarized state and Indigenous peasant communities, or as Antonia, a Mayan woman who helped refugees organize a weaving co-op and write a song for International Women's Day in the Zapatista autonomous *caracol*, Oventik, put it, "a battle between Goliath and David":

> I knew two people who died. One was Alonzo, a catechist. We weren't friends, just acquaintances. Nine days after the massacre, I went to Acteal to see where Alonzo and the other people died. There we saw their sandals and their necklaces thrown about on the ground.
> "What fault did these people have who died there?" I asked. The people who died in Acteal were only asking God for liberation, for peace. The men and women at Acteal were struggling for the wellbeing of our children who aren't born yet. The paramilitaries who came to kill at Acteal don't understand peace. They took the lives of children. That's why at times we can't forgive them....
> God isn't angry at those who defend their rights. It's like David did in the time of Jehovah. Do you know that there was a prophet David who defended his rights? There was this soldier named Goliath. I don't know in what text of the Latin American Bible it tells about this, but David confronted the government soldier. David was poor and little, a soldier of the poor people. The same thing is happening right now. We are acting like David. What else can we do?[61]

The mass wave of internally displaced persons from various Mayan peasant communities after the massacre, including Tsotsil, Tseltal, and Tojolabal communities, resulted in a large-scale humanitarian crisis. Meanwhile, the international media attention that the massacre received regenerated global interest in Chiapas. While camps were set up in the highlands and in San Cristóbal/Jobel—some of which were constructed at the center of INI—for the displaced who had lost their homes when the paramilitaries took them over, along with their lands and crops, international relief campaigns as well as governmental humanitarian aid and development programs flourished. This shift led to a boom in NGO formation[62] and activism that brought *Las Abejas* together again in their joint struggle for work, land, shelter, food, health care, education, independence, freedom, democracy, and peace. At the same time, nonetheless, the newly formed culture of aid organizations and gifts, which involved building houses, monetary help, and donations of computer equipment, furniture, cameras, Bibles, blankets, food, shoes, clothing, and other materials to Acteal—resources which even the EZLN had failed to secure[63]—created divisions within

Las Abejas. While those who were in favor of government aid left Las Abejas, those who refused "the gifts of enemies," as Hart observes, returned to Acteal to keep their membership in the social movement and the autonomous bases of the EZLN. By 2012, the original group of Las Abejas had split into four groups: *Sociedad Civil Las Abejas de Acteal* (Civil Society of Las Abejas of Acteal), *Unión de Pueblos Indígenas las Abejas de los Altos de Chiapas* (Union of the Indigenous People of Las Abejas of the Highlands of Chiapas), *Las Abejas*, and *Asociación Civil* (Civil Association). This chapter focuses on the commemorative practices of *Sociedad Civil Las Abejas de Acteal* that remained in the village.

In the face of international dismay over the massacre, the government arrested some low-level officials and then-President Ernesto Zedillo Ponce de León replaced prominent state governors and state secretaries.[64] The CDHFBC, in collaboration with several other national and international NGOs, continued their investigation of the massacre. In 2005, CDHFBC and the Civil Society of *Las Abejas of Acteal* presented in front of the Interamerican Commission for Human Rights (IACHR) a petition against the Mexican state for the assassination of forty-five Tsotsil Mayans.[65] In 2011, ten unnamed relatives of the victims filed a civil lawsuit against Zedillo in a Connecticut court in the US. At the time, Zedillo—an alumnus of Yale University—was serving as the director of the Yale Center for the Study of Globalization. The plaintiffs accused him of being the mastermind behind the Acteal massacre and demanded financial compensation exceeding ten million dollars. However, the Civil Society of Las Abejas of Acteal distanced itself from the case, issuing a *communiqué* stating that their demand was not centered on money, but rather on seeking justice and ending impunity. The *communiqué* affirmed that the Fray Bartolomé de Las Casas Center for Human Rights A.C. is their sole legal representative and emphasized that, in contrast to the anonymous plaintiffs in the US case, Las Abejas "have never acted anonymously."[66] In 2013, the case was dismissed after Zedillo's defense legal team claimed that he has immunity as a former governor of a sovereign nation.[67]

Painting Ṣumūd: Murals for Justice and Solidarity

To enter Acteal, one must go down a steep slope leaving behind the Acteal billboard covered by the green bushes and the dark sculpture with the twisted bodies, otherwise known as the "Pillar of Shame," a design gifted by the Danish artist Jens Glaschiøt that was installed at roadside up the hill leading to Acteal in 1999 to commemorate the second anniversary of the massacre.[68] Descending into the main entrance, one encounters colorful murals covering the façade of two buildings at the center of the village: a small white cement church and a green wooden building. While the former is covered with large portraits of solemn Mary and Jesus, the latter features an image of a cheerful young boy, a kite runner, floating over a bold text in Spanish; a quote from Octavio Paz's seminal book, *The Labyrinth of Solitude: The Other Mexico* (1965): "*Quien ha visto la Esperanza, no la olvida. La busca bajo todos los cielos y entre todos los hombres*" ("Whoever has seen hope does not forget it. He seeks it under all the heavens and among all men"). As one makes one's way into the small village, or "The Sacred Land of the Acteal Martyrs," as one writing on the walls describes it, the muddy path becomes more colorful with the bright murals covering the façade of almost all the single-room buildings along the way. Nearly all murals include a text either in Spanish or Tsotsil, and sometimes both, printed in bold style, graffiti, or stencils, corresponding to the function of the building they adorn. The atmosphere is calm and peaceful, or at least that is what the energy of the murals suggests. The humble spirit of the place is not too different from the evocative images of humility in the poems that were written in solidarity with Acteal by the Mayan poets Ruperta Bautista Vázquez (written in Tsotsil) and Juana Karen Peñate (written in Cho'l), the Chicano poet Juan Felipe Herrera, and many others.[69] The communal faucet and water buckets crowded in front of the murals are illustrative of the Mexican state's long-standing neglect of Chiapas and its structural impoverishment of Mayan villages. This landscape of Acteal vividly reflects why Acteal is widely considered as a turning point in the Indigenous struggle in Mexico, epitomizing the failure of the San Andrés agreement between the Zapatistas and the Mexican government signed in 1996.

This was my initial impression when I first arrived in Acteal in January 2016 on an educational tour. There was something hauntingly familiar in the quiet resilience of the scene. The tableau of neglect echoed the makeshift water points and crumbling infrastructure of unrecognized Palestinian villages in Israel and the refugee camps of the Occupied West Bank, where the daily struggle for dignity unfolds in the long shadows cast by state abandonment and military occupation. I arrived in Acteal with my students from Williams College within the framework of a course titled "Borderlands: Migration and Indigenous Cultures in Chiapas" that I cotaught with my colleague at the time, Jane Canova. Our visit to Acteal was organized by BorderLinks, a community-based organization with headquarters in Arizona that leads immersion educational trips to study the northern and southern borders from the borderlands of Arizona-Sonora to Chiapas-Guatemala. Our tour guides were two young people from the US, a light-skinned Mexican American woman and a white man, both of whom were fluent in Spanish. Our driver was a dark-skinned middle-aged mestizo man from a Zapatista community, who communicated with our hosts in Spanish. It did not take long for everyone in the group to notice that the racial composition of our team provided a unique educational insight into the limits of racial privilege within Zapatista communities, where political solidarity mattered more than skin color and the vision of a liberated world transcended color lines.

The first stop on our itinerary was a meeting with the *Mesa directiva*, the village's board, consisting of a group of elders from the community of *Las Abejas*. The meeting took place in a building called *Centro de consciencia* (center of consciousness). Sitting in a circle, we were surrounded by bookshelves, a desktop computer, a large poster of Ghandi, paper documents, and sacks filled with corn and coffee beans. After welcoming us into Acteal, members of the assembly began telling the story of the massacre by sharing testimonies of eyewitnesses and informing us in Spanish about the ongoing collective quest of the community for justice. Occasionally, a young member from the community would interject to translate from Tsotsil, and vice versa, words or complete sentences for members from the community who struggled relating their full testimony in Spanish. Most of our group spoke Spanish, but our chaperons translated from and to Spanish and English when needed.

Our next stop was a small chapel at the edge of the mountain where the massacre took place. As we made our way to the chapel, we passed through an open corridor that separated the main church from the other small buildings. The exterior side of the church displayed large portraits of three murdered community leaders: a bishop, a woman, and another man. The woman was positioned in the middle holding a big cross with the date of the massacre and wrapped in a banner that read Acteal. The three figures assumed a towering position, standing with a dignified tall posture, facial features defined, and eyes wide open. The row of brown-brick buildings across consisted of a store for the weaving cooperative, *Jolom Luch Maya* (Maya Weavers and Embroiderers), a media room, an autonomous health clinic, and dorms for the international volunteers who came from far away to stand in solidarity with the Zapatistas and the people of Acteal. The function of each building was conceptualized in the mural covering it. Going through this powerful visual portal, I was struck by the vibrancy of colors and the muralistic mapping of the space. I was struck, likewise, by the physical presence of foreign peace campers whose major role was to keep a record of the number of times per day that an army truck or convoy passes by. Again, I experienced a déjà vu from Palestine. The presence of foreign and international activists to protect civilians from a militarized occupier was too familiar. It resembled acts of solidarity carried out by outsiders in Palestine, such as the International Solidarity Movement (ISM) and Machsom Watch, or Checkpoint Watch). Whereas IMS volunteers often act like a human shield to protect the lives of Palestinians from the aggression of the Israeli military and the armed Jewish settlers, the Israeli Jewish women who form Machsom Watch monitor the conduct of Israeli soldiers at checkpoints and try to intervene to stop their systematic abuse of Palestinians crossing through checkpoints. To witness firsthand how Mayans and Palestinians needed foreign intervention to protect them from the Mexican and Israeli military, respectively, was a somber reminder of the commonalities between the Indigenous struggles in Chiapas and Palestine.

At the chapel, we were guided by a member from the community to observe the traces where the victims were killed. He pointed at the bullet holes and shrapnel marks on the walls and spoke with pride about how the community preserved the altar. Next, we were guided into a small room covered with a tin roof, called *El Museo* (The Museum). The atmosphere in the room oscillated between an unorganized storage and a messy archive. It was filled with a collection of framed posters produced during previous commemoration events alongside other ephemera and objects from the massacre, including bullets protected in a glass jar and a plastic miniature of a slain baby.

From the museum, we made our way back to the main entrance in the direction of the green wooden building. We proceeded into a large amphitheater with a tin roof to observe the arena where the community gathered for the monthly and annual remembrance events, which in recent years were broadcast live on *Las Abejas*'s Facebook page and other social media platforms. A tall sculpture of Christ on a cross took central stage. It was surrounded by white walls adorned with forty-nine short green wooden crosses, thus creating a replica of the chapel where the massacre took place. The bold black texts in Spanish that stood between the crosses reiterated the holiness of this open-space chapel: "*Bien venidos en la tierra sagrada de los martires de Acteal*" (Welcome to the sacred land of the Acteal martyrs) and "*Defender nuestra madre tierra, no cambiar en proyectos de mal gobierno*" (To defend our mother earth, and not to exchange it for projects of the evil government). The elevated 360-degree breathtaking view of the highlands complemented the holiness of the amphitheater with a similar effect of a sacred Eden.

Abandoning the fresh air and the idyllic mountain view, we descended into a crypt underneath. As soon as its metal door was unlocked, a flash of colorful light emanated from the inside. The walls of the crypt were covered with murals, against which were laid small colorful wooden crosses. Heavy silence fell in the room as our tour guide informed us that we were entering the burial ground for the forty-five massacred people. With no visible tombstones in sight, we were invited to take our time to look around, and to take pictures, if we wished, as if we were in an underground gallery.

The visual narration of the massacre was captured through the combination of the images of Mayan peasant refugees making their way to Acteal through a picturesque rural landscape and a depiction of their mournful faces as they roamed in grief afterward. An installed altar achieved a similar effect. It was decorated with a wooden panel designed like bee wings made of forty-five small yellow frames, each containing a painted image of a victim kneeling in prayer and surrounded by their name and date of birth. Faces of some victims could be seen, as some of them were painted from a side profile angle while others turned their back to the viewer. The unborn babies and children who were murdered were distinguished from the rest by turquoise-colored shapes of a womb or a bird containing their image, thus evoking safety, peacefulness, and serenity.

Whereas clusters of the topographical elements of rural Acteal, including imagery of a blue sky and green *milpas* edged by brown mountain summits, serve as the background for the murals, figures of bereaved Mayans, namely women and children, wandering in groups, are integrated into the vast landscape. Their strong visual presence is conveyed through the hue of the embroidery on their traditional clothing, the redness of threads and ceremonial designs that represent the square Mayan world woven into the women's *rebozos* and *huipils*, their deep-brown skin, and the braided black silky hair of women and little girls, all of which appear in harmony with the local colors of the vast landscape.

In comparison with the abstract cheerfulness of the murals above and the liveliness in the straight gaze of the victims depicted in the large mural on the main church, the murals here present a complex picture of *ṣumūd*, blending images of sorrow and hope. Whereas grief is vivid in the facial contour of the figures depicted in the murals by the main entrance, hopefulness is figured in the less colorful murals on the opposite side by the altar. Indeed, grief is evident in the hypervisualization of the solemn expressions of the women in the mural, which was painted in 2006 during *Semana Santa* (Holy Week). It is emphasized further in the thick lines of their forehead wrinkles, the long faces, the enormous, yet empty gazes of some men, and the closed lids and averted looks of older women and children. In contrast, in the murals on the opposite side, hopefulness is transmuted in the portraits of a crowd of Mayan marching. The distinctiveness of the community members participating in the march is conveyed through portraits of individuals with an accentuated emphasis on elements of hope: a big smile on a young man's face, a guitar in the hand of another, and an arm raising high a cross. It is also affirmed by text, in which the following words, capitalized, are printed in black over a red frame styled like a weaving pattern: *Justicia* (Justice), *Memoria*, (Memory), *Resistencia* *(Resistance)*, and *Autonomia* (Autonomy).

Figure 2. Acteal underground mural 1. Photo by Amal Eqeiq, 2016.

Figure 3. Acteal underground mural 2. Photo by Amal Eqeiq, 2016.

Leaving these murals behind and heading back to San Cristóbal / Jobel, we stopped on the way by *caracol* Oventik to learn more about the praxis of Indigenous autonomy in Zapatista educational systems. As we witnessed in Acteal, nearly all the walls here were covered with murals. We passed by the *To Exist Is to Resist* mural discussed in the first chapter. Although it was my second encounter with the mural, its message of *ṣumūd* resonated more poignantly this time. Coming from Acteal, the mural rendered the interrelatedness between affirming life and remaining steadfast on the land despite the atrocity of colonial violence and state terror as the core of Indigenous struggle. This was what I had witnessed in Acteal: The creative art on display was an integral part of life. It did not assume museumification or reproduce a language of victimization. The murals were there to honor both the dead and the living. Thus, the correlation between Indigenous existence and resistance echoed more than the rhythmic quality of the motto. They embodied a real sense of the *ṣumūd* of Indigenous Peoples, and a beautiful one, I would argue, against all odds. This holds true also for Kafr Qasem, where similar expressions of visual commemoration emerged in 2016.

In accordance with their decennial plan to mark the anniversary of the massacre with a special large project, the Public Committee for the Memorialization of the Kafr Qasem Massacre inaugurated a memorial space, called The Panorama. Given the committee's strong publicity efforts—a target that the committee set on its agenda to commemorate the sixtieth anniversary alongside launching a special Facebook page dedicated to the memory of the massacre[70]—the grand opening of the venue received wide media coverage in the local news as well as major Arab channels, such as *Al Jazeera*. This mobilization involved, likewise, a new public outreach program that offered educational tours for Palestinian and Jewish schools aimed at undoing the omission of the massacre from the Israeli curriculum in both Arabic and Hebrew.

Akin to the trip to the commemorative sites in Acteal, my first trip to The Panorama took place within an educational framework, though in a divergent context. In January 2017, I arrived there accompanied by three of my teenage kin, a niece and two nephews, who came along out of curiosity and a desire to spend time with their aunt who was visiting from the US. I, on the other hand, was keener on learning more about the structure of the new memorialization venue and the types of commemorative forms that the people of Kafr Qasem had deployed to narrate the story of the massacre. I had been before to *Matḥaf al-shuhadā /* متحف الشهداء (The Martyrs' Museum)—established in 2006 in commemoration of the fiftieth anniversary of the massacre—and so was eager to harness my knowledge of the massacre and to gain a better understanding of how this new addition to the museum, and the choice of the name

Panorama, contributed to the narration of the story of the massacre as told from the viewpoint of the local community.

It is worth pointing out here that as a Palestinian literary scholar from the Triangle, I have gained familiarity with the story through two main sources: First, oral historical accounts transmitted by the local community, teachers, and elders from the Triangle who recalled with profound sorrow the tragic misfortune that fell upon their neighbors in Kafr Qasem. Without exception, all the accounts I have heard described the massacre as a carefully planned attempt that the settler state executed to displace and transfer Palestinians across the so-called Green Line. The underlying fear of the occurrence of a similar massacre in the future was expressed explicitly by mentioning the vernacular Palestinian phrase, *Allāh yusturnā min allī jāy* (May God protect us from what is coming), thus speaking clearly to the precarious position of Palestinian citizenship in Israel as well as the position of the Triangle as a border area. Second, there is an oeuvre of literary works, namely Palestinian poetry and ethnographic accounts written by the first generation of post-Nakba writers, such as Darwish, al-Qasem, Habibi, and Zayyad, above all. This group of poets and writers, whom I identify as the generation that built the literary monument of the Kafr Qasem massacre,[71] provided valuable historical details and recorded testimonies about the massacre, conspicuously absent from my history books, which were assigned by the Israeli Ministry of Education. Samia Halaby's exhibit and book, *Drawing the Kafr Qasem Massacre* (2016),[72] complement this monument by illustrating the emotional and communal trauma of the massacre through a carefully curated visual archive. Drawing on recorded testimonies she collected in Kafr Qasem, as well as literature—most notably the work of Habibi—and other local art sources, Halaby privileges the Palestinian perspective by visually documenting the massacre without centering the perpetrators. In her critical analysis of Halaby's book, Rana Barakat identifies it as a form of Indigenous storytelling that offers a powerful alternative to conventional historical narratives rooted in settler colonial archives. Barakat further argues that, as an "epistemological intervention,"[73] Halaby's work demonstrates how Indigenous storytelling functions not only as a method of remembrance but also as a visual representation of Indigenous defiance. With this in mind, I approached the gates of The Panorama with my niece and nephews, in what felt like a collective educational journey for an intergenerational delegation of learners.

In contrast to the museum, which exhibited in silence archival documents, photos of the victims, aerial maps of Kafr Qasem that detailed the fragmented urbanization of the village and its shrinking residential areas and farmland, alongside artwork by Palestinian and Jewish artists with themes related to the massacre, The Panorama was an interactive space that offered an audiovisual reenactment of the massacre. While both spaces occupied the ground floor of a community center, they were separated by a large meeting hall, a storage room, *Muṣalla al-shuhadāʾ*/ مُصلّى الشهداء—a prayer room that was set up as a charitable contribution in memory of a local elder—and a set of stairs plus an elevator that connected with the upper floor. The entrance at the second floor opened with a corridor decorated with photo portraits of iconic Palestinian and Arab poets. At the end of the corridor, there were three educational spaces: *Al-ḥekma* (Wisdom) Public Library, *Matḥaf al-qarya* / متحف القرية (The Village Museum), and several classrooms. Whereas the main entrance of the library was marked by large colored photos of three deceased Kafr Qasemites, the main door of the adjunct museum displayed a collection of black-and-white as well as color photos of crowds of Kafr Qasemites marching in the streets or in public gatherings. At the center of the single-room museum, mannequins of two peasants, a man and a woman, dressed in traditional Palestinian embroidered attire, take the main stage. At their feet, various antique objects were scattered: clay pots, rusty farming tools, an old sewing machine, and other souvenirs from the village days of Kafr Qasem. In contrast to the futurist-looking high-speed internet at the library, the relics from the past in the museum conjured up a nostalgic representation of a slow and bygone peasant life. While the transparent glass barrier between the museum and the library dramatized this contrast, the double reflection of the colorful map of Historic Palestine engraved on the glass created harmony and continuity between both spaces and the entire two floors. The cohesiveness of this internal landscape was further emphasized by two metal installations on the patio outside: a visualization of the massacre narrated in a decorative metal panel glued to the exterior wall of the staircase, and a sculpture of three generations of male figures connected by a pickaxe, a briefcase, and a pencil. The three figures were ascending, holding each other's hands, through an open arched frame towards an elevated platform that overlooked a small park. The sculpture was adorned by two complementary elements that created a canvas of *ṣumūd*: a side bush of a green and thorny cactus plant, and verses from Darwish's 1967 poem "Kafr Qasem" engraved in calligraphic style on the panel of the frame:

علمتني ضربة الجلّاد أن أمشي على جرحي وأمشي.
ثم أمشي.
وأقاوم

(The executioner's blow taught me to walk over my wound.
And walk on / And then to stride / and resist.)[74]

The path to The Panorama passes through these words. When we arrived at the entrance, we were received by a group of local young and middle-aged volunteers who provided an explanation of how the self-guided tour inside works, in addition to a reminder that, once we were inside, the lights would go out for the show to begin. And so it happened. As soon as we stepped in, complete darkness fell upon the space, before a sudden strong light beamed into a diorama showcasing Kafr Qasem as a pastoral serene small village with white stone buildings, wooden windows, and fertile farmland. Peasant women in Palestinian embroidered dresses with colors and patterns specific to the area could be seen tending to their fields and animals, or carrying water jars on their heads. The vast luminous landscape suggested a tranquil atmosphere of everyday life. The maternal affect of the scene was accentuated by the sound of a chorus singing traditional Palestinian women's songs, though the songs were repeated by a group of men singers.

The following scene took place in the *mukhtār*'s house. The stone façade of the house was clearly outlined and so was the wide-open window where a Kafr Qasemite could be seen peacefully standing and gazing toward the fecund *ḥakura*, a vegetable garden, and the panoramic view of the green pastures. This romantic imagery, however, dissolved in the next scene. A single male voiceover

Figure 4. Kafr Qasem Panorama-Mural. Official picture from the Panorama website.

recited in an overly theatrical tone a militant poem by Zayyad about the massacre. At this point, it became clear that this voice would play the double role of an omnipresent narrator and the audio guide giving us cues to proceed to the next scene. Lights flash into the next scene and one could observe the presence of an armed Israeli Border Police pointing at the village's bewildered *mukhtār* and the hand of a woman closing her window to hide inside. What unfolded after that was a chronological three-dimensional visualization of the events of the massacre, including images of blood, injured and dead bodies lying on the ground, and horror in the eyes of surviving Kafr Qasemites trying to hide their grief in the *ṣulḥa* and the tribunal. The entire story unfolded in a total of six scenes and in less than fifteen minutes. No lights or sounds were used to signal that the show was over. Yet, the audience was expected to intuit that the story did not end with the tribunal. On their way out, they passed a mural featuring Kafr Qasemites walking in a ceremonial commemorative march.

The juxtaposition of collective grief and the ongoing struggle for justice against a colorful background showing the old Kafr Qasem was at the center of the mural. The familial connection between the collective participating in the memorial procession was conveyed in the intimate special proximity between them and the congregation of three generations of Kafr Qasemites, with

Figure 5. Kafr Qasem Panorama, Mural of the March. Photo by Amal Eqeiq, 2017.

a strong presence of women and children. The collective marched in the fields with heads held high and lighted candles in hands while their village loomed on a bright horizon. An elderly man dressed in a traditional Palestinian peasant outfit led the collective on a path illuminated by the glimmering silhouettes of their candles, the golden reflection of a wheat field ready to harvest, and a rocky olive grove.

The mural amplified the innocence of the villagers in two ways: first, through the image of a young man wearing a white shirt and holding a white flag with the words "We Will Not Forget"; and second, through the dominant presence of children and two veiled women, whose white-cloth veiling style resembles those worn by the veiled Madonna and Palestinian women peasants. Another striking visual element was the image of a pregnant woman standing in a towering position, while definitive lines of a halo highlight her veil and pregnant belly. She stood tall above everyone, fist held high and holding two white banners: "We Will Not Forgive" and "1956." The observable symmetry between the redness of the twilight in the sky and poppies flourishing from the land that engulfed the marching collective radiated a mix of communal solidarity and earthly warmth, thus piercing the complete darkness that overtook The Panorama and showing us the way out. As the unspoken final scene, the mural quietly insisted on remembrance, inviting us as viewers to reflect on the living memory of the massacre beyond the frame of the interactive performance that we had just experienced.

Exiting The Panorama, I experienced flashbacks from Acteal. I reached for my phone to look at photos that I had captured there a year before. My reaction to the visual resemblance between the two grieving communities was too visceral to ignore. I showed the images of the murals from Acteal to my niece and nephews and asked them if they saw the affinity that I saw. They pointed to the similarity in the facial features of the figures depicted in the murals and the earthy colors of the landscape. On our way home, we reflected on the history of Kafr Qasem that we had not learned and the stories of which we just saw. We also discussed the similarity between the murals in Acteal and Kafr Qasem: Were the murals fraternal or identical twins?

Apart from the murals, there is evidence of a sustained engagement with visual commemorative practices in Acteal and Kafr Qasem. Such practices include organizing coloring competitions, producing colored stories for children,[75] drawing the massacre, writing the names of the victims on walls,[76] and painting their coffins and tombstones in special colors,[77] in addition to designing posters and logos for the annual anniversaries. What stands out about all these works is their close engagement with the larger community as popular art, thus expanding the platform for diverse aesthetic expressions. These commemorative practices also apply to the appropriation of murals as an urban art form to tell a story about Indigenous peasant struggle. In the case of Acteal, for example, the idea of what to paint is debated within the community together with local and visiting artists. So, mural painting becomes an opportunity for bringing the community together in solidarity and unity. In Kafr Qasem, however, the murals were seen as an opportunity to educate the young generation about the history and story of the massacre by relying on a language that "speaks to them."[78] It is important to note here, however, that the team who painted the murals were not professional artists, but a group of skilled construction workers and a civil engineer from the neighboring towns Salfit and Al-Taybeh. The ultimate goal of painting what happened in Kafr Qasem, the team concurs, was motivated by a keen desire "to celebrate the fact that this village, which is at the edge of the Southern Triangle, did not fall. It is a story of hope."[79]

In a related vein, for Dyg'Nojoch—a San Cristóbal/Jobel-based Mayan visual artist and muralist from Chénalho—who has been painting murals in Acteal since 2016, the mural, or what he calls, word mural, takes both a physical and emotional space. It establishes solidarity and unity by allowing everyone to take part in the process of painting. He says:

> Even though the community in Acteal does not have resources, having murals is still considered an important part of the community's survival. The murals are organized through local initiatives. When I receive a call to come help with painting a new mural, I reach out to a woman leader in the community. She gathers donations from family members and friends of the victims to buy the material. I arrive and propose some ideas, but often follow what the community has in mind. Some have a figure or a poem in mind that they wish to turn into a mural. We then have a general discussion of how to paint it. Because my fluency in Tsotsil is limited, I often rely on children who take part in translating to the elders who do not speak Spanish. Throughout these years of collaboration, it became clear to me how the painting session became a collective effort to rebuild the community. As we paint figures, you will hear someone saying something along the lines of "This figure looks like the grandmother, or the *curandera* (healer) who lives over there." Our discussion also turns into reflections on the struggle, the malnourishment, the marches, the dialogues, and the ongoing act of *caminar para la justicia* (to walk toward justice). Unlike my murals in San Cristóbal/Jobel, which can be considered as a type of Mayan folk art, I feel that in Acteal, what I paint is more historical, because the space is that of struggle and resistance. The mural is for

them, a *word* mural. In the end, I feel that my role is to open the door toward another imagination. So, I ask myself, how can I paint this concept of walking?[80]

In a similar fashion, Ramy Amer, a fast-food restaurant owner and a community activist who has been involved in the memorialization of the massacre in Kafr Qasem for the past twenty years, explains how The Panorama transformed the commemoration scene in the village. In addition to attracting more visitors to the museum, the visualization of the massacre contributed to restoring the corporality of the people who were murdered. He notes:

I learned a lot from leading educational workshops at The Panorama. There is something powerful about seeing the massacre in the large scale of murals and in three dimensions. Yes, there was art before in Kafr Qasem, mainly by the artist Abdel Tammam. He painted picturesque scenes about the village, but The Panorama is different. In Kafr Qasem, we learn a new detail about what happened in the massacre almost every anniversary. People share more information about the people who were murdered, and we actively seek to document these untold details to create an archive. I am currently involved in a local project with some friends in the village to create a visual map of Kafr Qasem before the massacre based on the routes that the martyrs took. For example, the massacre took place near the old quarry where many martyrs worked. They needed a permit from the military government to go there. We want to remap Kafr Qasem according to these paths they took, because they are no longer there. We want people to remember the history of our village.[81]

It is almost impossible not to recognize in the testimonies of Dyg'Nojoch and Amer the critical significance of the murals as a visual expression of *ṣumūd* and cultural resistance. The communal making of these murals demonstrates how form and content embody the spirits of memory and resistance, culminating in acts of creative expression that narrate History, a history that overcomes erasure and denial.

To fully grasp the scope of this visual steadfastness and resistance, we must remember that the first commemorative events of the massacres in both Acteal and Kafr Qasem took place under heavy state surveillance that involved the deployment of military helicopters hovering over the commemorative stage or march,[82] the confiscation of megaphones,[83] and the blocking of access to the events for outsiders by setting up roadblocks and other disruptive techniques that speak to the state's militarized control tactics. So, the way the people in

Acteal and Kafr Qasem are reclaiming the space to tell the stories of the massacres is important. Moreover, as Dyg'Nojoch and Amer assert, painting the murals involved larger collaborations and created a space for community empowerment. For Amy Lonetree, practices such as these in museums, community centers, and local art sites in Indigenous communities can be spaces for healing from unresolved historical grief and the historical trauma of colonialism.[84] If we read these murals in a comparative Mayan and Palestinian framework of commemoration, we can observe, then, that this healing is not only possible, but is already under way. Through the tales of these two murals, separated by time and space, rises above all a distinct call of affinity and ṣumūd, a call that echoes the past, resonates across generations, and envisions a future shaped by collective resilience.

Conclusion: Unveiling with Affinity

Throughout the writing of this book and the past fifteen years of traveling back and forth between Mexico and Palestine, I have been guided by the vision of a recurring dream. It is lucid, yet unsettling: I am standing on a podium to deliver a lecture, in accented English, to a mixed academic audience consisting of students and scholars from Latin American studies and Middle Eastern studies. The theme of the lecture is the multifaceted South-South connections between Mexico and Palestine that I have been tracing over the years. The audience, whose members are unfamiliar with each other, is divided by a thick curtain that partitions the hall: Latin Americanists sit on one side, Middle Easterners on the other. I, in contrast, stand in the middle, at the border demarcated by the curtain. Here, I struggle to keep my balance as I switch between languages and classifications that seem to be intelligible to only one side of the hall at a time: *Conquista, mestizaje, ladino, kaxlan, literatura indigenista, testimonio, matanza, fue el estado, Zapatismo, pollero, muro,* ، جدار ، أوسلو مستوطنة ، محسايم، ، نكبة ، أدب الالتزام ، شعراء المقاومة، صمود، شهداء, مجزرة, إنتفاضة. As I pronounce these words, my eyes track the asymmetrical physical responses that my words elicit from either side of the room: nods of approval on one side, raised eyebrows on the other. As I observe these contradictory reactions, I am nudged by the lurking shadow of a mysterious figure. It hands me a small notebook whose cover in English reads, "This is for the glossary," before the figure disappears into the shadows, leaving me behind at the border, holding a basket of words in Palestinian Arabic, Palestinian Arabized Hebrew, Spanish, Mexican Spanish, Chiapanecan Spanish, and Tsotsil, along with the notebook.

After this dream, I always awake from deep sleep with a pounding heart and two nagging questions: *Who was that?! What about the curtain?!*

The lucid dream has stayed with me as both compass and lantern, illuminating the challenges that I have encountered as a comparatist. It vividly captures the epistemic and methodological stakes embedded in simultaneously speaking *from* and *to* different structures of knowledge situated across different geographies and disciplines. It does not vanish with waking. On the contrary, it lingers, guiding my work by orienting me toward Indigenous epistemologies, those rich relational imaginings that Tanana Athabascan poet and scholar Dian Million calls "Indigenous non-Western ways of knowing, with ceremony."[1] As a revelation, the dream has unconcealed the linguistic gap and questions of translatability across disciplines that have been constructed in the US academy, a third space in which both Latin American studies and Middle Eastern studies emerge against the backdrop of a parallel institutional history of Orientalism, colonialism, imperialism, and racism. As a source of critical insight, the dream has also brought to the surface a key question that I had been grappling with: How can a comparatist elucidate the connection between Chiapas and Palestine when there is a disciplinary and institutional barrier in the middle? While documenting the dream, I found that the noun "curtain" (*sitār* / ستار in Arabic) frequently appears with the verb *kashf* (كشف) and, together, they form the phrase *kashf al-sitār* (كشف الستار), which literally means "lifting the curtain." Whereas in theater this phrase gestures to the start of a show, for the Sufis, "lifting the curtain" represents an alternative way of knowing, not the knowing of the intellect but that of the heart. To lift the curtain, therefore, is to perform *kashf*, that is, to become familiar with things unseen behind the veil. It is only through this mystical state of knowledge attained by unveiling, *kashf*, that the borders between the human and the Divine are transcended.

Thus, guided by the vision of this dream, I use affinity as a lens through which to unveil the connection between Mayan and Palestinian narratives, shedding light on several unknown aspects about both literatures. In writing Chapter 1, which charts my journey in search of the translation of *'ulfa* (affinity) in Tsotsil, I discovered the limits of dictionaries in providing accurate ways to express embodied practices of knowing, belonging, and thinking from the heart. I also gained a new perspective on the meaning of *ṣumūd*, understanding it not only as a manifestation of hope but also as a commitment to the Good Life. This insight revealed how essential solidarity is for sustaining steadfastness.

In elucidating the strong link between language and land in Mayan and Palestinian poetry in Chapter 2, I observed a pivotal element of indigeneity. To write Indigenous literatures in Indigenous languages is not simply a matter of linguistic resistance, but rather an affirmation of *ṣumūd* in lands that are being forcefully disappeared by settler colonial regimes. In this regard, the *'ulfa-kuxlej/kuxlejal* between the deployment of Tsotsil by Mayan poets seeking to revive the history of the people of maize resonates with the image of the Palestinian poets who write in Arabic to reclaim a land where even the olive tree speaks Arabic.

As much as it can unveil the unseen, however, affinity, if not used with care, can also obscure the specific. Affinity does not simplify or force connections, but rather, it can help us consider ways to look more closely into the seemingly familiar. In this respect, working with the modality of *'ulfa-kuxlej/kuxlejal* was challenging. The structural differences between Arabic in Israel and Tsotsil in Chiapas, for example, or the racial divides across the rural-urban spatiality in Chiapas and Palestine '48 entailed internal complexities that necessitated a more focused lens. At the same time, the overlap of the familiar and the comparable embedded in the possible affinities promoted important reflections on the need for a deeper examination of the divergent local contexts of bilingualism in Chiapas and Palestine. It also highlighted the differing scales, dynamics, and ideological formations of racial segregation between Mayans and *ladinos* in Chiapas, and between Jews and Palestinians in Israel/Palestine. While this comparison revealed that unevenness of the local terrains, it also emphasized the significance of remaining attentive to the specificity and internal complexity of each context.

Propelled by the uncanny resemblance between the commemorative murals in Acteal in Chiapas and Kafr Qasem in Palestine, I set out to investigate further how affinity can unveil to both villages the *'ulfa-kuxlej/kuxlejal* between them. Between the summer of 2017 and the fall of 2019, I traveled twice back and forth between Acteal and Kafr Qasem. While it is beyond the scope of this work to delve into the details of these visits and the personal networks that I have developed in both villages as a result, it is sufficient here to mention two important encounters: an individual meeting with the *Mesa Directiva* in Acteal in August 2018 and an attendance of an organization meeting held by the Public Committee for the Memorialization of the Kafr Qasem Massacre in October 2019. During these encounters, I shared the pictures taken with my smartphone of the murals at both sites. As the device circulated in the room, from one hand to another, there were nods of approval and inquiries were made about the ongoing quest for justice at both sites. It was a true moment of *kashf*, of uplifting. In response to these questions, I shared information and links with members from each community through WhatsApp. I honor these connections and take my role as a messenger seriously. This brings me to the second encounter: María Vazques López from Acteal and Rose Amer from Kafr Qasem, each of whom had lost family members in the massacres. Both women are vocal feminist activists, and they assume organizational positions in the commemoration events. Whereas López works with weaving, Amer is a talented orator. During my last visit to Acteal, López gave me a scarf that she had woven to give to Amer. Amer was elated to receive López's gift and, in turn, gave me a set of key chains that she had helped codesign for the sixty-second anniversary of the massacre. The key chain's design includes a black circle with an olive tree, a lit candle, and the commemorative monument in the center. On one side of the circle, the text in Arabic reads: *"This is our home. Arabic is our language."* On the other side, the bold text in Arabic reads: *"Glory and eternity to our martyrs."* "Take this to María," Amer said. I promised that I would—and then the Covid pandemic struck. I still have the key chains in my house, stored in a safe space. Every time I see them, I imagine López and Amer conversing together or marching side by side united by a solidarity born from similar stories of mourning and a common quest for justice in two sister villages from parallel geographies of Indigenous struggle. Maybe we can see by means of affinity, after all. For if so, the potential conversations to be had can be boundless and will unveil more and more solidarity while bringing to light, from behind the curtain, seemingly disparate cultures and political landscapes from the Global South and beyond.

Postscript: *Indigenous Affinities after the Gaza Genocide*

The original manuscript of this book was completed in Palestine in August 2023, but most of the revisions were done between February and May 2024 during trips to Palestine and Spain. Throughout the course of those three months, I was deeply immersed in the editorial process of the revisions: revamping sections, connecting dots, and tweaking sentences to convey in the clearest way possible the affinities between contemporary Mayan and Palestinian narratives and what they tell us about the shared aspects of the Indigenous struggles in Chiapas and Palestine. The writing did not happen against a quiet library backdrop or static surroundings. Rather it unfolded against the backdrop of Israel's genocide in Gaza, which was raging in full force, despite the ongoing global protests, the growing worldwide calls for a ceasefire, the recognition by several European countries (Norway, Spain, and Ireland) of Palestinian statehood, and the orders from the International Court of Justice in The Hague to Israel for an immediate halt of its military assault on Rafah. This border city, located along the borders of Egypt and the Gaza Strip, had become the last refuge for more than half of Gaza's two million people who were forcibly displaced from their homes because of Israel's continuous multipronged attacks from the air, the sea, and the ground since October 7, 2023. Though differing in intensity, these events deeply resonated with the comparative framework of Indigenous struggles and solidarity, settler colonialism, and ongoing Nakba(s) that contours this book as well as key themes, historical moments, and several individuals that it draws attention to. At the same time, every sentence revised or newly added felt haunted by the immediacy of unfolding violence just beyond the page, a violence perpetrated by a settler colonial state waging ethnic cleansing in Gaza with full impunity. In this text, I offer some reflections on these resonances and the ways in which they impact (or not) the original version of the book in terms of framing, content, and context. To chart these reflections, I will not adhere to a chronological timeline of the genocide in Gaza, but rather follow a conceptual map that captures its intersection with the narrative arc of the book. Crucially, these current events compelled me to reconsider Indigenous affinities, not merely as a comparative framework, but more importantly, as a catalyst for solidarity. At its core, affinity insists on relationality, mutual recognition, and the ethical imperative to stand with others in struggle. In these urgent times, Indigenous affinities offer not only a lens for analyzing the familiar across comparative settler colonial histories in the Global South, but also a practice of global solidarity grounded in shared resistance to colonialism, imperialism, and fascism.

Indigenous Affinities is anchored in the solidarity between Chiapas and Palestine. As I show in the first chapter, my conceptualization of affinity as an affective modality inextricably tied to solidarity is rooted in my close reading of the Zapatista mural of solidarity with Palestine. Historically, this mural together with the political discourse of the Zapatistas in respect to Palestine have been solidly entwined with Gaza. To put it differently, Gaza has been the bedrock of Indigenous solidarity between Chiapas and Palestine. Since its emergence in 1994, the Zapatista Indigenous rebel movement evoked Gaza as a parallel epicenter of Indigenous struggle.[1] A prime example is the explicit allusion to Gaza in the Inauguration of the First Exchange of Indigenous Peoples of Mexico with Zapatista Peoples in 2014, two years before the election of Hamas and the subsequent Israeli blockade of Gaza. During this meeting, Comandante Tacho drew a poignant analogy between the struggle of the Palestinian people in Gaza and Indigenous Peoples in Mexico. He stated:

> When we say these two words so well known by our peoples—these words of death and destruction—our heart and our gaze go to the PALESTINIAN people. We hear and read what they say about "the conflict in Gaza," as if there were two equal forces confronting each other, and as if saying "conflict" would hide the *death* and *destruction* such that death would not kill and destruction would not destroy. But as the Indigenous People that we are, we know that what is happening there is not a "conflict" but a MASSACRE, that the government of Israel is carrying out a war of extermination of the PALESTINIAN people. Everything else is just words to try to hide reality.[2]

By using the colonial legacy of the systematic extermination of Indigenous Peoples in reference to Gaza, Comandante Tacho not only recognizes Israel's long record of destruction in Gaza as an act of colonial extermination, but also predicts the current massacres as a foretold genocide. The spirit of this strong correlation between the genocidal violence in Chiapas and Gaza animates several expressions of solidarity that the Zapatistas have issued in their press releases over the past eight months, including one from November 2023, in which the Capitan emphasizes that the Zapatistas refuse to live in "concentration camps like Gaza."[3]

In conjunction with the Zapatista's affirmation of affinity with Gaza, there has been a dramatic surge in cultural manifestations of solidarity with Gaza at several locations in Chiapas and throughout Mexico. In San Cristóbal / Jobel, for instance, a new solidarity collective called *Acción Palestina Chiapas* (Chiapas Palestine Action) was formed in December 2023. Bringing together activists, artists, librarians, local and international community members— Zapatistas and non-Zapatistas alike—this collective organized a set of activities advocating for a ceasefire in Gaza as well as calling for Boycott, Divestment, and Sanctions (BDS) and the liberation of Palestine. Their rich program of public events involved not only a presentation of cultural and historical material on Palestine that was an introduction for many in Chiapas, but also creative performances envisioning different paths of solidarity. Apart from organizing public lectures and film festivals on the Nakba, the collective hosted a Palestinian poetry night and a screening of the Palestinian documentary *Slingshot Hip Hop* (dir. Jackie Reem Salloum, 2008), which was followed by a live hip-hop performance by the local rappers Mr. Tonalli, Psicolexia, Shinigami Garcias Nataren, and Can of Wormz. They also hosted a discussion with Dr. Aldo Rodríguez, who volunteered with Doctors Without Borders in Gaza, as well as a conversation about the similarities between the anticolonial struggles in Ireland and Palestine led by an Irish activist who goes by the name of Lonko Nahuel and who, like numerous international activists, had moved to Chiapas in the mid-1990s to be in solidarity with the Zapatistas. In addition, the collective staged several street performances to commemorate the death of innocent Palestinian civilians. These performances included a collective painting of a mural for Palestine, a one-day fast to protest Israel's use of starvation as a weapon of war, and a silent march to protest the US's unconditional support of Israel that involved holding signs in front of a famous US burger chain restaurant. Similar types of activities took place across Mexico. In Mexico City, for example, the black, white, green, and red colors of the Palestinian flag were strongly present in the solidarity altars that were set up during the Day of the Dead celebrations. The four colors were also flaunted in hand-painted Palestinian flags that were carried by the protesters in the massive street demonstrations and the student encampments at the Universidad Autónoma de Mexico (UNAM). They were even laid over graphic designs featuring the patterned black-and-white Palestinian *kuffiyeh* in posters announcing academic roundtables on decolonizing Palestine and on feminism and liberation in Palestine. The same aesthetics were used in brochures at the *Museo Nacional de las Culturas del Mundo* (The National Museum of World Cultures), where an exhibit on Palestinian embroidery and a new project of painting murals for Palestine in collaboration with the artists Gustavo Chavéz Pavon (the Zapatista artist who painted the mural discussed in Chapter 1), Eduardo Rivas, and Antonio Gritón were curated.

Although taking place in different spaces under different organizational structures, these manifestations of solidarity engaged a wide range of audiences through a common incorporation of Palestinian iconography of cultural resistance blended with Indigenous Mexican art. The colorful multilingual and multivalent texture of this solidarity, which developed in response to the genocide in Gaza on an unprecedented scale, echoes the point made in Chapter 1 about decoloniality embedded in the Indigenous affinity between Chiapas and Palestine as the lands of global Intifadas. Indeed, the South-South solidarity that foregrounds this affinity not only valorizes the connection between Indigenous struggles in Chiapas and Palestine, but also demonstrates how a periphery-periphery conversation within the Global South can ignite a global anticolonial and anticapitalist movement that reshapes the boundaries of global indigeneities.

Curiously, in early January 2024, an unexpected player joined the growing solidarity with Palestine: the Mexican state. The Mexican state has a documented record of buying weapons from Israel to arm paramilitaries in Chiapas and of sponsoring special training sessions for Mexican soldiers and police with Israeli military forces, aimed at sharing techniques to suppress Indigenous insurgency (as noted in Chapters 1 and 4), in a close collaboration over decades. Yet, the Mexican state, together with the Chilean state, filed a lawsuit with the International Criminal Court (ICC) against the state of Israel, accusing it of committing war crimes in Gaza. In late May, Mexico took another step toward solidarity with Palestine by filing a declaration of intervention in solidarity with South Africa's genocide case against Israel before the International Court of Justice (ICJ). While it is not clear as of this writing whether this decision will culminate in severing diplomatic ties with Israel, as was the case with other Latin American countries like Colombia, Bolivia, Chile, and Brazil, this dramatic shift in the relationship between the Mexican state and its military ally could potentially have significant implications for reconfiguring the latitudes of the affinity between Chiapas and Palestine, for Mexico's own relationship to its own Indigenous Peoples, and—above all—for the armed struggle of the Zapatistas and Mayan People. In this regard, it is important to indicate that in its application to the ICJ the Mexican state accused Israel of violating the UN's 1948 Genocide Convention by referring to Israel's obstruction of humanitarian assistance in Gaza and citing Article II(b) of the Convention that outlines the destruction of cultural heritage:

> It is Mexico's position that the massive destruction of cultural property and the eradication of any cultural symbol related to a group can be construed as acts aimed to accomplish the severe harming of a group, diminishing or even destroying the connection between culture and the self-determination and identity of a population, in terms of Article II(b) of the Convention.[4]

When it comes to the Indigenous struggle in Chiapas, Mexico's position on the genocide in Gaza displays a thorny paradox, if not a political irony, that merits attention. By recognizing the connection between culture, identity, and self-determination, the Mexican state not only affirms its commitment to the Geneva Convention, but also endorses, albeit indirectly, Indigenous cultural rights as human rights. This principle was a key demand that the Zapatistas had put forward in their uprising thirty years ago. As observed in the analysis of Mayan cultural spaces in San Cristóbal / Jobel in Chapters 2 and 3, this principle continues to be an important factor in engineering Mayan cultural autonomy. Moreover, it plays a pivotal role in the ongoing Indigenous mobilization across the Yucatán Peninsula against the Tren Maya, Mexico's new tourism mega project that destroys Indigenous lands and resources on a scale that resembles earlier colonial violence of conquest and cultural genocide.

On the other hand, borders, specifically the racialized and militarized internal settler colonial borders, are a main component of the affinity between Chiapas and Palestine. As I have detailed in Chapters 2, 3, and 4, the materiality of internal borders, in both their linguistic and territorial extensions, undergirds the configuration of indigeneity in alphabetical and visual Mayan and Palestinian texts across genres. Whether it is in the poetry of $ṣumūd$ written in Tsotsil and Arabic, in fictional and theatrical accounts of border crossing in San Cristóbal / Jobel and Haifa, or in commemorative murals of state-sanctioned violence against Mayan and Palestinian peasants, the imagery of internal borders as structures of land theft, racial segregation, and militarization are similarly evident in Mayan and Palestinian texts. Working on the revisions of the book while staying with my parents in my border hometown of Al-Taybeh from early February to early May of 2024 only amplified this notion of borders. Over the course of these three months, I witnessed firsthand Israel's rapid physical transformation and accelerated militarization of the so-called Green Line along the Triangle Area and its bordering Palestinian villages and towns in the Occupied West Bank. The imprints of this transformation on the geographical and political topography of the landscape of the border(s) were visible both on land and in the sky. The following series of reflections, excerpts from my "Diaries of a Hedgehog Feminist" creative nonfiction book in progress, offers a lived glimpse and a quiet testimony to how the expansion of Israel's Zionist settler colonial project and the consolidation of its fascist regime are intertwined with the genocide in Gaza and the intensification of the ongoing Nakba across Historic Palestine.

February 29, 2024

"It has been almost a month since I arrived home. Everything feels different this time. Even the silence of my elderly parents who have withdrawn deeper into their grief about the war and their rage about the horrific images of the genocide in Gaza that live streams on Al-Jazeera's channel on their big flat-screen TV. During our morning coffee together, we debrief about the latest updates from Gaza that circulate on social media and WhatsApp, their profound fear for the future of Palestine, and how much they miss their weekly grocery shopping trips to the neighboring village of Shufa at the southeastern outskirts of Tulkarm across the 'border,' an activity that they stopped doing after Israeli military forces had closed the road with concrete blockades and flying checkpoints since October 7. Despite speaking nostalgically about the ripeness of the local vegetables of Shufa, the prime taste of its free-range chicken, and the lush air of rural Palestine, they refuse to risk going there. Meanwhile, many other relatives and people in our hometown and in neighboring towns have continued to make the journey by following alternative bypass routes that they have jointly paved along with people of Shufa. They navigate these paths using a system of ad hoc signs—handwritten in Arabic and hung on olive trees or placed on rocks—and directions passed along by word of mouth. After midnight, our exchange focuses on my responses to their inquiries about my progress on the book revisions and ways to combat our common insomnia, which has exacerbated over the past month because of the night raids of the Israeli drones on Tulkarm and its adjacent Nur Shams refugee camp. My mother and I compare notes on the frequency of these drones and the difference between the hollow buzzing noise that they make in contrast to the thick noise of the military helicopters that Israel deployed during the Second Intifada in its airstrikes on Tulkarm. Sometimes, our after-midnight small talk would not end until the muezzin announces the dawn call to prayer. Then, my mother would say a collective prayer for the people of Gaza while the three of us remain wondering how they could have possibly survived all these years with the Israeli drones hovering over their heads, day and night.⁵ After a short sleep, we would wake up to the growing realization that 'the border' that separated us from Tulkarm has *become* Gaza."

April 29, 2024
"Today was the last session in my father's treatment at the hydrotherapy pool in the Palestinian town of Jatt in the northern Triangle. For the past two months, we have been commuting twice a week along the so-called Green Line to this pool so that my father could receive the physical therapy that his Jewish female neurologist in the hospital in Tel-Aviv recommended. 'We can't stop your Parkinson disease, but you can delay its degeneration by exercising regularly and remaining active,' his attentive neurologist reassured him with a thick Russian accent in Hebrew. Throughout these commutes, my father and I would jointly comment on how the Palestinian villages of Irtah and Far'un at the hills near Tulkarm across the Line were being gradually disappeared from our horizons as the Apartheid Wall was being extended further north. In fact, the erection of tall cement barriers topped with barbwire was going at such a fast pace that we would increasingly arrive late to the pool due to the traffic jams that congested our path more and more with construction trucks and military jeeps patrolling the erection of more walls. Nevertheless, when we would approach the green valley area between Jatt and the Palestinian villages of Zeita and Dayr al-Ghusun across the Line, my father would ask for a few minutes of solitude so he could relish the picturesque view of the landscape. Today, on our way back home, my father waved at his favorite view, which he called 'The Little Switzerland of Palestine,' and asked me to admire with him the fleeting colors of spring before he delved into a linguistic journey into the Palestinian farmer's lexicon: 'Did you know that our ancestors had a name for the land after harvest? I bet you never heard of it! It is called *al-shilf*.' I asked if he knew the etymology of the word. He did not, but he did repeat the word putting more emphasis on the intonation of the letter '*sh*' before proceeding with more excitement to teach me another word from the language of the Palestinian *fellaheen*. 'Do you know what *al-libish* is?' I shook my head for the second time while keeping my foot on the brake in order not to collide with the border police car that was driving in front of me. '*Al-libish* is the green vine that sends out long runners along the soil where watermelons grow.' Once again, my father emphasized the '*sh*' and repeated the two words to make sure that I won't forget them. I promised him that I won't, especially during these days when the watermelon has blossomed into a global symbol of Palestinian cultural resistance and its iconography, not botany, has branched out into

colorful manifestations of solidarity with Palestine worldwide, including Mexico where it adorned murals and posters that celebrated the slogan 'From Palestine to Mexico All Walls Have Got to Go. *Palestina Libre!*'"

May 28, 2024
"This morning Spain officially approved the recognition of the State of Palestine. Except for a slight increase in the temperature this afternoon, nothing seems out of the ordinary in the quiet residential neighborhood in Madrid where I have been staying for the past ten days. I am also not certain if the tall flags of Palestine that are spread at the entrance of the cultural center of Casa Árabe are from today or were left behind after the Star of Palestine embroidery exhibit traveled back to their headquarters in Cordoba. I saw the Star there earlier this month when I visited that city: hanging like a chime in the conference room with its colorful weaving patterns swinging in slow motion following the light breeze that sneaked from the open door that led to the Andalusian-style garden. Being in Spain for a few weeks now, I can observe that the country has prepared for this historic day for quite some time. This was my impression when I first landed at the airport in Madrid when the immigration officer flipped the Israeli passport that I handed him with a scornful look that revealed his clear reluctance to stamp it. The same behavior would reoccur with another Spanish immigration officer at the border crossing-point in Gibraltar a few days later. That time, I waited patiently before I was given a soundless cue to proceed to the British checking point where I received a strikingly different welcome as soon as I handed him my blue passport. 'You guys should have won the Eurovision!' the British officer declared with utter frustration. 'What do you mean?' I asked. 'My grandfather is Jewish,' he replied. 'And I am Palestinian,' I said firmly while waiting anxiously for him to allow me to cross. It was a long journey from Cordoba to this transcontinental frontier zone, which I was eager to see in person for the first time after teaching about it in my border literature courses and was truly hoping that he would not ask me to turn back to where I came from. The commanding tone that reverberated in his voice did not alleviate my anxiety. Instead, it reminded me of the violently loud voice of Israeli soldiers at the checkpoints in Palestine. I do not remember how long it took him to examine my name and picture in the passport, but it seemed like a long time because I heard a car honking in the queue that trailed behind me. 'Carry on,' he finally said before turning to his colleague to complain about how ungrateful Palestinians are."

Given the unprecedented escalation of pace at which Israel's physical and human destruction of Gaza and Palestine is unfolding, it is impossible to predict the ways in which the arguments made in *Indigenous Affinities* about affinities and borders will evolve by the time this book is out in the world. The drone airstrikes and land invasion of the Israeli army into Nur Shams refugee camp near Tulkarm mentioned in the diary excerpt above have not ceased over the past three months, and as I write these words there is growing evidence from news reports on the ground that show that the camp has turned into a "Mini Gaza."[6] Moreover, Israel has imprisoned two notable anticolonial Palestinian feminists mentioned in this book since the manuscript was completed last August: Ahed Tamimi and Nadera Shalhoub-Kevorkian. Tamimi, a celebrated activist referred to in the introduction in the context of the Zapatistas commemoration of her release from an Israeli prison in 2018, was rearrested in November 2023 on the pretext of inciting violence and terrorism on her social media. She was released later that same month within an agreement with Hamas that involved the release of Israeli hostages captured on October 7 in exchange for freeing Palestinian captives in Israeli prisons.[7] Shalhoub-Kevorkian, a feminist scholar and activist cited in Chapter 3 for her insightful work on how Palestinians from the third generation of the Nakba resist spatial erasure in Palestinian urban spaces, was suspended from her position as a professor of criminal law at the Hebrew University in Jerusalem in March 2024 after being accused by the university administration of violating the Zionist mission of the university by identifying Israel's crimes in Gaza as genocide. The public campaign to reinstate her did not prevent the Israeli police from arresting her in April 2024 for charges related to her academic work.[8] Although she was released from prison a day later, her imprisonment represents an antidemocratic turning point in the apparatus of the state of Israel and the strong emergence of political surveillance, silencing of critical voices that speak against the ruling power, and the policing of freedom of speech.

Although this book was written before the ongoing Gaza genocide, reading it in retrospect, especially through the lens of the "To Exist Is to Resist" traveling mural that the Zapatistas painted in Palestine on the Apartheid Wall in Occupied Bethlehem in 2004, suggests that the Zapatistas had already foreseen the coming genocide at that time. On this mural, which forms the kernel of South-South Indigenous solidarity between Chiapas and Palestine as I have elucidated in this book, the Zapatista artist Gustavo Chávez Pavón signed the following words: "*Viva Palestina libre abajo el muro facsista*" [Long live Palestine under the *facsista* wall]. The artist's play on the words "fuck" and "fascist" in Spanish and English, through his coining of the word *facsista*, leads me to conclude that this was more than a bilingual pun aimed at conveying irony. Perhaps, after all, what we see in this mural is how Indigenous affinities time travel in the Global South, carrying with them the persistent echoes of settler colonial violence that stretches across a shared historical continuum of colonial dispossession and Indigenous resistance. These affinities, forged across time and space, embody the temporality of South-South connections: a nonlinear solidarity rooted in shared histories and affective ties, where struggles in different geographies and moments speak to and sustain one another through mutual care, forming a global network that defies colonial borders in the pursuit of collective liberation.

Madrid, Spain / May 31, 2024

Acknowledgments

This book is the culmination of a journey that has taken nearly fifteen years. It builds on archival research, personal interviews, and ethnographic fieldwork conducted in four languages across four continents. Gathering this material and writing the actual book evolved slowly and, for long periods of time, even painfully, due to the onset of serious health issues and the outbreak of a series of global crises that had a direct effect on my main research sites in Palestine and Chiapas, Mexico, the most recent of which include the construction of the tourism megaproject El Train Maya (The Maya Train) across the Yucatán Peninsula and Israel's genocidal war in Gaza. Despite the challenges posed by this context, the completion of the book was a monumental labor of love. I am deeply grateful to the immense support and comradeship of countless mentors, colleagues, interlocutors, students, healers, friends, and family members who patiently and graciously accompanied me along this journey by sharing their time, knowledge, and resources, and at the same time teaching me important lessons about kindness, solidarity, grief, dignified rage, and the power of resisting collectively. The following list is very partial, and I apologize for those I have inevitably missed.

The seeds for this book were originally planted in 2006 when I was first exposed to contemporary Mayan literature in Cynthia Steele's graduate course on literature from Chiapas in the Comparative Literature Department at the University of Washington. In this course, we read Mayan literature in translation and watched documentaries about the Zapatistas. The similarities between the heavy presence of military tanks and checkpoints in Chiapas and Palestine and the parallels between the Indigenous resistance movements in both geographies and the global solidarities that they garnered were so obvious to me that I could not but delve into investigating this connection with passion and curiosity. Embracing my keen interest in this South-South comparison, Cynthia took me under her wing. With devoted, rigorous, and compassionate mentorship, she supervised a dissertation that I wrote on the literary history aspect of this comparison, thus preparing me to write this book. I am very appreciative of her generosity and her ongoing support of my professional development as a scholar and a teacher.

I began writing this book during my Assistant Professor Leave in Summer/Fall 2019 through Spring 2021. With the help of the Palestinian American Research Center (PARC) NEH/FPIRI award, I was fortunate to spend a semester in Palestine, where I could deepen my engagement with the oral archive of Palestinian literature and solidify my scholarly and personal connections with my local interlocutors across the so-called Green Line. Thanks to kind invitations from Omar Tesdell at Bir Zeit University and Jamil Khader at Bethlehem University, I had the opportunity to share my work with Palestinian students from the Occupied West Bank. Through these exchanges, I gained profound insight into the enduring challenges of studying Palestine across internal borders. I am especially grateful to the team of the PARC office in Ramallah for unwavering support during my time there.

Generous support from the Forum Transregionale Studien in Berlin allowed me to participate in two academic encounters in Berlin and Mexico City: The Transregional Academy "Minor/Small Literature(s): Perspectives on World Literature from Elsewhere" (Berlin, July 2019) and The Transregional Academy "Spaces of Art: Concept and Impact in and Outside Latin America" (Mexico City, October–November 2019). The overlap of these collaborations with the initial writing stages of this book was perfect timing. Thanks to the invaluable feedback that I received in both academies, I gained a more acute understanding of the intricacies of the South-South framework that I was seeking to develop in the book. More importantly, I identified the specific threads that I needed to use to weave the connections across disciplinary, geographical, linguistic, and cultural borders. Special thanks to the art historians Laura Karp Lugo and Élodie Vaudry for taking the time to provide additional feedback on my comparative analysis of murals in Chiapas and Palestine after our meeting in Mexico City. I benefited a lot from their expertise on Latin American art and their methodological approaches to reading the history of art objects comparatively.

The Hellman Fellowship and Class of the 1945 World Fellowship from Williams College were another vital source of support. As a recipient of both fellowships, I was able to travel to Mexico and Palestine for ethnographic research in 2018 and 2019, respectively. The Class of the 1945 World Fellowship granted me the opportunity to participate in the CES Summer School "Archives of the Present: Racism, Activism and Remembrance" at the University of Coimbra in Portugal in September 2019 and refine my argument about the significance of embodied archives in Indigenous commemorative practices in Chapter 4. Additionally, the fellowship supported two visits to Brussels (in October 2019 and in March 2020), where I presented sections of this book at two cultural spaces that foster South-South dialogues: Maison de l'Amérique Latine and Lagrange Points. I wish to extend my great appreciation to Luís Martínez Andrade, Feras Abo Dabboseh, and Dima Issa-Daibes for facilitating these visits and for inviting me to be in conversation with the Latin American and Arab communities in Belgium. Moreover, the fellowship gave me the exceptional opportunity of spending eighteen months in Berlin. Unfortunately, my residency coincided with the unexpected outbreak of the Covid-19 pandemic and the onset of several serious health setbacks in my own household. Managing these hardships in a city that I was not familiar with during a prolonged lockdown was truly challenging. Thankfully, I was blessed with three research affiliations in academic institutions and projects that were populated by a supportive community. I profusely thank Georges Khalil, the director of Europe in the Middle East–The Middle East in Europe (EUME) at the Forum Transregionale Studien for going out of his way to establish a joint affiliation for me at EUME and the Lateinamerika-Institut of Freie Universität Berlin (LAI), where I had the opportunity to engage with German scholarship on Latin America and present my work in Susanne Klengel's scientific colloquium.

Another special affiliation in Berlin emerged from the kind invitation of my friend and interlocutor Refqa Abu-Ramileh to collaborate with her research team in the digital humanities project PalREAD—Country of Words: Reading and Reception of Palestinian Literature from 1948 to the Present (also at the Freie Universität Berlin). The meetings with PalREAD's research team were truly rewarding. The discussions with astute peers on historical and methodological aspects of Palestinian literature opened my eyes to the subtleties of the tension between nationalism and indigeneity in Palestinian literary history. Equally rewarding were the follow-up conversations that Refqa and I shared during memorable walks in the park with Gertude, the punkiest dog in Berlin! A particularly fruitful outcome of the collaboration with PalREAD was the organization of the workshop "Unwriting Literary History: Palestinian & Indigenous Literary Imaginaries" in February 2020. In this workshop, the first of its kind in Berlin, the participants read texts that map literary histories of Palestinian, Native American, and Mayan literatures. They also listened to presentations by leading scholars in Mayan and Native American literatures: Rita M. Palacios (Liberal Studies, Conestoga College), Paul M. Worley (Appalachian

State University), and Eman Ghanayem (University of San Diego). The well-attended workshop generated dynamic discussions about decolonial literary history and translating indigeneity across continents that contributed in vital ways to improving my formulation of the affinity between Mayan and Palestinian literatures within a Global South framework. In addition to expanding my thinking about Indigenous literatures from the work of these esteemed colleagues, I have learned a lot from their intellectual generosity and their deep political commitment to developing decolonial paths to study Indigenous literatures. In a related context, I want to thank Paul once more. We had several exchanges when I was writing Chapter 1 about correct translations of words in Tsotsil, and later after I received the reports from the external reviewers. Paul's enthusiastic endorsement of the project and his valuable comments on the original draft that I submitted to the press were extremely helpful in getting the book published in its current format.

Moreover, I want to thank friends and colleagues in Berlin who welcomed me into their community and offered kind support during difficult times: Adi Yassin, Lina Yassin, Amna Abdel Kader, Rita Pokorny, Anne-Marie McManus and Adrian, Avinoam Shalem, Diana Abbani, Muhammad Jabali, Himmat Zoubi, Hanan Toukan, Angelina Saule, Alexandra Handal, Dr. Franziska Musharbash, Alia Mossallam, Nora Parr, and Isis Nusair. Special thanks to Zahiye Kundus for modeling intellectual and familial sisterhood, to Antonio Ungar for the conversations we shared on Palestinian literature in Colombia, and to the beautiful talented children of both for brightening my times with their joy and creativity. I am also grateful to the formidable Fouad Abdelnour for sharing his private archive and expertise on the local history of the Galilee and the Triangle in Palestine, as well as to Islam Dayeh for his insightful suggestions for primary readings on affinity in Islamic theology.

The writing of this book would not have been possible without the incredible support of my communities in Chiapas and Mexico City. Since my first trip to Chiapas in 2010, I have been welcomed with open arms into the home of Carmen Martinez Estrada. Señora Carmen, or *abuelita*, as I was asked to call her, was more than my host. Until her death in 2022, *abuelita* Carmen was an inspirational teacher. She taught me important lessons about the struggle of young labor migrant women from Mexico City who arrived in Chiapas in the early 1940s to work in coffee plantations, which houseplants to use as a remedy for an injury caused by a dog bite, why watching ants at work matters, how to soak in the brilliance of the last star in the sky before dawn, and the secret of familial connections that transcend bloodlines and continents. My deep appreciation goes as well to Señora Amelia Gonazales Sanchez, with whom I stayed in summer 2018. Señora Amelia was eager to learn more about Palestine,

Islam, and Mayan languages. During our daily lunch meals together, I would share updates about my Tsotsil classes and the latest news from the Holy Land. In fact, these conversations together with Señora Amelia's visit with me to the Chamula Muslim community that summer enhanced my understanding of linguistic, ethnic, and religious borders in Chiapas. In Fall 2019, Patricia Velasco graciously offered her entire house for me to stay with a group of friends who joined me on my fifth trip to San Cristóbal / Jobel. Another set of thanks goes to Ámbar Past, Carlota Duarte, John Burstein, Nancy Cruz Dávila, and Beatriz Deangoitia for hosting me at different cultural events and personal gatherings in which they shared critical insights about Indigenous cultural production in Chiapas and the political aspects of *ladino/a* and Mayan interactions in San Cristóbal / Jobel.

Apart from my encounter with the Muslim community in 2010, my participation in the *Escuelita Zapatista* (The Zapatista Little School) in 2013, and the close collaboration with Mayan teachers, writers and artists, and community members in San Cristóbal / Jobel and Acteal that I have had over the past decade were transformative experiences that left a personal and an intellectual imprint on me and the book. I wish to convey my sincerest gratitude to Linda Quiquivix (Quiqui) for her comradeship, leadership, and facilitation during my time at the school and beyond. I also thank my two classmates from the Palestinian delegation who participated in the *escuelita*, Beesan Ramadan and JJ Mitchell, for the debates that we shared together with Quiqui about the future of Zapatismo in Palestine. Special thanks to Sylvia Marcos for her generous hospitality in Cuernavaca, and for opening both her home and her vast intellectual archive to our delegation. Her critical insights and personal reflections on Zapatista feminisms in Chiapas offered us a rare and profound lens through which to think across geographies of struggle.

I consider my relationship with the Muslim community in Chiapas especially privileged. Juana Gómez Hernández, or *hajja* Nora, welcomed me (and the many friends that I brought along) into her house during Friday prayers, Eid celebrations, and casual family gatherings. Her older son, Abdulhafid, treated me with equal warmth and reached out frequently via social media and WhatsApp to inquire about my health and the safety of my family in Palestine. My friendship with the younger son, Imam Chechev, grew into a vital intellectual collaboration as we navigated together a path toward an Arabic-Tsotsil translation of the word affinity. Thanks to meetings with valued members of the community, including Adela Muneera Bonilla Vidal and Carlos Abed El-Raheem Jimenz (*Allah yerhamu*), as well as individuals who were close to them, such as Gaspar Morquecho Escamilla, I acquired a more nuanced understanding of the local history of Muslims in Chiapas and Mexico, more broadly.

In a related vein, I want to acknowledge the debt I owe to members of my Tsotsil-speaking community. They were indispensable to my thinking about the connection between Indigenous struggles in Chiapas and Palestine. They also contributed substantially to this project by sharing with me their own intellectual work, valuable resources on Tsotsil language, culture, and art, plus personal accounts of what they perceived as similar aspects of our common struggle against settler colonial states and racialized second-class citizenship. My appreciation goes to the staff and students at CIDECI-UniTierra for their guided tours of the school and the dialogues at the monthly seminars. Jose Mendoza Lopez, my dedicated Tsotsil teacher, answered many questions that I had about Tsotsil with care and patience. Without his physical presence with me in Acteal during my first fieldwork trip and his active participation as a witness and a translator, I would not have been given access to the community. When Jose could not join me in future trips because of his teaching commitments, he insisted that I go with Ignacio Hernandez, a trusted member of his own family and a competent translator. Because of Jose and Ignacio's chaperoning, I was given a personal guided tour of the massacre site in Acteal and was allowed to record intimate testimonies of the grieving community. The muralist Dyg'Nojoch played a crucial role in this project by taking the time to talk to me about the history of murals in Acteal and his own work with the community of Las Abejas and other Mayan communities in San Cristóbal / Jobel. The poet and translator Xun Betan played an equally important role in this project by providing incisive feedback on possible translations of the concept of affinity in Tsotsil. Thanks to the personal interviews I conducted with members of La FOMMA in 2010, I was able to gain a better understanding of the evolution of Mayan theater and performance in the 1980s, as well as the intersection of the personal and the political in the movement of Mayan writers and artists across rural-urban spatial and cultural divides. These interviews have deeply informed my thinking about internal borders in Chapter 3. I hope that in this project I was able to present accurately the multifaceted cultural landscape of the Tsotsil-speaking Mayan literature and the Indigenous struggle in Chiapas more broadly. I also hope that I was able to amplify the voices of this struggle with the respect, honor, and solidarity they deserve. To everyone, *Kolaval*!

Colleagues and friends in the Colegió de Mexico (COLMEX) and the Universidad Autónoma de Mexico (UNAM) in Mexico City supported this project by sharing their own work on South-South connections and extending invitations to present parts of earlier drafts of this book. *Alf shukr / mil gracias* to Shadi Rohana, Gilberto Conde, Silvana Rabinovich, Fernando López de la Torre, and Janet Calderon. I am especially thankful to Heather Harper for translating parts of my work into Spanish and for accompanying me in my journey toward somatic healing. Thanks to her, I discovered the depth of writing from my body and the healing that comes with the release of stories and testimonies that it had stored. My valued friendship and rich collaboration with Ghadeer Abu-Sneineh and Shadi Rohana, two Palestinian translators who introduced contemporary Mexican and Latin American literatures to Arab readership and broadened my perspective on the larger history of the encounter between Arabic and Latin American literatures. As contributors to South-South connections, both Ghadeer and Shadi offered illuminating comments on my contextualization of the history of solidarity with Palestine in Mexico and Central America. I am especially grateful to Gustavo Chavéz Pavón for his generosity as a person and an artist. In addition to giving me unconditional access to his complete archive that contains rare images of his murals and artwork in Palestine and Mexico, Gustavo refused to accept any monetary compensation for using the image of the mural "To Exist Is to Resist" on the cover of this book. His commitment to the Zapatistas' strong belief that public art—particularly artworks of solidarity movements that are emerging from below and to the left—belongs to the people, and *not* market capitalism, affected the way I position this book as a project that, concurrently, *is inspired by solidarity* and *is thinking alongside solidarity*.

Among the many individuals from whose enthusiasm for interdisciplinary conversations I have benefited the most over the years, I would like to mention several colleagues and friends at Williams College who have read and commented on various early drafts of this book: Rashida Braggs, Nelly Rosario, VaNatta Ford, Marshall Green, and Radhiyah Ayobami. Their thoughtful criticism and encouragement during our monthly "Writing Exchange with Care" meetings, especially during Covid, were a true anchor. I also owe particular thanks to the Oakley Center for the Humanities and Social Sciences for granting me the opportunity to organize a manuscript review workshop with leading scholars in Middle Eastern studies, anthropology and sociology, latino/a studies, and creative writing to discuss the first skeleton of this book. I was very privileged to spend an entire day reflecting on the different conceptual and structural elements of the book with Nadia Yaqub, Michael Vicente Pérez, Christina Simko, and Nelly Rosario, who have constantly encouraged me integrate my creative writing voice into my academic projects. The interdisciplinary feedback of these esteemed colleagues pushed me to think deeply about affinity, borders, memory, and my positionality in the South-South conversation that this book seeks to create.

A heartfelt thanks goes as well to members of my tenure evaluation committee, Gail Newman, Kashia Pieprzak, Magnús Bernhardsson, Jennifer French, Lama Nassif, and Brahim El-Guabli, for their dedicated mentorship and the many ways in which they have been instrumental in my growth as a scholar and a teacher. I have been enormously fortunate to work in a very supportive department, and cobuilding a uniquely interdisciplinary Arabic Studies Department alongside Lama Nassif and Brahim El-Guabli has been the highlight of my time at Williams College. I wish to acknowledge the important lessons I learned from Armando Vargas, one of the pillars of Arabic Studies at Williams. He was a foundational figure in the department when it was still a program, before his departure. His passion for Arabic and South-South connections left a lasting impression on me. In addition to being a pioneer in the study of cultural production among Arab migrants in Latin America, particularly Arabs in Brazil, he is also a remarkably kind human being. As an unofficial mentor, Dorothy Wang offered important guidance and great support. I would like to express gratitude to the following librarians for answering my queries and helping me gain access to material stored in obscure library repositories across the world: Christine Ménard, Alison Roe O'Grady, and Karen Bucky. I would also like to acknowledge the security staff at the Clark Art Institute library for the stimulating conversations about art and politics that we shared during my late-night writing sessions at the library. Likewise, I wish to extend my gratitude to the following colleagues, cohorts, and comrades for creating a true sense of community in the remote Williamstown. Saadia Yacoob, Zaid Adhami, Aparna Kapadia, Monica Mackey, and Christi Kelsey have sustained me most during stressful times. Shaina Adams-El Guabli, Aly Corey, Nimu Njoya, Carlos Macías Prieto, Sidra Mahmood, Hajar Al-Dirani, Maha Bouhnin, Rene R. Cordero, and Radwa El Barouni exemplified true solidarity. I thank Sophie Saint-Just, Christopher Koné, Man He, Jackie Hidalgo, Sourena Parham, Lucy Green, and Andrea Massar for their care and collegiality. Special thanks go to Jane Canova, who continued to be a valued member of this community after her retirement. Just as I was putting the finishing touches on this manuscript, I had the pleasure to stay for three weeks with Jane in her house in Madrid, where I wrote both the postscript and these acknowledgments. Writing both texts under a tight deadline and a nonstop flood of breaking news from Israel's genocidal war in Palestine was emotionally demanding. In addition to giving me the space to write, Jane was a gracious host. Thanks to her comforting home-made food and invigorating excursions into Madrid's parks, I was able to recharge and keep writing.

Although this book was produced within the course of my teaching at Williams College, the continuous support of numerous benevolent people across the US, including those whom I met during my graduate studies in the Pacific Northwest between 2004 and 2013 before moving to teach in western Massachusetts, has been truly extraordinary. I thank Razan Francis, Dima Ayoub, Eman S. Morsi, and Manar Shabouk for many moments of joy, laughter, and deep conversations about politics, art, literature, Arab feminism, and revolutions in the

Middle East and beyond. I extend my gratitude to Juliane Hammer for her annual gift of a solidarity calendar and the many ways in which she has inspired my thinking about Sufism, feminism, and the wisdom of the heart. Many thanks as well to Cemil Aydin for his friendship. I cherish the critical debates we shared and the warm hospitality I received from him and Juliane, both at UNC and in their home. I am grateful to Adile Aslan and Ian Almond for their friendship and for the stimulating conversations we had on reading world literature from the Global South. My friend Carol Smith from NYC taught me memorable lessons about magic: to look for the shooting star and to trust serendipitous encounters. Carol was a Jewish Voice for Peace activist who was deeply involved in transnational antiwar, antiracist, and antifascist struggles from Chile, to New York, to Palestine. She continued to march and distribute flyers in support of these causes until her death in August 2022 at the age of eighty-one. Four days before her death she wrote an email wishing me a happy birthday and asking if she could read the introduction. My response came too late. I hereby dedicate the introduction of this book to her memory and the beautiful legacy she left behind. I also thank her partner, Joe Esposito, for his friendship and hospitality. My friends, host families, and mentors in Eugene, Portland, and Seattle continue to remind me of the home that I have away from home. Many thanks to Lillian Darwin-López, Jeanne and Kent Henriksen, Maha, Maya, and Ian Barrett, Analisa Taylor, Nour Chida, Zakaria Chida, Mounir Ghattas, Aisha Kaba, Sahera Bleibleh, Fatima Bahloul, Nobuko Yamasaki, Maged Zaher, Ebtihal Shedid, Ziad Zaghrout, Haneen Ahmad, María Santizo, Yasmine Bouagga, Sarah Guthu, Erin Salokas, Daniela Ahmed, Cathlin Starke, Akila Estrella, Yuko Mera, Cuate Mexica, and Anjali Vats. My mentors at UW, Terri DeYoung, Leroy Searle, Tony Lucero, and María Elena García were instrumental in my intellectual and personal growth throughout graduate school and beyond. Special thanks to Ella Habiba Shohat, Samah Selim, Sinan Antoon, and Ibtisam Azem for many fruitful exchanges and their gracious hospitality during my visits in NYC.

This version of the book is the result of extensive critical exchanges with scholars, writers, and editors who contributed to its revisions in meaningful ways. I give credit to Samer Al-Saber, a dear friend and a cohort from The Seattle School, as I call it, for encouraging me to prioritize writing with rigor over paying too much attention to disciplinary politics, especially when it comes to serving Palestine as a cause. Susan Eisenberg modeled how to attend thoughtfully to the personal and the political in writing and organizing. I am also thankful to Susan for graciously hosting me at her home in Jamaica Plain, where I was not only nourished with meals cooked with love, but also pampered with flowers from her Garden Café and the privilege of being the first one to read/listen to her poems. Chadwick Allen and Sherene Seikaly read early drafts of the book prospectus and provided constructive comments. Ussama Makdisi brought my attention to the political significance of affinity in nineteenth-century Syria. I hereby thank all three of them for their generative feedback. I also want to thank the anonymous reviewers for their enlightening input and comments. Special thanks to Thomas Lay, my editor at Fordham University Press, for championing this project from the beginning and for guiding it with remarkable enthusiasm, generosity, and patience through the press. I am also deeply grateful to Nancy Basmajian, my copyeditor, for her insightful and meticulous reading of the manuscript. Thanks as well to Kem Crimmins, Assistant Managing Editor, for his support during the production of the book. All oversights are mine.

I am blessed to have the inspiration and support of four people who made this book eminently more readable than it otherwise might have been. I am forever grateful to Souhail Chichah for his phenomenal intellectual support. In addition to helping me resolve several conceptual impasses, Souhail provided sharp critique of the epistemological framework of the book and constantly encouraged me to think outside the box, especially when it comes to decoloniality. Pia Kohler deserves applause for patiently and skillfully coaching me through the preparation of the manuscript for my tenure-review package and the press. In addition to making important stylistic corrections, Ibrahim Muhawi contributed to the translations from Arabic, and called my attention to leaps, gaps, and missing connections. The current version of the book is much stronger because of his input. On a personal level, I wish to acknowledge that his compassionate mentorship and deep love for Palestinian literature have been a constant source of inspiration for my growth, both as an individual and as a Palestinian literary scholar. Since I wrote my dissertation in 2013, Jacinthe Assaad has been my best reader and proofreader. She has contributed significantly to my intellectual and creative growth. This book (and the rest of my writings) is enriched by her creative formulation of metaphors and titles. I treasure our sisterhood and the critical support she has offered as the doula of this book! Once again, I profusely thank all four of them and hope that when they recognize their own insights in the pages which follow they will take notice of the great influence that they have had on me!

My family, relatives, friends, former students, and members of my extended community in Palestine have sustained me the most since I left home twenty years ago to embark on an academic research journey that yielded this book. By sharing their resources, memories, time, ideas, advice, prayers, contacts, food, care, and love, all contributed in some vital ways to the intellectual, social, and familial milieu in which I wrote this book. I would like to acknowledge with deep gratitude my best friend Alaa Yousef as well as this list of cherished childhood friends for their sisterhood and for cheering me up along the path that I pursued, as if it were achieving a shared collective dream: Heba Baloum, Samar Gbara, Yumna Shehadeh, Linda Azem, Farida Gbara, Wasna Azem, Shatha Massarweh, Salam Baransi, Nasreen Baransi, Nasreen Haj Yehia, Suha Jaber, Nadia Massarweh, Enas Haj Yehya, and Hoda Haj Yehya. My research trips to Palestine were made more pleasant because of the reunion meetings with Salim Abu Jabal, Rabab Haj Yehya, Hazar Alhadi, Zakiya Asali, Manar Makhoul and Aida Fahmawi. To Issac Meller, my former orthopedic oncologist surgeon and current fellow writer, I am indebted twice: first, for the miracle of walking on two feet; second, for the surprising fact that I have not lost my fluency in Hebrew. I must make special acknowledgment to members of the bereft community in Kafr Qasem, especially Rose Amer and Ramy Amer, for their time and for facilitating my access to the oral archive of the Kafr Qasem massacre.

I wish to recognize three beloved family members who passed away while I was writing this book: My maternal uncle Mu'in Massarweh (1959–2019), my step-grandmother Fehmiyya Massarweh (1948–2020), and my cousin Ilham Eqeiq (1968–2021). It is beyond the scope of these acknowledgements to delve into their memory and how it intersects with the colonial dispossession of Palestine, but I must record here my gratefulness to them. They were generous and warm soulful people who believed in me. Their frequent visits to me in my dreams and my subsequent attempts to decipher these dreams together with other family members have illumined my understanding of the significance of ancestors, orality, and the unseen in Indigenous narratives.

Finally, I would like to acknowledge with infinite gratitude my parents Samiha and Thabet Eqeiq. I could never put in words or reward them adequately for their unconditional love, sacrifices, generosity, kindness, patience, and faith in me. They could not have imagined that my trip to the US for two years to pursue an MA in comparative literature would extend into a permanent residency in a faraway foreign continent where they have no family or relatives. Despite their strong resistance to brain drain, both of my parents were indispensable to my success abroad. In addition to creating a nurturing space for me to write at home during my annual summer visits, they helped me thrive in my research by abundantly sharing their resources and welcoming international friends and colleagues. I also owe much to my beloved siblings, Yousef, Reem, Lubna, and Akram, their partners, and my thirteen nieces and nephews for showering me with love and invitations to special meals, and vacations that sustained my physical and emotional well-being. Many thanks as well to my family members in Belgium, Fatima El Bouanani, Chorok Chichah, and Majda Chichah for their support, prayers, Belgian chocolate, Moroccan delights, and much more, sent all the way from Brussels! Since the book is officially (and finally!) completed, we can dance together now and sing the family's favorite song: "We submitted the book!"

A substantial portion of this book was written in Williamstown, located on the ancestral homeland of the Stockbridge-Munsee Band of Mohican Indians, known as the People of the Waters That Are Never Still. My words are infused with their living memory. May it inspire readers to honor their histories, and to walk the path of reparation, justice, and liberation—past, present, and future.

The final revisions of this book were completed while Israel's genocide in Gaza was raging in full force. Despite all the unfathomable horror, destruction, death of family members, and forced displacement, my friend in Gaza, Amal Al Haj, continued to inquire about my well-being and the progress of the book. The postscript, drawn from both the hope her name carries and the roots of the orange and avocado trees that her mother, Fatima Al Haj, and my brother, Akram Eqeiq, planted at the same time in the early days of the genocide, is dedicated to her. Despite the devastation in Gaza and the ongoing Nakba in Palestine, these trees continue to exist, their roots growing deeper into the land and mirroring the enduring hope that we will one day share their fruits together in a free Palestine.

Text Permissions

I gratefully acknowledge the generosity of the following authors, translators, and publishers for granting permission to reproduce their poems in this book, in the following order: Mariano Reynaldo Vázquez López for *Nichim vayichetik / Orquídea de sueños* (Unidad de Escritores Mayas-Zoques, 2006); Xun Betan for the poems "Jme'tik ta bats'i k'op / La madre luna Tsotsil," originally published in *Insurrección de las palabras: Poetas contemporáneos en lenguas mexicanas*, edited by Hermann Bellinghausen (Fondo de Cultura Económica, 2023), as well as "Semillas de esperanza / Seeds of Hope" and "Flores para el corazón / Flowers for the Heart," translated by Sean S. Sell and originally published in *North Dakota Quarterly* 86, no. 3/4 (2019); and Manu Pukuj for the poem "Vovijel," in *Snichimal Vayuchil: Experimental Poetry in Bats'i K'op*, edited and translated by Paul M. Worley (University of North Dakota Press, 2018). Many thanks to Tawfiq Zayyad's family and the Tawfiq Zayyad Institute in Nazareth for their kind permission to translate and reproduce the poem "Hunā bāqūn" (Here We Shall Remain, 1965) from *Dīwān Tawfīq Zayyād* (Dār al-'Awda, 2000). I also wish to thank the *Journal of Palestine Studies* for granting permission to republish selections from Amal Eqeiq's article "From Haifa to Ramallah (and Back): New/Old Palestinian Literary Topography," originally published in *Journal of Palestine Studies* 48, no. 3 (2019).

Glossary

Adab al-Iltizām, Literature of Commitment—An Arabic model of politically committed literature that flourished in the early days of nation-building in the postcolonial Arab world. The Palestinian cause was a central topic among writers in this movement. أدب الالتزام

Intifāḍa, uprising—The first Palestinian Intifada took place in 1987. انتفاضة

al-Jidār, the Apartheid Wall. الجدار

Maḥasīm, Arabic broken plural of the Hebrew word *Maḥsom,* checkpoint. مَحاسيم

Majzara, massacre. مجزرة

Mustawṭana, a settlement—Zionist colony. مُستوطنة

Nakba—An Arabic word for "catastrophe." It refers to the ethnic cleansing and destruction of Historic Palestine in 1948. نكبة

Oslo—An abridged reference to the Oslo Peace Accords in 1993. The current Palestinian authority is often mocked as the Oslo State. أوسلو

Shu'arā' al-muqāwama, Resistance Poets—A literary movement of Palestinian poets in Israel who recited militant anti-Zionist poems and participated in fierce public performances in poetry festivals organized in the 1950s and 1960s despite the martial law that the apparatus of the Israeli military rule imposed between 1949 and 1966. Samih Al-Qasim, Mahmoud Darwish, and Tawfiq Zayyad were prominent figures in this movement. The poems they performed from that era are still popular and widely remembered. شعراء المقاومة

Shuhadā', martyrs. شُهداء

Ṣumūd, steadfastness—A Palestinian notion of steadfast perseverance by remaining on the land and resisting Zionist occupation. صُمود

Conquista	The Spanish conquest of the Americas.
El muro	The fence wall across the US-Mexico borderlands.
¡Fue el estado!	"It was the state!": A popular phrase referring to state-sanctioned violence. The phrase is often disseminated in graffiti and banners in street marches across Latin America to express a public protest against state terror, disappearances, and massacres.
Kaxlan	A Tsotsil and Tseltal term designated specifically for mestizos/as. The word literally means "hen." It is often used to make fun of mestizos/as.
Ladino/a	*Ladino/a* is a term used by Mayan communities in Chiapas to refer to non-Indigenous Peoples, including foreigners. It also describes assimilationist mestizos/as who are culturally and politically aligned with European ideals and the dominant norms of mainstream Mexican society.
Literatura indigenista	A body of literary works by non-Indigenous authors with a paternalistic view of the Indigenous. These works are often motivated by a mestizo ideology of Indian assimilation, and produced a romanticized and ahistorical image of the Indian.
Matanza	Slaughter.
Mestizaje	The miscegenation of European and Amerindian race and culture post conquest.
Pollero	A term used in Chiapas as a synonym for *coyote*, the person who smuggles migrants across the border.
Testimonio	A nonfiction narrative account of a subaltern eyewitness who tells their story for an anthropologist or a journalist. Ricardo Pozas's *Juan Pérez Jolote: Biografía de un tzotzil / Juan Pérez Jolote: An Ethnological Re-creation of the Life of a Mexican Indian* (Chiapas, Mexico, 1952) and Esteban Montejo's *Biografía de un Cimarrón / Biography of a Runaway Slave* (Cuba, 1966) are two foundational texts in this genre.
Zapatismo	The political philosophy of the Zapatista armed rebellion in Chiapas in 1994. Identifying with the agrarian socialism of Emiliano Zapata, the leader of the 1910 Mexican revolution, Zapatistas demand Indigenous autonomy in addition to more basic needs like land, work, healthcare, education, and cultural rights.

Notes

Introduction: On Conversations Yet to Be Had

1. *Subcomandante Insurgente* Marcos, *Our Word Is Our Weapon: Selected Writings*, ed. Juana Ponce de León (Seven Stories, 2001), 417.
2. Mark LeVine, *Why They Don't Hate Us: Lifting the Veil on the Axis of Evil* (Oneworld, 2005), 253.
3. Sylvia Marcos and Linda Quiquivix, "Chiapas and Palestine, Together and Side by Side," *NACLA Report on the Americas* 56, no. 4 (2024): 443, https://doi.org/10.1080/10714839.2024.2427986.
4. Amal Eqeiq, "Of Borders and Limits: Comparative Indigeneity in Mexico and Palestine," *Jadaliyya*, August 27, 2018, https://www.jadaliyya.com/Details/37898.
5. Leslie Quintanilla and Jennifer Mogannam, "Borders Are Obsolete: Relations Beyond the 'Borderlands' of Palestine and US-Mexico," *American Quarterly* 67, no. 4 (2015): 1041, https://doi.org/10.1353/aq.2015.0066.
6. Charles Pinderhughes, "Toward a New Theory of Internal Colonialism," *Socialism and Democracy* 25, no. 1 (2011): 236, https://doi.org/10.1080/08854300.2011.559702.
7. Rosaura Sánchez and Beatrice Pita, "Rethinking Settler Colonialism," *American Quarterly* 66, no. 4 (2014): 1043, https://doi.org/10.1353/aq.2014.0065.
8. Elia Zureik, *The Palestinians in Israel: A Study in Internal Colonialism* (Routledge & K. Paul, 1979).
9. M. Bianet Castellanos, "Introduction: Settler Colonialism in Latin America," *American Quarterly* 69, no. 4 (2017): 778.
10. Patrick Wolfe, "Settler Colonialism and the Elimination of the Native," *Journal of Genocide Research* 8, no. 4 (2006): 388, https://doi.org/10.1080/14623520601056240.

11. Cecilia Baeza, "Palestinians and Latin America's Indigenous Peoples: Coexistence, Convergence, Solidarity," *Middle East Report*, no. 274 (2015): 34–36.

12. Baeza, "Palestinians," 36.

13. Chadwick Allen, *Trans-Indigenous Methodologies for Global Native Literary Studies* (University of Minnesota Press, 2012), xviii, xiii.

14. Munir Akash was another pioneering figure who examined Palestinian and Native American literatures through a comparative framework. In this earlier scholarship in this field, which appeared in Arabic, he argues that the fact that the British conquest of North America was rooted in the narrative of mythical Israel, and that the Puritan settlers treated Native Americans as if they were Canaanites, speaks more to the similarity between the British Puritan settlers and the Zionists as executioners. As for the two victims, Akash insists, the distinctions are striking. In addition to their differences in time, place, history, geography, thought, culture, lifestyle, and most importantly, resistance to invasion, Palestinians occupy a different position than Native Americans. Whether long or short, he argues, there is no future for a Zionist entity in Palestine, and hence Palestinians are more likely to prevail. In 2015, when Akash was interviewed about his book *Dawla Filasṭīniyya li-l-Hunūd al-Ḥumr / An Indian Canaan* (Riyāḍ al-Rayyis lil-Kutub wa-al-Nashr, 2015), he was asked: "If you had the opportunity to write a study with a title heralding the victory of the Palestinians, which historical people would you choose to compare the Palestinian people to?" His response was: "Palestinians are *not* red Indians. They should be *compared* to themselves." Emphasis is mine. See Munir Akash, interview by the cultural section of *al-ʿArabī al-Jadīd*, August 18, 2015, "Munīr ʿAkash: Al-Filasṭīniyyūn laysaū Hunūdan Ḥumran" (Munir Akash: The Palestinians Are Not Red Indians), https://www.alaraby.co.uk/منير-عكاش-الفلسطينيون-ليسوا-هنوداً-حمراً-0, accessed May 24, 2025.

15. Steven Salaita, *The Holy Land in Transit: Colonialism and the Quest for Canaan* (Syracuse University Press, 2006), Kindle, chap. 2, loc. 510.

16. Steven Salaita, *Inter/Nationalism: Decolonizing Native America and Palestine* (University of Minnesota Press, 2016), 2–4.

17. Lauren Tynan, "What Is Relationality? Indigenous Knowledges, Practices and Responsibilities with Kin," *Cultural Geographies* 28, no. 4 (2021): 600, https://doi.org/10.1177/14744740211029287.

18. Matt Wildcat and Daniel Voth, "Indigenous Relationality: Definitions and Methods," *AlterNative: An International Journal of Indigenous Peoples* 19, no. 2 (2023): 478.

19. Wildcat and Voth, "Indigenous Relationality," 481.

20. Dana M. Olwan, "On Assumptive Solidarities in Comparative Settler Colonialisms," *Feral Feminisms*, no. 2 (Winter 2013): 100.

21. For more on these networks of solidarity and the interest of Palestinian prisoners in Latin American revolutionary thinking, see Carlos Fernando López de la Torre, "The Cuban Poster and Palestine: Solidarity and Third Worldism in Images," *Middle East Studies Association Annual Meeting*, November 17, 2018, San

Antonio, TX, conference paper; Jessica Stites Mor, "Rendering Armed Struggle: OSPAAAL, Cuban Poster Art, and South-South Solidarity at the United Nations," *Jahrbuch für Geschichte Lateinamerikas* 56 (2019): 42–65; Robert Austin Henry, "Global Palestine: International Solidarity and the Cuban Connection," *Journal of Holy Land and Palestine Studies* 18, no. 2 (2019): 239–62; Lena Meari, "Reading Che in Colonized Palestine: On Analyzing and Drawing Inspiration from Revolutionary Latin American Texts," *NACLA Report on the Americas* 50, no. 1 (2018): 49–55; and Fernando Camacho Padilla and Jessica Stites Mor, "Presence and Visibility in Cuban Anticolonial Solidarity: Palestine in OSPAAAL's Photography and Poster Art," in *Palestine in the World: International Solidarity with the Palestinian Liberation Movement*, ed. Sorcha Thomson and Pelle Valentin Olsen (I. B. Tauris, 2023), 167–96, https://doi.org/10.5040/9780755647026.ch-007.

22. Shadi Rohana, "Latin America in the Palestinian Journal *Al-Karmel*," *Middle East Studies Association Annual Meeting*, November 17, 2018, San Antonio, TX, conference paper.

23. Sebastian Haug, Jacqueline Braveboy-Wagner, and Günther Maihold, "The 'Global South' in the Study of World Politics: Examining a Meta Category," *Third World Quarterly* 42, no. 9 (2021): 1929, https://doi.org/10.1080/01436597.2021.1948831.

24. Abya Yala, "Continent of Life," or "land in its full maturity" in the language of the Kuna peoples of Panama and Colombia. It is a term used to describe Latin America from Indigenous perspectives. For further details on the history of the term and its critical use in decolonial Indigenous thought, see Arturo Escobar, *Pluriversal Politics: The Real and the Possible* (Duke University Press, 2020).

25. Moisés Garduño García, "Resonancias del zapatismo mexicano y la resistencia palestina: Dos ejemplos de autonomía en el Sur Global," *Espiral (Guadalajara)* 23, no. 65 (2016): 111.

26. Gloria Elizabeth Chacón, *Indigenous Cosmolectics: Kab'awil and the Making of Maya and Zapotec Literatures* (University of North Carolina Press, 2018), 14.

27. Camelia Suleiman, *The Politics of Arabic in Israel: A Sociolinguistic Analysis* (Edinburgh University Press, 2017), 165.

28 Kashua's writing in English is mainly creative nonfiction and TV sitcoms. Although officially he did not stop writing in Hebrew, his last novel, *Aḳov aḥar ha-shinuyim*, which he wrote in 2017 after moving to the United States and which was translated into English in 2020 by Mitch Ginsburg as *Track Changes*, includes an entire section in a mix of Palestinian vernacular Arabic and modern standard Arabic that is left untranslated into Hebrew.

29. Anton Shammas, "Can the Bilingual Speak?," *Markaz Review*, May 15, 2022, https://themarkaz.org/can-the-bilingual-speak-thoughts-on-the-arabic-hebrew-mind/.

30. In an interview for *The New York Review of Books*, Kashua recalls his memories as the only Palestinian student in a Jewish school and the colonial logic embedded in his choice to write in Hebrew. He states:

> In the new school, there was a library the like of which we had never had in our school or town, but there were no books in Arabic. There, in West Jerusalem, I experienced as a teenager the meaning of being a minority, a stranger with heavy accent: a threat, a primitive Arab, a Palestinian in a Jewish state. As a teenager (not yet familiar with Frantz Fanon's writing), I really wanted to belong, or at least to prove to my friends and maybe to myself that I was no less than them. To prove their assumptions about me wrong, I had to work on my language, my accent, my taste in music, art, and literature. Even as I internalized my "primitivity" as the Arab Other, I wanted to adopt the "superior" Western/Hebrew culture. . . .
>
> But my Hebrew was always different, accented even while writing, trying to challenge the "legitimate" Hebrew writers. This complicated relationship—struggling with the language, hating it, loving it, trying to make room for myself in it while fighting it—became essential to my writing. At times, I wonder how writers can write at all in their mother tongues. It makes no sense to me when people write in languages they already understand.

For the complete interview, see Sayed Kashua, "Advanced Hebrew with an Arabic Accent," interview by Matt Seaton, *New York Review of Books*, August 14, 2021, https://www.nybooks.com/online/2021/08/14/advanced-hebrew-with-an-arabic-accent/.

31. Sayed Kashua, "My Palestinian Diaspora," *New York Review of Books*, August 7, 2021, https://www.nybooks.com/online/2021/08/07/my-palestinian-diaspora/.

32. Pascale Casanova, *The World Republic of Letters*, trans. M. B. DeBevoise (Harvard University Press, 2004), 203.

33. Rita M. Palacios, "Maya Literature," in *Oxford Research Encyclopedia of Literature* (Oxford University Press, 2022).

34. Gloria Anzaldúa, *Borderlands/La Frontera: The New Mestiza* (Aunt Lute Books, 1987), 25.

1. On Affinity and Affiliative Comparison

1. Chávez Pavón painted the mural in Oventik in collaboration with the local Zapatista community at the *caracol* before leaving for Palestine in October 2004. He arrived there together with Juan Erasto Molina Urbina, from Chiapas, and Alberto Aragón Reyes from Oaxaca. They were officially invited by the Lutheran Bishop of Jerusalem, Dr. Munib Younan, to participate in an international artists' residency and give lectures and children's art workshops at the International Center of the Evangelical Lutheran Church in Jerusalem. For more information about this mural, see Amal Eqeiq, "Aesthetics of Indigenous Affinity: From Chiapas to Palestine in the Traveling Murals of Gustavo Chávez Pavón," *Transmotion: An Online Journal of Postmodern Indigenous Studies* 5, no. 1 (July 2019): 152–65, https://journals.kent.ac.uk/index.php/transmotion/article/view/761.

2. The word *facsista* is a playful twist in Spanish of the words "fuck" and "fascist" in English. The irony is intended by the artist.

3. In 1984, the Syrian visual artist Burhan Karkoutly (1932–2003) used a similar technique in his famous poster "Long Live Zapata, Long Live Abed Al-Qadir al-Husayni." Karkoutly, who was involved with the cultural mission of the PLO in the late 1960s, which called for galvanizing international solidarity with Palestine through dissemination of Palestinian art and cultural production, traveled to Mexico in 1980. Inspired by Mexican revolutionary art, particularly the murals of David Siqueiros (1896–1974), he designed several posters that center Palestinian landscape and Palestinian peasants as Indigenous icons. In this black and white poster, he positions the images of two revolutionary figures from Mexico and Palestine: Emiliano Zapata (1879–1919) and Abed Al-Qadir al-Husayni (1907–1948). The images of the two men, who are celebrated as national heroes, occupy an equal space in the poster. They stand tall, side by side, with aligned juxtaposition of the *sombrero* and the *kuffiyeh* on their heads, arms carried in their hands, and special lines that accentuate their similar facial features, most notably their thick mustaches. For more on the poster and its significance in the archive of early solidarity between Mexico and Palestine see, Amal Eqeiq, "Of Borders and Limits: Comparative indigeneity in Mexico and Palestine," *Jadaliyya*, August 26, 2018.

4. Khaled Jarrar, in the film *Khaled's Ladder* (2016), my emphasis. For more on the film, see "Khaled's Ladder," *Culturunners*, accessed May 20, 2025, https://www.culturunners.com/films/khaleds-ladder.

5. Apart from the chorus, "This border control ... call," the translation of the lyrics in Arabic and Spanish are mine. See 47Soul, "Border Ctrl. ft. Shadia Mansour x Fedzilla," *YouTube*, August 20, 2020, https://youtu.be/iL11uPXsS4U.

6. Brahim El Guabli, "Where Is Amazigh Studies?," *Africa Is a Country*, May 8, 2023, https://africasacountry.com/2023/05/where-is-amazigh-studies.

7. Maurice Ebileeni, *Being There, Being Here: Palestinian Writings in the World* (Syracuse University Press, 2022).

8. Refqa Abu-Remaileh, "Country of Words: Palestinian Literature in the Digital Age of the Refugee," *Journal of Arabic Literature* 52, no. 1–2 (2021): 72.

9. According to official records of the Mexican government there are twelve Mayan languages in Chiapas. However, the most prevalent ones are Tsotsil, Tseltal, Cho'l, Tojolabal, Zoque, Mam, and Lacandon.

10. Arturo Arias, *Recovering Lost Footprints: Contemporary Maya Narratives*, vol. 2 (State University of New York Press, 2017), 178.

11. An illustrative example appeared recently in the magazine *The Funambulist*, which dedicated a special issue to the topic of "Decentering the U.S." In the introduction, Editor-in-chief Léopold Lamber remarks: "The question that motivates this issue is simple: how come so many of us outside the settler colony called the United States of America, are so deeply influenced by, and interpret our own contexts through the political 'software' created by U.S.-based academics and activists? The goal here is less to disqualify this U.S. political framework, than to

demonstrate that the successful ways through which it analyzes its own context may not be as useful when analyzing other situations." For further reading on how the contributors to this issue address this question, see Léopold Lambert, "Decentering the U.S.," *Funambulist*, no. 41 (May–June 2022), https://thefunambulist.net/shop/41-may-june-2022-decentering-the-u-s.

12. Walter D. Mignolo, *Local Histories/Global Designs: Coloniality, Subaltern Knowledges, and Border Thinking*, Princeton Studies in Culture/Power/History (Princeton University Press, 2000), 266.

13. Arias, *Recovering Lost Footprints*, 2:193–94.

14. Unless mentioned otherwise, I rely on Muhammad Asad's translation of the Quran. However, my comparative analysis of different translations of the verses I am citing here, including those done by Yusuf Ali, Mustafa Khattab, and Tarif Khalidi, yielded similar meanings. Whereas Ali translates the verb *'allafa*, ألّف as "putting affection between their hearts," Khattab opts for "have united their hearts." Likewise, Khalidi uses "brought their hearts together," and "reconciled them with one another." For a more detailed account of other translations and a comparative view of the translations of this verse, see Alim.org, "Compare Surah 8. Al-Anfal, Ayah 63," https://www.alim.org/quran/compare/surah/8/63/.

15. Muhammad Asad, *The Message of the Qur'an* (Dar Al-Andalus, 1980), 345.

16. Asad, *Message of the Qur'an*, 372.

17. According to the *Doha Historical Dictionary of Arabic*, the concept of *'ulfa* as a core principle of union and affability was already evident in pre-Islamic Arabic poetic texts that date to the sixth century in the work of Marthad al-Khayr bin Yankaf al-Himyari [Marṭad al-Khayr bin Yankaf al-Ḥimyarī]. For further details, see *Doha Historical Dictionary of Arabic*, "الألفة," accessed April 8, 2025, https://www.dohadictionary.org/dictionary/%D8%A7%D9%84%D8%A3%D9%84%D9%81%D8%A9.

18. Asad, *Message of the Qur'an*, 372.

19. Alim.org, "Compare Surah 8. Al-Anfal, Ayah 63."

20. My emphasis.

21. Imam al-Ghazali, *The Duties of Brotherhood in Islam*, trans. Muhtar Holland (Kube, 2012), 82.

22. Ali ibn Ahmad ibn Hazm, *The Ring of the Dove: A Treatise on the Art and Practice of Arab Love*, trans. Arthur John Arberry (Luzac, 1953), 23. Emphasis is mine.

23. Ibn Hazm, "Ring of the Dove," 30.

24. Butrus al-Bustani, *The Clarion of Syria: A Patriot's Call Against the Civil War of 1860*, trans. Jens Hanssen and Hicham Safieddine (University of California Press, 2019), 95.

25 Ahmad Faris al-Shidyaq, *Leg over Leg, or, The Turtle in the Tree Concerning the Fāriyāq*, ed. and trans. Humphrey Davies (New York University Press, 2015), 287–89, my emphasis.

26. Mahmoud Darwish, *In the Presence of Absence*, trans. Sinan Antoon, 1st Archipelago Books ed. (Archipelago Books, 2011), 21.

27. Yásnaya Elena Aguilar Gil, *Ää: Manifiestos sobre la diversidad lingüística*, Ensayo (Tabla Rasa Libros y Ediciones) (Almadía Ediciones, 2023). The quotation here is cited from the English translation of the letter published in the e-zine *Specimen* published on August 8, 2022. For the complete letter visit https://www.specimen.press/articles/las-lenguas-indigenas-escriben-su-carta-a-los-reyes-magos-from-aa-manifiestos-sobre-la-diversidad-linguistica/.

28. According to Robert M. Laughlin and John Beard Haviland, the authors of *The Great Tzotzil Dictionary of Santo Domingo Zinacantán*, an anonymous Dominican friar compiled a Tsotsil dictionary at the end of the sixteenth century. Although the complete manuscript of this dictionary disappeared during the Mexican Revolution, a copy of 351 pages survived. For more, see Robert M. Laughlin and John Beard Haviland, *The Great Tzotzil Dictionary of Santo Domingo Zinacantán, with Grammatical Analysis and Historical Commentary, vol. 1, Tzotzil-English* (Smithsonian Institution Press, 1988).

29. My discussion with Betan was fruitful for reviewing and synthesizing the different possible translations that the others have provided. Having engaged in translation from and to Spanish and Tsotsil, including a publication of his own translation of selected texts of José Martí, the national poet of Cuba and the visionary champion of antcolonial Latin American and Caribbean thought into Tsotsil, Betan was particularly attuned to syntax and figurative language. Our very recent exchange was conducive for formulating a more accurate and encompassing translation of *'ulfa* in Tsotsil.

30. Paul M. Worley and Ellen Jones, "'Tequio Literario': Translating Indigenous Literature as Communal Labor," in *The Routledge Handbook of Latin American Literary Translation*, ed. Delfina Cabrera and Denise Kripper (Taylor & Francis, 2023), 241.

31. Worley and Jones characterize *"tequio literario"* with one of the following traits: "the involvement of more than one translator, as well as consultants, mentors, or community advisors; close attention to and involvement with the community from which the text has emerged; more than one 'source' text, including oral or performed versions of the text; working 'translingually' across an Indigenous language and Spanish; dual or triple-language publications; free online publication; poor or no financial remuneration for the various actors involved" (244). For more see Worley and Jones, "'Tequio Literario.'"

32. During my first research trip to Chiapas in 2010, Chechev was in Spain. He had just started his studies of Arabic and Islam in Granada together with his brother. Our first meeting took place in 2018 in the mosque adjunct to his family's house in the neighborhood of Nueva Esperanza in San Cristóbal / Jobel, where he leads the prayers in Arabic, Tsotsil, and Spanish.

33. Ibrahim Chechev, text message to the author on March 5, 2023. (Original in Spanish: *"Dame chance para poder encontrar las palabras cercana. Le preguntare a mi padre."*)

34. Mary Louise Pratt, "Arts of the Contact Zone," *Profession* (1991): 34.

35. Mary Louise Pratt, *Planetary Longings* (Duke University Press, 2022), 225.

36. Ngũgĩ wa Thiong'o, *The Language of Languages: Reflections on Translation* (Seagull Books, 2023), 4.

37. Linda Quiquivix, *Palestine 1492: A Report Back* (Wild Ox Books, 2024), 66.

38. In 2021, the website *al-Hamesh* (*The Margin*), a digital platform dedicated to the history of social movements and resistance movements, published a dossier titled "The Zapatistas: Twenty Years." The dossier features Arabic translations of six Zapatista communiques from 1994 to 2020. See https://al-hamish.net/11574/.

39. Sandra Cañas Cuevas, "The Politics of Conversion to Islam in Southern Mexico," in *Islam and the Americas* (University Press of Florida, 2015), 163.

40. I personally witnessed these dynamics during my first visit with the Maya Muslim community in January 2010 during a memorial service for one of the community members. I was invited to attend the memorial by the American poet Ámbar Past, who lived in San Cristóbal / Jobel at the time and had close ties with the larger Maya community of writers as a fluent speaker of Tsotsil, a translator, and a cultural activist who published Mayan texts in English translation. Past's relationship with the Muslim community, however, occurred in a more personal context, as the deceased had worked in a carpentry shop together with a group of her close *ladino* friends. During the ceremony, which was organized by the Spaniard missionaries, Muslim rituals of reciting the Quran, making *dhikr*, and feeding the guests to honor the memory of the deceased were followed. Nonetheless, the food that was served included lamb chunks and liver. When I asked a non-Mayan guest why the lamb was left untouched, I was told that in some Tsotsil Mayan communities lamb is considered a sacred animal representing God on Earth. Therefore, they refrain from killing it though they use its wool to weave traditional clothes. For detailed accounts and personal testimonies by members of the Tsotsil-speaking Muslim Mayan community on the cultural racism they experienced at the hands of the Spanish missionaries, see Cañas Cuevas, *Politics of Conversion*, 172, and the film by Ouissem Satouri, Dhia Ben Naser, and Gabriel Marchand, *Somos Musulmanes* (France, 2019).

41. As mentioned earlier, my first meeting with the Tsotsil-speaking Muslim community took place in January 2010. In addition to visiting personally with *Hajja* Nora after the memorial service, I visited the community's first small wooden-structure mosque, *al-Kawthar*, in the neighborhood Peje de Oro, which is in the vicinity of the current location of the community. Between 2010 and 2014, I have stayed in touch with *Hajja* Nora's family through regular contact over Messenger with her oldest son Marcos Abdel Hafeeth Chechev. I remained in contact with the family in the following years through other forms of social media and informal visits during my research trips to Chiapas.

42. For a detailed explanation of the spelling rule of neologism in Tsotsil, see Óscar Díaz López, *Smelolal sts'ibael bats'i k'op tsotsil: Norma de escritura de la lengua tsotsil* (Instituto Nacional de Lenguas Indígenas [INALI], 2011), 109–10.

43. Laughlin and Haviland, *Great Tzotzil Dictionary*, 232.

44. The expression appeared on a banner waved by a young, veiled girl from the Tsotsil-speaking Muslim community during a solidarity protest with Palestine after Israel's war in Gaza in 2014. The script literally reads: "*La comunidad Musulmana indigena de San Cristóbal de Las Casas Apoya al Pueblo PALESTINO!*" (The Indigenous Muslim community in San Cristóbal de Las Casas supports the Palestinian people), with a hashtag at the corner: *#PalestinaLibre* (Palestine is Free). An image of the girl with the banner circulated on social media, and despite extensive search, I was unable to locate its source or the photographer.

45. This is a verbatim translation from a WhatsApp exchange in Spanish with the author on March 27, 2023.

46. Steven Rendall, trans., "The Translator's Task, Walter Benjamin (Translation)," *TTR* 10, no. 2 (1997): 154.

47. Samah Selim, "Nation and Translation in the Middle East: Histories, Canons, Hegemonies," *Translator* (Manchester, England) 15, no. 1 (2009): 10, citing his translation of Hassam Wahbi, "La part du semblable," in *La traduction des sciences humaines et sociales dans le monde arabe contemporain*, ed. Richard Jacquemond (Fondation du Roi Abdul-Aziz Al Saoud pour les Etudes Islamiques et les Sciences Humaines, 2008), 104.

48. Selim, "Nation and Translation," 10.

49. It is important to point out here that by envisaging a nonhierarchical encounter between Arabic and Indigenous languages, I do not ignore the fact that Arabic exists in a dominating relationship with minoritized and Indigenous languages in the Arabic-speaking worlds, namely Tamazight, Kurdish, and Nubian. On the contrary, it is my hope that the encounter between Arabic and Tsotsil contributes to undoing these power dynamics that involve Arabization and forced linguistic and cultural assimilation. For more on this see Brahim El Guabli, "(Re)Invention of Tradition, Subversive Memory, and Morocco's Re-Amazighization: From Erasure of Imazighen to the Performance of Tifinagh in Public Life," *Expressions maghrébines* 19, no. 1 (2020): 143–68; H. L. Murre-van den Berg, Karène Sanchez-Summerer, and Tijmen C. Baarda, eds., *Arabic and Its Alternatives: Religious Minorities and Their Languages in the Emerging Nation States of the Middle East (1920–1950)* (Brill, 2020); Mary Youssef, *Minorities in the Contemporary Egyptian Novel* (Edinburgh University Press, 2018); and Andrew D. Magnusson, "Ethnic and Religous Minorities," in *The Cambridge Companion to Modern Arab Culture*, ed. Dwight Fletcher Reynolds (Cambridge University Press, 2015), 36–53.

50. For a fuller picture on Apter's theory of "checkpointization" and translation, see Emily Apter, "Translation at the Checkpoint," *Journal of Postcolonial Writing* 50, no. 1 (2014): 56–74 (72).

51. These are the words of Evon Z. Vogt as they appear in a note from his memoir *Fieldwork among the Maya: Reflections on the Harvard Chiapas Project* (University of New Mexico Press, 1994), 373. Elaborating on why *The Great Tzotzil Dictionary of*

Santo Domingo Zinacantán (1988) stands as a monumental achievement in American Indian linguistics and lexicography, Vogt notes that this two-volume work builds upon the foundational efforts of Laughlin and Haviland's earlier *Great Tzotzil Dictionary of San Lorenzo Zinacantán* (1975), which documented over 35,000 Tsotsil words and was the result of more than a decade of meticulous fieldwork and data analysis. The *Santo Domingo* edition expands the historical and regional scope of Tsotsil lexicography by focusing on the variety spoken in Zinacantán during the late sixteenth century. Vogt also emphasizes the critical role played by Tsotsil speakers from Zinacantán, who were brought as native informants from Chiapas to Laughlin's offices in Santa Fe and Washington to assist in the translations. In terms of scope, the *Santo Domingo* dictionary surpasses even other major reference works in the field. For instance, Young and Morgan's *The Navajo Language* (1980), often regarded as one of the most extensive and technically detailed dictionaries of a North American Indigenous language, contains about 17,000 entries and is praised for its rich grammatical detail and extensive example sentences. While the Navajo dictionary excels in morphosyntactic representation, Laughlin and Haviland's work stands out for its unparalleled lexical breadth and historical depth. For a comparative assessment of both dictionaries, see James Kari and Jeff Leer, "Review of *The Navajo Language: A Grammar and Colloquial Dictionary*," *International Journal of American Linguistics* 50, no. 1 (1984): 124–30, http://www.jstor.org/stable/1265203; and Vogt, *Fieldwork among the Maya*, 373–74.

52. The full verses are "Laj taj une, xi laj yal ti Dios ti ja' Ajvalile: Mu lecuc ti yuni tuc ti vinique. Ja' lec ta jmeltsanbe junuc yuni *chi'il* yo' jech oy buch'u ta xcoltaun" and "Xi laj stac' ti Esaue:—Mo'oj unbi, cuni *chi'il* ta voq'uel, mu jc'an. Yu'un ti vu'un eque, oy ep cu'un. Ja' yu'un, q'uelo tuc'ulano atuc ti c'usitic ja' avu'une." (Emphasis by the author.) These verses are retrieved from the online version of the Bible in Chamula Tsotsil. For more information, visit https://www.bible.com/bible/334/GEN.2.TZC00.

53. Asad, *Message of the Qur'an*, 372.

54. This is a verbatim translation from a WhatsApp exchange in Spanish between Xun Betan and the author on April 19, 2023.

55. Betan, WhatsApp exchange with author, April 19, 2023.

56. Gilles Deleuze and Félix Guattari, *What Is Philosophy?*, trans. Hugh Tomlinson and Graham Burchell, European Perspectives (Columbia University Press, 1994), 17–18.

57. Ming Xie, *Conditions of Comparison: Reflections on Comparative Intercultural Inquiry* (Bloomsbury, 2015), 8–12.

58. Felipe Reyes-Escutia and Carmen Yolanda Quintero Reyes, eds., *Trazos del tiempo: Hacia una escuela sustentable e intercultural* (Secretaría de Educación de Chiapas y UNACH, 2017).

59. The Tseltal-speaking anthropologist María Patricia Pérez expands on this model by including the dimensions of doing, feeling, and thinking, hence *ser-ester-hacer-sentir-pensar*. In affirming the centrality of the heart in Tseltal philosophy and

ethics, Pérez observes its figurative and metaphoric symbolism in relation to solidarity: "When it is said that a person's heart is too good, it is because his daily life is kind and supportive" (123). It is important to point out here that in the original text in Spanish Pérez uses the word *solidario*, which derives from *solidaridad* (solidarity) to convey the idea of a supportive heart. For a more detailed review of the Tseltal philosophy of the heart, see María Patricia Pérez Moreno, *Corazón: Una forma de ser-estar-hacer-sentir-pensar de los tseltaletik de Bachajón, Chiapas, México* (Ediciones Abya-Yala, 2014).

60. Felipe Reyes-Escutia, "The Living Interculturality of Chiapas to Recreate the Modern University Towards Sustainability Horizons," in *Sustainable Development Research and Practice in Mexico and Selected Latin American Countries*, ed. Walter Leal Filho et al. (Springer International, 2018), 48.

61. María Eugenia Santana E., "El buen vivir, miradas desde dentro," *Revista pueblos y fronteras digital* 10, no. 19 (2015): 194–95. For a nuanced discussion of the radical and decolonial politics of the concept of good living and its implications for promoting an Indigenous ideal of climate justice and plurinationalism across Abya Yala, see *Salvador Schavelzon, Plurinacionalidad y Vivir Bien/Buen Vivir: Dos conceptos leídos desde Bolivia y Ecuador post-constituyentes* (CLACSO, 2015).

62. Arias, *Recovering Lost Footprints*, 2:29.

63. Paul M. Worley and Rita M. Palacios, *Unwriting Maya Literature: Ts'íib as Recorded Knowledge* (University of Arizona Press, 2019), 19.

64. Worley and Palacios, *Unwriting Maya Literature*, 23–24.

65. Manuel Bolom Pale, "Didáctica de la resistencia desde el Lekil Kuxlejal del Pueblo Originario y la educación intercultural en contextos educativos pluriculturales," in *Razos del tiempo: Hacia una Escuela sustentable e intercultural*, ed. Felipe Reyes Escutia and Carmen Yolanda Quintero Reyes (Secretaría de Educación de Chiapas y UNACH, 2017), 110-111.

66. Lola Cubells, "La Justicia del Corazón: Sabiduría tseltal-maya sobre la vida buena," *El Salto* (blog), October 9, 2018, https://www.elsaltodiario.com/el-rumor-de-las-multitudes/la-justicia-del-corazon-sabiduria-tseltal-maya-sobre-la-vida-buena.

67. Rosalva Aída Hernández Castillo, "'Putting Heart' into History and Memory: Dialogues with Maya-Tseltal Philosopher, Xuno López Intzin," *Memory Studies* 13, no. 5 (2020): 809.

68. Shu-mei Shih, "Comparison as Relation," in *Comparison: Theories, Approaches, Uses*, ed. Rita Felski and Susan Stanford Friedman (Johns Hopkins University Press, 2013), 81.

69. Shih, "Comparison as Relation," 95.

70. Walter D. Mignolo, *The Politics of Decolonial Investigations* (Duke University Press, 2021), 559.

71. Mignolo, *Politics of Decolonial Investigations*, 559.

72. Cutcha Risling Baldy and Melanie K. Yazzie, "Introduction: Indigenous Peoples and the Politics of Water," *Decolonization: Indigeneity, Education & Society* 7, no. 1 (2018).

73. Smith's model is a revision of the original framework put in place in the first edition of her seminal book *Decolonizing Methodologies: Research and Indigenous Peoples* (Zed Books, 1999). In a new chapter in the second edition entitled "Choosing the Margins: The Role of Research in Indigenous Struggles for Social Justice," Smith (2012) outlines the five conditions or dimensions that have framed the struggle for decolonization: 1. Critical consciousness, "an awakening from the slumber of hegemony"; 2. Reimagining the world, "what enables an alternative vision and "dreams of alternative possibilities"; 3. The coming together of disparate ideas, the events, the historical moment, which "creates opportunities" and "provides the moments when tactics can be deployed"; 4. Movement or disturbance, "counter-hegemonic movements or tendencies, the competing movements which traverse sites of struggle, the unstable movements that occur when the status quo is disturbed"; 5. Structure, "the underlying code of imperialism, of power relations that reproduce "material realities" (201). For an elaboration on this model, see Linda Tuhiwai Smith, *Decolonizing Methodologies: Research and Indigenous Peoples*, 2nd ed. (Zed Books, 2012).

74. Smith, *Decolonizing Methodologies*, 3.

75. Jodi A. Byrd et al., "Predatory Value: Economies of Dispossession and Disturbed Relationalities," *Social Text* 36, no. 2 (2018): 5.

76. Peter Wade, "Afro-Indigenous Interactions, Relations, and Comparisons," in *Afro-Latin American Studies: An Introduction*, ed. Alejandro de la Fuente and George Reid Andrews (Cambridge University Press, 2018), 92–129.

2. Topographies of Affinities: Writing Erasure and Borderlands

1. The shorter versions of the city name San Cristóbal de las Casas (San Cristóbal or San Cris) as well as Jobel are widely, and sometimes interchangeably, used among Mayans in Chiapas. Therefore, I will henceforth refer to the city as San Cristóbal/Jobel.

2. My translation. Unless indicated otherwise, all translations from Arabic and Spanish are my own. Moreover, given that Mayan poets often translate their own work into Spanish or are closely involved in the translation process, I have chosen to present the Tsotsil poems side by side with the Spanish versions whenever that was the case, or whenever the Spanish versions were available. This decision reflects the poets' bilingual authorship and honors their voice in both languages. The English translation appears in run-in form to maintain readability while also foregrounding the Tsotsil and Spanish texts. With this formatting choice, I seek to highlight for readers the significance of visual and linguistic dimensions in representing Indigenous languages while affirming their aesthetic and epistemic integrity.

3. Hannah Burdette, *Revealing Rebellion in Abiayala: The Insurgent Poetics of Contemporary Indigenous Literature* (University of Arizona Press, 2023), 11.

4. The recent surge in political tourism in Chiapas has transformed the commercial center of San Cristóbal/Jobel. In addition to the Zapatista-owned

independent shops that were constructed in the late 1990s, several high-end shops owned by wealthy *ladinos* were constructed in the 2020s along the main promenade. Unlike the Zapatista stores that follow a solidarity trade model by selling coffee, art, and crafts from autonomous Mayan communities, the newly opened boutiques target international tourists. They sell original Mayan textiles and crafts at prices that exceed the local market value. These shops also tend to display fragments of Mayan languages as part of their marketing strategy. For further reading on tourism and the commercial consumption of the Zapatista uprising see Florence E. Babb, "Remembering the Revolution: Indigenous Culture and Zapatista Tourism," in *The Tourism Encounter: Fashioning Latin American Nations and Histories* (Stanford University Press, 2020), 92–120.

5. With the establishment of the State of Israel in 1948, two segregated schooling systems were put in place: one for the (Hebrew-speaking) Jewish majority and one for the (Arabic-speaking) Palestinian minority. While the former was built as "a *nationalizing* apparatus for Jews, the latter was constructed as a *denationalizing* apparatus for Palestinians" (Awayed-Bishara, 2). This segregation was enforced in the formation of two separate curriculums that served the dual role of promoting the Zionist narrative and erasing the Palestinian national identity. In this model of educational segregation, the state institutionalized its control over Arabic to dissolve Palestinian identity and secure the individual and collective subjugation of Palestinians. For further details on the sociolinguistics of Arabic as a colonized language see Muzna Awayed-Bishara, "*Sumud* Pedagogy as Linguistic Citizenship: Palestinian Youth in Israel Against Imposed Subjectivities," *Language in Society* (2023): 1–23; and Ismail Nashef, *A Language of One's Own: Literary Arabic, the Palestinians and Israel* (Edinburgh University Press, 2023), 3.

6. Although the great majority of Palestinian writers continue to write in Arabic, the novels written in Hebrew by Anton Shammas (1950–) and Sayed Kashu (1975–) have provoked debate about the subversive potential of minor literature, translation, and linguistic cross-fertilization between Arabic and Hebrew, on the one hand, and the tension between Palestinian memory and Jewish memory, on the other hand. For further reading on this debate and its generational and ethnic dimensions, see Camelia Suleiman, *The Politics of Arabic in Israel: A Sociolinguistic Analysis* (Edinburgh University Press, 2017); Manar H. Makhoul, *Palestinian Citizens in Israel: A History Through Fiction, 1948–2010* (Edinburgh University Press, 2020); Sadia Agsous, *Derrière l'hébreu, l'arabe: Le roman palestinien en hébreu* (Classiques Garnier, 2022); Gil Z. Hochberg, *In Spite of Partition: Jews, Arabs, and the Limits of Separatist Imagination* (Princeton University Press, 2007); Lital Levy, *Poetic Trespass: Writing Between Hebrew and Arabic in Israel/Palestine* (Princeton University Press, 2014). As for the politics of bilingualism in the work of Mayan writers where it is more common to write in both Spanish and a Mayan language or to engage in auto-translation, critics have praised the creative act embedded in such practices. Gloría E. Chacón, for example, considers bilingualism in Mayan literature as a manifestation of a movement between languages that is deeply rooted in the

Mayan notion of *kab'awil* (double gaze). As a counteract of forgetfulness, *kab'awil*, she argues, is "a reminder that memory is constantly activated by the seemingly erased 'Indian body'" (14). For more on the theory of *kab'awil* in Mayan writing in Chiapas, see Gloria Elizabeth Chacón, *Indigenous Cosmolectics: Kab'awil and the Making of Maya and Zapotec Literatures* (University of North Carolina Press, 2018), 75–92.

7. Evon Z. Vogt, *Fieldwork Among the Maya: Reflections on the Harvard Chiapas Project*, 1st ed. (University of New Mexico Press, 1994), 146, 345.

8. Elaborating on why *The Great Tzotzil Dictionary of Santo Domingo Zinacantán* (1988) stands as a monumental achievement in American Indian linguistics and lexicography, Evon Z. Vogt notes that this two-volume work builds upon the foundational efforts of Laughlin and Haviland's earlier *Great Tzotzil Dictionary of San Lorenzo Zinacantán* (1975), which documented over 35,000 Tsotsil words and was the result of more than a decade of meticulous fieldwork and data analysis. The *Santo Domingo* edition expands the historical and regional scope of Tsotsil lexicography by focusing on the variety spoken in Zinacantán during the late sixteenth century. Vogt also emphasizes the critical role played by Tsotsil speakers from Zinacantán, who were brought as native informants from Chiapas to Laughlin's offices in Santa Fe and Washington to assist in the translations. In terms of scope, the *Santo Domingo* dictionary surpasses even other major reference works in the field. For instance, Young and Morgan's *The Navajo Language* (1980), often regarded as one of the most extensive and technically detailed dictionaries of a North American Indigenous language, contains about 17,000 entries and is praised for its rich grammatical detail and extensive example sentences. While the Navajo dictionary excels in morphosyntactic representation, Laughlin and Haviland's work stands out for its unparalleled lexical breadth and historical depth. For a comparative assessment of both dictionaries, see James Kari and Jeff Leer, "Review of *The Navajo Language: A Grammar and Colloquial Dictionary*," *International Journal of American Linguistics* 50, no. 1 (1984): 124–30, http://www.jstor.org/stable/1265203; and Vogt, *Fieldwork Among the Maya*, 373–74.

9. Donald H. Frischmann, "New Mayan Theatre in Chiapas: Anthropology, Literacy, and Social Drama," in *Negotiating Performance: Gender, Sexuality, and Theatricality in Latin/o America*, ed. Diana Taylor and Juan Villegas (Duke University Press, 1994), 216.

10. Jan Rus and Diane L Rus, "The Taller Tzotzil of Chiapas, Mexico: A Native Language Publishing Project, 1985–2002," in *Decolonizing Native Histories: Collaboration, Knowledge, and Language in the Americas*, ed. Florencia E. Mallon (Duke University Press, 2012), 141.

11. Rus and Rus, "Taller Tzotzil," 151.

12. For a more detailed account of this history see Arturo Arias, *Recovering Lost Footprints: Contemporary Maya Narratives*, vol. 2 (State University of New York Press, 2017), 175–223.

13. In 1562, the Franciscan friar Diego de Landa ordered the burning of twenty-seven Mayan folded books and idols in the town of Maní in the Yucatan to implement Catholicism. This cultural genocide involved torture of nearly four thousand Maya and the death of many others. Appointed as a bishop later, Landa would compile records documenting information about the Maya and their language and customs. For further details on this see Dennis Tedlock, *2000 Years of Mayan Literature* (University of California Press, 2010).

14. Elaborating on the auto-da-fé that Fray Pedro Bariento staged in 1554 in the main plaza of Ciudad Real (what is now San Cristóbal / Jobel) against Mayas who moved away from the city to practice their traditional religious ceremonies in secret locations, Arturo Arias speculates that given the brutality of the persecution, there is a likelihood of the "existence of documents burned on that occasion" (181). For further details, see Arias, *Recovering Lost Footprints*, 2:180–81.

15. Chacón, *Indigenous Cosmolectics*, 33.

16. Tedlock, *2000 Years of Mayan Literature*, 246.

17. For further information on the attempts to assimilate Indigenous communities into the modernizing mestizo nation and the ensuing problematic social dynamics, mainly due to unresolved race and class differences, see Alexander S. Dawson, *Indian and Nation in Revolutionary Mexico* (University of Arizona Press, 2004); and Stephen E. Lewis, *Rethinking Mexican Indigenismo: The INI's Coordinating Center in Highland Chiapas and the Fate of a Utopian Project* (University of New Mexico Press, 2018).

18. Aníbal Quijano, "El 'Movimiento Indígena' y las cuestiones pendientes en América Latina," *Argumentos (México, D.F.)* 19, no. 50 (2006): 51–77.

19. Guillermo Bonfil Batalla and Philip Adams Dennis, *México profundo: Reclaiming a Civilization,* 1st ed. (University of Texas Press, 1996), 55.

20. The name El ciclo de Chiapas was coined by Joseph Sommers in 1964. It refers to *indigenista* literature written in and about Chiapas in the period between 1948 and 1962. It includes the narrative work of six authors: Ramón Rubín, Rosario Castellanos, Carlo Antonio Castro, María Lombardo de Caso, Eraclio Zepeda, and Ricardo Pozas. The cycle opens with *Juan Pérez Jolote* by Pozas, originally published in 1948, and ends with *Oficio de tinieblas* (*Book of Lamentations*) by Castellanos, published in 1962. For more, see Joseph Sommers, "El ciclo de Chiapas: Nueva corriente literaria," *Cuadernos Americanos* 133, no. 2 (1964): 246–61.

21. Estelle Tarica, *The Inner Life of Mestizo Nationalism* (University of Minnesota Press, 2008), xi.

22. Cynthia Steele, "Power, Gender, and Canon Formation in Mexico," *Studies in 20th & 21st Century Literature* 20, no. 1 (1996): 25, http://dx.doi.org/10.4148/2334-4415.1381.

23. Paul M. Worley, *Telling and Being Told: Storytelling and Cultural Control in Contemporary Yucatec Maya Literatures* (University of Arizona Press, 2013), 24.

24. Analisa Taylor, *Indigeneity in the Mexican Cultural Imagination: Thresholds of Belonging* (University of Arizona Press, 2009).

25. Yásnaya Elena Aguilar Gil, Gloria Anzaldúa, and Ruperta Bautista, *Lo lingüístico es político*, 3rd ed. (Ediciones OnA, 2020), 44–45.
26. Arias, *Recovering Lost Footprints*, 2:181.
27. Javier Castellanos Martínez, "El escritor indígena," *Ojarasca*, July 2013, 3.
28. Martínez, "El escritor indígena," 3.
29. Martínez, "El escritor indígena," 3.
30. PEN International, "Writing the Future in Indigenous Languages," https://www.pen-international.org/news/kl7hgawijzo3vvftq8iehuw60olukn. Emphasis mine.
31. Burdette, *Revealing Rebellion in Abiayala*, 6.
32. Ámbar Past et al., *Incantations: Songs, Spells and Images by Mayan Women* (Cinco Puntos, 2005), 30.
33. Aguilar Gil, Anzaldúa, and Bautista, *Lo lingüístico es político*, 54.
34. ta Chikinib, "Conversatorio 'Kojtikinbetik xch'ulel li Jk'optike-Reconozcamos la esencia de nuestra lengua,'" December 5, 2022, https://www.tachikinib.com/post/conversatorio-kojtikinbetik-xch-ulel-li-jk-optike-reconozcamos-la-esencia-de-nuestra-lengua.
35. Paul M. Worley and Rita M. Palacios, *Unwriting Maya Literature: Ts'íib as Recorded Knowledge* (University of Arizona Press, 2019), 31.
36. Aguilar Gil, Anzaldúa, and Bautista, *Lo lingüístico es político*, 46.
37. Mariano Reynaldo Vázquez López, *Nichim vayichetik / Orquídea de sueños* (Unidad de Escritores Mayas-Zoques, 2006), 2–3.
38. CELALI is a cultural affairs program of the state of Chiapas established specifically for Indigenous Peoples. Since its foundation in 1996, it has organized a range of activities that support Indigenous languages and literary production. In addition to organizing literary and drama workshops and publishing works by emerging Mayan writers, CELALI has hosted exhibits of Mayan arts, including sculpture and paintings. The main office is in San Cristóbal / Jobel, but there are eighteen cultural centers in the villages to promote women weavers, art workshops, and music.
39. The English translation of the poem is mine.
40. Vázquez López translated the poem himself, which is a prevalent trend among Mayan writers. As Mikel Ruiz points out, it is very common for Mayan authors to translate their own work from one language to the other, or to alternate between the two (Spanish and Maya). The process, however, starts from the following premise: "Each author assumes a political and aesthetic position when writing and self-translating. The Spanish versions that they share are only for clarification purposes." Mikel Ruiz, "La literatura en Tsotsil (1996–2017)," in *Enciclopedia de la literatura en México* (2019), http://www.elem.mx//buscador?sitesearch=http%3A%2F%2Felem.mx%2F&bus=tsotsi.
41. Xun Betan, "Jme'tik ta bats'i k'op / La madre luna Tsotsil," in *Insurrección de las palabras: Poetas contemporáneos en lenguas Mexicanas*, ed. Hermann Bellinghausen (Fondo de Cultura Económica, 2023), 294.
42. Xun Betan, "Semillas de esperanza / Seeds of Hope" and "Flores para el corazón / Flowers for the Heart," trans. Sean S. Sell, *North Dakota Quarterly* 86, no. 3/4 (2019): 221–22.

43. In the original publication, the poem appears in Spanish and Tsotsil side by side on the page. I am reversing the order here to align with the formatting in the previous poem, and thus make it easier for the reader to follow. The English translation of the poem is mine.

44. There are only two versions of the poem here, because it was originally written in both Tsotsil and Spanish.

45. It is worth mentioning here that Arabic has thirty-eight synonyms for the word heart. Remarkably, this is another example of the commonality between Arabic and Tsotsil in respect to the significance of the epistemology of the heart, and thus the cross-cultural affective dimension of *'ulfa–ko'olajel*.

46. Arias, *Recovering Lost Footprints*, 2:180.

47. Yasir Suleiman, "A Language in Conflict: Arabic in Israel and Palestine," *Journal of Sociolinguistics* 24, no. 3 (2020): 389.

48. Ibrahim Mahfouz Abdou and Refqa Abu-Remaileh, "A Literary *Nahda* Interrupted: Pre-Nakba Palestinian Literature as *Adab Maqalat*," *Journal of Palestine Studies* 51, no. 3 (2022): 23.

49. In addition to the destruction of entire institutions, printing presses, periodicals, bookshops, cultural organizations, and associations, the authors observe the scale of the cultural loss that resulted from looting, plundering, and forcibly evacuating literary clubs and cafes. The profound scale of the loss, they add, involved the death and exile of writers and cultural figures as well. For further reading see Abdou and Abu-Remaileh, "Literary *Nahda* Interrupted," 23.

50. Nur Masalha, *The Palestine Nakba: Decolonising History, Narrating the Subaltern, Reclaiming Memory* (Zed Books, 2021), 26.

51. Masalha, *Palestine Nakba*, 24.

52. Yasir Suleiman, *Arabic in the Fray: Language Ideology and Cultural Politics* (Edinburgh Universtiy Press, 2013), 17.

53. Zachary Lockman, *Comrades and Enemies: Arab and Jewish Workers in Palestine, 1906–1948* (University of California Press, 1996), 91.

54. Levy, *Poetic Trespass*, 27; emphasis in the original

55. Levy, *Poetic Trespass*, 14–15.

56. Levy, *Poetic Trespass*, 10.

57. Amira Hass, "To Expel Palestinians Efficiently, Learn Arabic," *Haaretz*, June 6, 2023.

58. There is now a plethora of innovative research on the shifting status of Arabic in Israel vis-à-vis the asymmetry with Hebrew, nationalism, and globalization. While these studies observe how these dynamics situate Arabic at different battlefronts, there is a general contention among the scholars that Arabic remains in a subaltern position. For more see Yasir Suleiman, *Arabic in the Fray*; Yonatan Mendel and Abeer AlNajjar, *Language, Politics and Society in the Middle East: Essays in Honour of Yasir Suleiman* (Edinburgh University Press, 2018); Camelia Suleiman, *The Politics of Arabic in Israel*; Muhammad Amara, *Lughati Huwiyyatī: Naḥwa Siyāsa Lughawiyya Shumūliyya Limuwājahat Taḥaddiyāt al-Lugha al-ʿArabiyya fī Isrāʾīl* (*My Language Is My Identity: Towards a Comprehensive Language Policy to Meet the Challenges of*

Arabic in Israel) (Dār al-Hudá, 2020); Muhammad Amara, *Arabic in Israel: Language, Identity and Conflict*, Routledge Studies in Language and Identity (Routledge, 2018).

59. Nashef, *Language of One's Own*, 5.

60. Yonatan Mendel, *The Creation of Israeli Arabic: Security and Politics in Arabic Studies in Israel* (Palgrave Macmillan, 2016), 6.

61. Mendel, *Creation of Israeli Arabic*, 8.

62. For further reading on the ethnoracial national vision of the law, which is a culmination of decades of transformation in Israeli Zionist settler colonial values, policies, and practices that perpetuated an expansionist Zionist agenda, see Honaida Ghanim, "Israel's Nation-State Law: Hierarchized Citizenship and Jewish Supremacy," *Critical Times* 4, no. 3 (2021): 565–76.

63. Sheila Hattis Rolef, trans., "Basic-Law: Israel—the Nation State of the Jewish People," ed. The Knesset (2018).

64. Fouzi Asmar, *To Be an Arab in Israel*, 2d ed., Reprint Series no. 8 (Institute for Palestine Studies, 1978), 47–48.

65. Ella Shohat, *On the Arab-Jew, Palestine, and Other Displacements: Selected Writings* (Pluto, 2017), 357.

66. Shira N. Robinson, *Citizen Strangers: Palestinians and the Birth of Israel's Liberal Settler State* (Stanford University Press, 2020), 10.

67. Mahmoud Darwish, *Journal of an Ordinary Grief*, trans. Ibrahim Muhawi, 1st Archipelago Books ed. (Archipelago Books, 2010), 50.

68. Tamir Sorek, *The Optimist: A Social Biography of Tawfiq Zayyad* (Stanford University Press, 2020), 38.

69. Mahmud Ghanayim, *The Quest for a Lost Identity: Palestinian Fiction in Israel* (Harrassowitz, 2008), 1–17.

70. Adina Hoffman, *My Happiness Bears No Relation to Happiness: A Poet's Life in the Palestinian Century* (Yale University Press, 2009), 290.

71. Hanna Abu-Hanna, "Al-'Arḍ wa-al-Lugha," *al-Ṣanāra*, March 29, 1990.

72. While writing poetry and creative nonfiction essays in English has been more common, the novel *Haifa Fragments* by Khulud Khamis was published in 2015. It was translated into Italian by Ester Borgese in the same year.

73. Levy, *Poetic Trespass*, 185.

74. Maha Nassar, *Brothers Apart: Palestinian Citizens of Israel and the Arab World* (Stanford University Press, 2017), 184.

75. Nassar, *Brothers Apart*, 108.

76. Since 1976, Palestinians have been commemorating this territorial dispossession and Israel's killing of Palestinian protesters during the mass demonstrations in the Galilee. The commemorations take place on March 30 and include a general strike and national events to honor the land and the martyrs. On the historical significance of Land Day as a turning point in the militarized encounter of Palestinian citizens in Israel with the state, see Ilan Pappé, *The Forgotten Palestinians: A History of the Palestinians in Israel* (Yale University Press,

2011); Amal Jamal, *Arab Minority Nationalism in Israel: The Politics of Indigeneity* (Routledge, 2014).

77. Mundhir ʿĀmir ʿAwaḍ Aḥmad Rafiq, Liyāna Badr, and Zakariyyā Muḥammad, "Imīl Ḥabībī: Al-Ḥiwār al-Akhīr—Anā Māniʿat al-Ṣawāʿiq al-Filasṭīnīya," *Majallat Mashārif* 9 (1996): 12–27.

78. Tawfīq Zayyad, *ʿAn al-Adab wa-al-Ādāb al-Shaʿbī fī Filasṭīn* (Dār al-ʿAwdah, 1970).

79. Hanna Abu-Hanna et al., "Ḥannā Abū Ḥannā: Riḥlat al-Adab wa-al-Siyāsa wa-al-Muqāwama," *Journal of Palestine Studies*, no. 105 (2016): 99.

80. Ghassan Kanafani, *Resistance Literature in Occupied Palestine 1948–1966* (Rimal, 2013).

81. Makhoul, *Palestinian Citizens in Israel*, 62.

82. Nashef, *Language of One's Own*, 14.

83. Nashef, *Language of One's Own*, 262.

84. Arias, *Recovering Lost Footprints*, 2:31.

85. Susan Slyomovics, *The Object of Memory: Arab and Jew Narrate the Palestinian Village* (University of Pennsylvania Press, 1998), 73.

86. For further reading on the pivotal role that the Palestinian communist press played in creating a countercultural sphere, see Nassar, *Brothers Apart*; Ṣāliḥ Sayf al-Dīn Abū, *Al-Ḥaraka al-Adabīya al-ʿArabīya fī Isrāʾīl: Ẓuhūruhā wa-Taṭawwuruhā min khilāl al-Mulḥaq al-Thaqāfī li-Jarīdat al-Ittiḥād bayna al-Sanawāt 1948–2000* (Majmaʿ al-Lugha al-ʿArabīya, 2010).

87. Abu-Hanna et al., "Ḥannā Abū Ḥannā," 108.

88. Khaled Furani, *Silencing the Sea: Secular Rhythms in Palestinian Poetry* (Stanford University Press, 2012), 293.

89. Furani, *Silencing the Sea*, 294.

90. Tawfīq Zayyad, *Dīwān Tawfīq Zayyād* [Diwān Tawfīq Zayyad] (Dār al-ʿAwdah, 2000).

91. The English translation of the poem is mine.

92. In the original in Arabic, Zayyad uses the word ناب/ *nāb*, which means cuspid. However, since the speaker in the poem addresses his colonizing oppressor with an emotionally charged languagage that points out the wildness of his actions, I opted for using the word *fang*. It clearly conveys the metaphor of wildness because of its connotation of the tooth that dogs use to tear into flesh. Special thanks to Ibrahim Muhawi for his insightful suggestions on the translation.

93. Darwish, *Journal of an Ordinary Grief*, 26.

94. Darwish, *Journal of an Ordinary Grief*, 49.

95. Darwish, *Journal of an Ordinary Grief*, 27.

96. Helit Yeshurun, "Exile Is So Strong Within Me, I May Bring It to the Land," a Landmark 1996 Interview with Mahmoud Darwish, *Journal of Palestine Studies* 42, no. 1 (2012): 52.

97. Yeshurun, "Exile," 60.

98. *Yucatán Magazine*, "Mayan Train Project Ignites Anger Among Zapatistas," https://yucatanmagazine.com/mayan-train-project-ignites-anger-among-zapatistas/.

99. IsraelArabic(@IsraelArabic), "Al-Lugha al-'Arabiyya fī Isrā'īl," # "Bimunāsabat al-Yawm al-'Ālamī li-l-Lugha al-'Arabiyya ilaykum Ḥaqā'iq Mufāji'a 'an al-Lugha al-'Arabiyya fī Isrā'īl" (Twitter, December 18, 2022), 2:56 AM.

100. The Arabic language is commonly referred to by Arabs as the language of Ḍād' to indicate its uniqueness.

101. It is worth mentioning here that the second half of the twentieth century witnessed the emergence of a discourse across the Arabic-speaking world about Arabic being in danger. However, unlike the threat for Arabic in Israel resulting from the structural erasure of Zionist settler colonialism, the fear for Arabic in the Arabic-speaking world is related to the economic domination and cultural imperialism of English and French. Those concerned about the future of Arabic also point to the decline in proficiency in formal Arabic, *fuṣḥa,* among the youth, and the concurrent rise of *'amiyya* that is gaining more prevalence in the public cultural sphere because of technology, media, and globalization. This shift, they argue, may lead to a loss of cultural heritage. For more on this issue see Kristen Brustad, "The Question of Language" in *The Cambridge Companion to Modern Arab Culture*, ed. Dwight Fletcher Reynolds (Cambridge University Press, 2015), 19–35.

3. Border Crossers and City Dwellers: Narratives of Indigenous Urban Culture

1. Sections from this chapter, namely the parts on Azem's novel and La FOMMA, appeared in the following publications: the discussion of Azem's work was included in both Amal Eqeiq's article, "From Haifa to Ramallah (and Back): New/Old Palestinian Literary Topography," *Journal of Palestine Studies* 48, no. 3 (2019): 26–42, and the dissertation "Writing the Indigenous: Contemporary Mayan Literature in Chiapas, Mexico and Palestinian Literature in Israel" (ProQuest Dissertations, 2013); the discussion of La FOMMA appeared only in the dissertation.

2. Leanne Betasamosake Simpson, *As We Have Always Done: Indigenous Freedom Through Radical Resistance* (University of Minnesota Press, 2017), 152.

3. Eve Tuck and K. Wayne Yang, "Decolonization Is Not a Metaphor," *Decolonization: Indigeneity, Education & Society* 1, no. 1 (2012): 7.

4. Jan Rus and Gaspar Morquecho Escamilla, "The Urban Indigenous Movement and Elite Accommodation in San Cristóbal, Chiapas, 1975–2008: 'Tenemos que vivir nuestros años'/'We Have to Live in Our Own Times,'" in *Enduring Reform: Progressive Activism and Private Sector Responses in Latin America's Democracies*, ed. Jeffrey W. Rubin and Vivienne Bennett (University of Pittsburgh Press, 2015), 81–82.

5. Amandine Desille and Yara Sa'di-Ibraheem, "'It's a Matter of Life or Death': Jewish Migration and Dispossession of Palestinians in Acre," *Urban Planning* 6, no. 2 (2021): 33, https://doi.org/10.17645/up.v6i2.3676.

6. Rus and Morquecho Escamilla, "Urban Indigenous Movement," 82.

7. Another vivid example of this trend is the documentary *Tote-Abuelo*, directed by the Tsotsil-speaking filmmaker Maria Sojob in 2019. Narrated in Tsotsil, the film

chronicles the reunion of an Indigenous Tsotsil woman who grew up in Jobel and returns to her village to reconnect with her heritage through her grandfather, an elderly man who has kept his culture and language alive despite enduring the hardships of being an Indigenous *campesino* and migrant labor worker in the virulently racist and classist Jobel in the 1950s and 1960s. Given the focus in this chapter on written texts, I won't delve into this film, but will note its significance in providing a visual account of the rural-urban divide through a story about a reverse migration back to the village to trace an intergenerational family history of racialized encounters with Jobel and the perils of cultural assimilation.

8. Unless indicated otherwise, all translations from this play are by the author.

9. The editor notes: "In regard to the indigenous way of speaking Spanish in Chiapas, the author reflects, in the characters' conversations, many disagreements in gender, number, etc. Note that, in Chiapas, a peculiar form of using "Castilian" has developed, which has a great deal to do with the native languages. A specific analysis of speech is outside the purview of this book. However, the readers can notice it throughout the work and draw their own conclusion." Anna Albaladejo, ed., *La risa olvidada de la madre: 10 años de Fortaleza de la Mujer Maya (Fomma)* (La Burbuja, 2005), 101. (This quote is my translation from the original in Spanish.)

10. Albaladejo, *La risa olvidada*, 112.

11. Albaladejo, *La risa olvidada*, 121.

12. Pierre L. van den Berghe, *The Quest for the Other: Ethnic Tourism in San Cristóbal, Mexico* (University of Washington Press, 1994), 123.

13. van den Berghe, *Quest for the Other*, 124.

14. This text appears on a large pad installed at the entrance of the gallery. In 2020, the gallery published a 203-page catalogue featuring the artists, their bios, and details about different exhibitions hosted in the space. In his reflection on the history of the gallery and its work over the years, John Burstein, the gallery's principal curator and a longtime Tsotsil speaker and interlocutor who moved to Jobel in the 1970s to conduct research in linguistic anthropology, emphasizes the pluricultural landscape of MUY and its disruption of the exoticized gaze: "To conjugate in MUY, then: '*They* paint'; '*we* (that is we-inclusive: the painters and the gallery) exhibit'; and, then, 'we-all regard.'" ("Arte contemporáneo Maya y Zoque de Chiapas," ed. Galería MUY (Galería MUY, 2020), 202.

15. Mikel Ruiz, *Ch'ayemal nich'nabiletik / Los hijos errantes / The Errant Children: A Trilingual Edition*, trans. Sean S. Sell, SUNY Series, Trans-Indigenous Decolonial Critiques (State University of New York Press, 2023), 127.

16. For further reading on the centrality of *ch'ulel* in Mayan culture and its metaphysical and social meanings, see Linda King, "Learning Through the Soul: Concepts Relating to Learning and Knowledge in the Mayan Cultures of Mexico," *International Review of Education* 45, no. 3/4 (1999): 367–70.

17. Ruiz, *Errant Children*, 103.

18. Ruiz, *Errant Children*, 83.

19. Hannah Burdette, *Revealing Rebellion in Abiayala: The Insurgent Poetics of Contemporary Indigenous Literature* (University of Arizona Press, 2023), 45.

20. Manu Pukuj, "Vovijel," in *Snichimal Vayuchil,* trans. Paul M. Worley (Digital Press at the University of North Dakota, 2018), 11–12.

21. Doris Sommer, *Proceed with Caution, When Engaged by Minority Writing in the Americas* (Harvard University Press, 1999), 9.

22. Salman Abu Sitta, *Atlas of Palestine, 1917–1966* (Palestine Land Society, 2010).

23. For a detailed personal account of the political, historical, and architectural significance of the city of Beersheba, including a vivid description of its sophisticated Ottoman urban planning schemes, see Salman Abu Sitta's *Mapping My Return: A Palestinian Memoir* (American University of Cairo, 2016). For a deep historical analysis of the modern political economy of Palestinian cities and the ways in which they were incorporated into a capitalist world system, see Sherene Seikaly, *Men of Capital: Scarcity and Economy in Mandate Palestine* (Stanford University Press, 2016).

24. Nadeem Karkabi, "How and Why Haifa Has Become the 'Palestinian Cultural Capital' in Israel," *City & Community* 17, no. 4 (2018): 1168–88.

25. Naama Blatman and Areej Sabbagh-Khoury, "The Presence of the Absence: Indigenous Palestinian Urbanism in Israel," *International Journal of Urban and Regional Research* 47, no. 1 (2023): 120–21.

26. Gloria Anzaldúa, *Borderlands: The New Mestiza / La Frontera* (Spinsters/Aunt Lute, 1987), 2–3.

27. Ibtisam Azem, *Sāriq al-Nawm: Gharīb Ḥayfāwī* (Manshūrāt al-Jamal, 2011), 9. This section of the novel was translated by Diyala Najjar and shared courtesy of the author before it became available online in 2012.

28. Azem, *Sāriq al-Nawm,* 9.

29. Azem, *Sāriq al-Nawm,* 32–33.

30. Azem, *Sāriq al-Nawm,* 66.

31. Azem, *Sāriq al-Nawm,* 67.

32. Azem, *Sāriq al-Nawm,* 51.

33. Mark LeVine, "The 'New-Old Jaffa': Tourism, Gentrification, and the Battle for Tel Aviv's Arab Neighbourhood," in *Consuming Tradition, Manufacturing Heritage: Global Norms and Urban Forms in the Age of Tourism,* ed. Nezar AlSayyad (Routledge, 2001), 240–72.

34. Azem, *Sāriq al-Nawm,* 95.

35. Sheikha Helawy, "The Braid," trans. Aicha Yassin, *World Literature Today* 95, no. 3 (2021): 41–42.

36. Helawy, "Braid," 41.

37. Ahmad al-Jammal, "Ḥulaywī, Shaykha: Lahjatī al-Badawiyya Ghuyyibat 'an al-Adab al-Filstīnī," *Independent Arabia,* January 23, 2023.

38. For more on this see Hashem Abu Shama's essay "The Palestinian City, the Song, and Settler Colonial Gentrification: On 'Better than Berlin' by Faraj Suleiman and Majd Kayyal," *Jadaliyya,* January 8, 2021, https://www.jadaliyya.com/Details/42216.

39. Layla AlAmmar, "'Cached Memories': Spatiotemporal (Dis)ruptures and Postmemorial Absence in *Palestine +100*," *MOSF Journal of Science Fiction* 4, no. 2 (2021): 68–69.

40. In the original text, the father uses the plural possessive pronoun *our*; "swallows our children to over there, to the other over there" (45). I used *Palestinian* here instead to convey the collectiveness alluded to in the original quote. 41. Majd Kayyal, "N," trans. Thoraya El-Rayyes, in *Palestine + 100: Stories from a Century After the Catastrophe*, ed. Basma Ghalayini (Comma, 2019), 45.

42. Kayyal, "N," 45.

43. Kayyal, "N," 50.

44. Kayyal, "N," 59.

45. Abu Nawwas (756–814) was an Arab poet renowned for his *khamriyyat* (wine poetry) and for writing sensual poems on pleasure and sexuality.

46. Kayyal, "N," 57.

47. Manar H. Makhoul, *Palestinian Citizens in Israel: A History Through Fiction, 1948-2010* (Edinburgh University Press, 2020), 180–82.

48. Nadera Shalhoub-Kevorkian and Himmat Zoabi, "Al-Nafī fī al-Waṭan wa-al-Numū ilā al-Judhūr," *Majallat al-Dirasat al-Filastiniyya*, no. 93 (2013): 50–65.

49. Anzaldúa, *Borderlands*, 3.

50. Anzaldúa, *Borderlands*, 25.

51. Audra Simpson, *Mohawk Interruptus: Political Life Across the Borders of Settler States* (Duke University Press, 2014), 116. (Emphasis in the original.)

52. Simpson, *Mohawk Interruptus*, 116. (Emphasis in the original.)

53. Aileen Moreton-Robinson, *The White Possessive: Property, Power, and Indigenous Sovereignty* (University of Minnesota Press, 2015), xii.

4. Murals, Marches, and Metaphors: Performative Commemoration in Rural Chiapas and Palestine

1. Officially, Israel has no borders, so by using the term *border* here, my intention is not driven by a recognition of the 1949 Armistice Line as an official border, but rather an alignment with the standardized use of the term in academic scholarship, namely history. That said, among the vernacular references to it among Palestinians, it is often called the Green Line, and sometimes, simply, the Line.

2. In the 1990s, the welcoming sign at the entrance was "*Kufur Qāsim, Balad al-shuhadā*'" (Kafr Qasem, Village of Martyrs).

3. Amy Sodaro, *Exhibiting Atrocity: Memorial Museums and the Politics of Past Violence* (Rutgers University Press, 2018), 17.

4. Sodaro, *Exhibiting Atrocity*, 24.

5. On the recent surge in memory studies, memorials, and the cultural memory of trauma, see Mieke Bal, Jonathan V. Crewe, and Leo Spitzer, eds., *Acts of Memory: Cultural Recall in the Present* (Dartmouth College Press, 1999); Paul Harvey

Williams, *Memorial Museums: The Global Rush to Commemorate Atrocities* (Berg, 2007); Julian Bonder, "On Memory, Trauma, Public Space, Monuments, and Memorials," *Places* 21, no. 1 (2009): 62–69.

6. As of now, I am not aware of any documentation of the history of the memorial site in Acteal. In the case of Kafr Qasem, however, in "Palestinian Remembrance Days and Plans: Kafr Qasim, Fact and Echo," in *Modernism and the Middle East: Architecture and Politics in the Twentieth Century*, ed. Sandy Isenstadt and Kishwar Rizvi (University of Washington Press, 2011), 186–217, Waleed Khleif and Susan Slyomovics discuss the history of the museum that was inaugurated in 2006, though they do not provide an account of the interactive memorial that opened after the publication of their article in 2011. Likewise, in his book *Palestinian Commemoration in Israel: Calendars, Monuments, and Martyrs* (Stanford University Press, 2015), Tamir Sorek offers a reading of Palestinian commemoration in Israel focusing on the monuments and the discursive formation of collective memory. In 2020 a collective of Palestinian youth associated with Tishreen Association, an NGO based in the Triangle, led tours in collaboration with artists, architects, and the art historian Raoof Haj Yehia to record the history the monuments and memorial sites in the area, including Kafr Qasem. This project culminated in curating an exhibit titled *Complex Space*.

7. Adel Manna, *Nakba and Survival: The Story of Palestinians Who Remained in Haifa and the Galilee, 1948–1956* (University of California Press, 2022), 250.

8. Abner Cohen, *Arab Border-Villages in Israel: A Study of Continuity and Change in Social Organization* (Manchester University Press, 1965), 16.

9. Benny Morris, *Israel's Border Wars, 1949–1956: Arab Infiltration, Israeli Retaliation, and the Countdown to the Suez War*, rev. ed. (Oxford University Press, 1997), 126.

10. Honaida Ghanim, "Once upon a Border: The Secret Lives of Resistance—the Case of the Palestinian Village of Al-Marja, 1949–1967," *Biography* 37, no. 2 (2014): 502.

11. Ghanim, "Once upon a Border," 497.

12. Morris, *Israel's Border Wars*, 147.

13. Manna, *Nakba and Survival*, 286.

14. Mustapha Azem, interview by Amal Eqeiq, January 28, 2017.

15. Ghanim, "Once upon a Border," 493.

16. Morris, *Israel's Border Wars*, 123.

17. Ilan Pappé, *The Forgotten Palestinians: A History of the Palestinians in Israel* (Yale University Press, 2011), 27.

18. Rosalva Aída Hernández Castillo, *La otra palabra: Mujeres y violencia en Chiapas, antes y después de Acteal* (CIESAS, 2008), 42.

19. Hernández Castillo, *La otra palabra*, 44.

20. Gustavo A. Hirales Morán, *Camino a Acteal* (Rayuela Editores, 1998), 20.

21. June C. Nash, *Mayan Visions: The Quest for Autonomy in an Age of Globalization* (Routledge, 2001), 99.

22. Hernández Castillo, *La otra palabra*, 51.

23. Nash, *Mayan Visions*, 165.

24. Human-environmental interactions are prevalent in Mayan cosmology and literatures. The close spiritual connection between humans and animals is a recurring motif in canonical Mayan creation books, such as the *Popol Vuh*, as well as contemporary poetry, folktales, and novels; see Micaela Morales López, *Raíces de la ceiba: Literatura indígena de Chiapas* (Universidad Autónoma Metropolitana, 2004); Fredy Rodríguez-Mejía and James D. Sexton, "Depiction of Animals in the Popol Vuh and Current Mayan Folktales," *Latin American Indian Literatures Journal* (2010): 1–26; Sean S. Sell, "The Chiapas Jaguar as Symbol of Maya Resintencia—Resistance and Intention," *Latin Americanist* 65, no. 1 (2021): 105–22.

25. Marco Tavanti, *Las Abejas: Pacifist Resistance and Syncretic Identities in a Globalizing Chiapas* (Taylor & Francis, 2002), 4–5.

26. Maria Ramona Hart, "'The Gifts of Enemies': The Acteal Massacre, Sociedad Civil Las Abejas and Mexico's Ejército Zapatista de Liberación Nacional and Humanitarian and Development Aid During the Low-Intensity War, 1997–1999" (ProQuest Dissertations Publishing, 2020), 54.

27. Hart, "'Gifts of Enemies,'" 59.

28. Gardenia Mendoza, "The Sinaloa and Jalisco Cartels Wage an Intense Battle in Chiapas Territory," trans. *Schools for Chiapas*, April 20, 2023, https://schoolsforchiapas.org/the-sinaloa-and-jalisco-cartels-wage-an-intense-battle-in-chiapas-territory/.

29. In *Memory for Forgetfulness,* Palestinian poet Mahmoud Darwish reminds us that wars are always declared on the border: not only the ones between Israel and the Arab world, but also those of writing itself. See Ibrahim Muhawi's introduction to the book. Mahmoud Darwish, *Memory for Forgetfulness*, August, Beirut, 1982, trans. and intro. by Ibrahim Muhawi; new foreword by Sinan Antoon (University of California Press, 2013), xi.

30. Jimmy Johnson and Linda Quiquivix, "Israel and Mexico Swap Notes on Abusing Rights," *Electronic Intifada,* May 21, 2013, https://electronicintifada.net/content/israel-and-mexico-swap-notes-abusing-rights/12475.

31. Aracely Cortés-Galán, *El papel de Israel en la militarización de México* (Stop the Wall y Para Leer en Libertad AC, 2019), 17.

32. José Rabasa, *Without History: Subaltern Studies, the Zapatista Insurgency, and the Specter of History* (University of Pittsburgh Press, 2010), 238.

33. Both journalists and scholars have documented this collaboration highlighting the growing demand for the security services and surveillance technologies that Israeli military manufacturers, such as Elbit Systems, Magal Security Systems, and NICE Systems, export to the US and other countries building fences. For further details, see Brittany Dawson and Gabriel Schivone, "Interview with Gabriel Schivone: U.S. Borderlands, Israel's Latest Surveillance Technology Laboratory," *Journal of Palestine Studies* 47, no. 4 (2018): 57–68; and Andréanne Bissonnette and Élisabeth Vallet, eds., *Borders and Border Walls: In-Security, Symbolism, Vulnerabilities* (Routledge, 2021).

34. Shira N. Robinson, *Citizen Strangers: Palestinians and the Birth of Israel's Liberal Settler State* (Stanford University Press, 2020), 104.

35. Robinson, *Citizen Strangers*, 160.

36. Emile Habibi, "Kufur Qāsim: Al-Majzara—al-Sīyāsa," *Majallat Mashārif* (1995): 99.

37. Habibi, "Kufur Qāsim," 24.

38. Samia Halaby, *Drawing the Kafr Qasem Massacre* (Schilt, 2016), 171.

39. The citation here comes from the English version of the pamphlet, p. 21. In the Arabic version, there is a similar, yet more poetically poignant, description and the additional sentence: "إنفجرت كفر قاسم تبكي بصوت شجي، وتشكو إلى الله ظلم الظالمين/" "Infajarat Kufur Qāsim tabkī bi-ṣawtin shajiyyin wa-tashkū ilā Allāh ẓulma al-ẓālimīn" (Kafr Qasem burst into tears, its plaintive voice crying out in complaint to God against the oppression of the oppressors) (16).

40. Helwa Saleem Taha, interview by Amal Eqeiq, February 21, 2021.

41. Khleif and Slyomovics, "Palestinian Remembrance Days," 193.

42. Mahmoud Darwish, *Journal of an Ordinary Grief*, trans. Ibrahim Muhawi, 1st Archipelago Books ed. (Archipelago Books, 2010), 76.

43. Shira N. Robinson, "Commemoration Under Fire: Palestinian Responses to the 1956 Kafr Qasim Massacre," in *Memory and Violence in the Middle East and North Africa*, ed. Ussama Samir Makdisi and Paul A. Silverstein (Indiana University Press, 2006), 104.

44. Robinson, *Citizen Strangers*, 154.

45. Robinson, *Citizen Strangers*, 175.

46. Robinson, *Citizen Strangers*, 172.

47. Halaby, *Drawing the Kafr Qasem Massacre*, 55.

48. Robinson, *Citizen Strangers*, 170.

49. Danny Orbach, "Black Flag at a Crossroads: The Kafr Qasim Political Trial (1957–58)," *International Journal of Middle East Studies* 45, no. 3 (2013): 505.

50. Adam Raz's book was translated into Arabic in 2019.

51. Pappé, *Forgotten Palestinians*, 53.

52. Hermann Bellinghausen, *Acteal: Crimen de Estado*, Los Nuestros (La Jornada Ediciones, 2008).

53. Tavanti, *Las Abejas*, 13.

54. Richard Stahler-Sholk, "Massacre in Chiapas," *Latin American Perspectives* 25, no. 4 (1998).

55. Information about the arms trade between Chiapas and Guatemala was conveyed to me off the record in a personal interview with a local anthropologist during a meeting in San Cristóbal / Jobel in November 2019.

56. See José Rabasa, *Without History: Subaltern Studies, the Zapatista Insurgency, and the Specter of History* (University of Pittsburgh Press, 2010). Here, Rabasa points to the federal and state governments' refusal to accept responsibility for the massacre, citing their proposed scenario that "the deaths were the result of a legitimate battle between equals—insurgents and self-defense groups—thereby undermining the

testimony given by survivors and witnesses that the paramilitaries plotted and executed a massacre" (232–33). On the logic of massacres and collective forgetting, Rabasa refers to Pierre Vidal-Naquet's citation of Amnon Kapeliouk's essay "Inquiry into a Massacre," which appears in *The Jews: History, Memory, and the Present*, edited by Vidal-Naquet himself: "For a few weeks, the massacre, followed by the Israeli reactions, the establishment of a commission of inquiry, and the first meetings of this commission were front-page news, before disappearing into the common grave of forgetfulness, where massacres are buried." Pierre Vidal-Naquet, *The Jews: History, Memory, and the Present* (Columbia University Press, 1992), 228–29. Drawing parallels between the responses to Sabra and Shatila and to Acteal, Rabasa further observes that the Mexican government's attempt to suppress the massacre failed when the international media exposed the event and prominent foreign governments voiced their condemnation, causing embarrassment for Ernesto Zedillo Ponce de León's administration.

57. G. M. Joseph and Timothy J. Henderson, *The Mexico Reader: History, Culture, Politics* (Duke University Press, 2002), 667.

58. As Tavanti points out, the urgent rush to perform autopsies was motivated by the Mexican state's desire to absolve itself from responsibility: "As a result of the autopsies, the Procuraduría General de la Republica (Mexican Attorney General, or PGR) declared that the deaths at Acteal had been the result of either a family conflict or perhaps community strife. According to the CDHFBC, this interpretation was later used to justify the military buildup that followed in the municipality of Chenalhó and in other Zapatista areas of Chiapas." Tavanti, *Las Abejas*, 14.

59. Nick Higgins, dir., *A Massacre Foretold* (First Run / Icarus Films, 2008).

60. Higgins, *Massacre Foretold*.

61. Christine Eber and "Antonia," *The Journey of a Tzotzil-Maya Woman of Chiapas, Mexico: Pass Well over the Earth*, Louann Atkins Temple Women & Culture Series 26 (University of Texas Press, 2011), 70–80.

62. Hart notes that in 1997, there were upwards of nine hundred NGOs in San Cristóbal / Jobel alone. Hart, "'Gifts of Enemies,'" 54.

63. Hart, "'Gifts of Enemies,'" 56.

64. Stahler-Sholk, "Massacre in Chiapas," 66.

65. Luis Hernández Navarro, "Acteal: Impunidad y memoria," *El Cotidiano*, no. 172 (March–April 2012): 100.

66. For the full communiqué see Comunicado 22 de septiembre de 2011, https://acteal.blogspot.com/2011/09/comunicado-22-de-septiembre-de-2011.html.

67. Navarro, "Acteal," 101.

68. The eight-meter-tall obelisk-like sculpture was staged first in Chapultepec Park in Mexico City. It was included in the First of May demonstrations before being transported to Acteal later in a caravan arranged by the *Centro de Libre Experimentación Teatral y Artística* (The Free Theatrical and Artistic Experimentation, CLETA) festival in collaboration with the artist and the *Congreso Nacional Indígena* (National Indigenous Congress of Mexico, CNI). In

fact, the sculpture is part of a series of similar sculptures that the artist designed to commemorate other acts of state terror against innocent citizens in Hong Kong, China, and Brazil. For more information see the following press release by the artist, AIDOH: Art In Defense of Humanism, "The Pillar of Shame in Mexico City," news release, 24-4-1999, http://www.aidoh.dk/news_releases/pos/mexico/ukposmexnews03.htm.

69. Ruperta Bautista Vázquez and Juana Karen Peñate Montejo, both Indigenous Mayan poets writing in Tsotsil and Ch'ol respectively, responded to the Acteal massacre through powerful poetic reflections composed in the immediate aftermath of the event. See Ruperta Bautista Vázquez, *Xchamel Ch'ulel: El Telar del Alma* (Editorial Pluralia, 2013), and Juana Karen Peñate Montejo, *Isoñil ja'al: Agua que llueve* (Consejo Estatal para las Culturas y las Artes de Chiapas, 2013). Both poems can be found online at https://launidadmorelos.blogspot.com/2009/10/cantares-de-acteal-poesia-chol-y.html. Chicano poet Juan Felipe Herrera also composed a bilingual poem sequence in homage to the victims in *Thunderweavers / Tejedoras de rayos* (University of Arizona Press, 1999).

70. This information was gathered from the minutes of the committee's meeting in August 2016. The committee shared with the author the minutes from their meetings and other archival material, a gesture that allowed the author to gain access to otherwise unavailable documents.

71. In a previously published article, "Literary Historical Intersections: Indigenous Ethnography and Rewriting History from Mexico to Israel/Palestine," I discuss the literary ethnogamy of Tawfiq Zayyad in Kafr Qasem in the first decade following the massacre as an example of the attempts of Palestinian writers to document the untold story of the massacre. In a current article in progress, I argue that despite the considerable attention that the massacre received in Palestinian poetry, it remains iconized, but not narrated. For more on Zayyad's ethnography, see Amal Eqeiq, "Literary Historical Intersections: Indigenous Ethnography and Rewriting History from Mexico to Palestine," in *Routledge Companion to World Literature and World History*, ed. May Hawas (Routledge, 2018), 122–34.

72. Samia Halaby's *Drawing the Kafr Qasem Massacre* (Schilt, 2016) is a seminal book in the historical documentation of the massacre.

73. Rana Barakat, "How to Read a Massacre in Palestine: Indigenous History as a Methodology of Liberation," *Al-Muntaqa* 5, no. 2 (September/October 2022): 41.

74. Mahmoud Darwish, "Azhaar al-damm" ("Roses of Blood"), in *Dīwān Maḥmūd Darwīsh* (The Collected Works of Mahmoud Darwish) (Dār al 'Awda, 1971), 523–40.

75. Martínez González Rocío Noemí's *Totik, Metik, Kanal: Dos años de Acteal* (2000), for example, asked children from Acteal to draw the massacre while reflecting on words in Tsotsil to help them find a way to express their grief.

76. In a report about a visit for Kafr Qasem in 1963, a journalist from the Arabic daily newspaper *Al Ittiḥād* notes that one of the manifestations of mourning in the village was writing the names of the victims on the walls of houses alongside slogans

of solidarity with struggles in Asia and Africa. In a related vein, in the graphic narration of the massacre in the Palestinian villages of Khan Younes near Gaza on the border with Egypt, which took place two weeks after the Kafr Qasem massacre, Joe Sacco records a similar practice. This is the testimony of Omm Nafez, the wife of Abdullah El-Sa'doni, who had to bury her children after the Zionist gangs shot them: "I covered all the house with ash from the oven with my hands. . . . I made the house black. [In Islam] . . . you are not supposed to mourn more than three days." See Joe Sacco, *Footnotes in Gaza* (Metropolitan Books, 2009), 111.

77. In one of the first studies about the commemoration practices in Kafr Qasem, Waleed Khleif and Susan Slyomovics point out that in 2006, the memorialization event included a youth project to "paint all the martyrs' coffins green, so their numbers and location are visually prominent to mourners." Waleed and Slyomovics, "Palestinian Remembrance Days," 207.

78. Al Jazeera Mubasher, "ʾAwal Panorama Tuḥākī Majzarat Kufur Qāsem," https://www.youtube.com/watch?v=dlBU4j6A1fE.

79. Al Jazeera Mubasher.

80. Dyg'Nojoch, interview by Amal Eqeiq, June 25, 2023.

81. Ramy Amer, interview by Amal Eqeiq, October 26, 2022.

82. Lynn Stephen, "The First Anniversary of the Acteal Massacre in Chiapas," *Cultural Survival Quarterly* 23, no. 1 (1999): 27.

83. Robinson, "Commemoration Under Fire," 116.

84. Amy Lonetree, *Decolonizing Museums: Representing Native America in National and Tribal Museums* (University of North Carolina Press, 2012), 124–25.

Conclusion: Unveiling with Affinity

1. Dian Million, "Intense Dreaming: Theories, Narratives, and Our Search for Home," *American Indian Quarterly* 35, no. 3 (Summer 2011): 316, https://doi.org/10.1353/aiq.2011.0031.

Postscript: *Indigenous Affinities* after the Gaza Genocide

1. Perhaps one of the earliest public statements about Gaza was made in 2009 when the spokesperson of the Zapatistas at the time, Subcomandante Marcos, delivered a talk titled "Gaza Will Survive" in which he described Israel's Operation Cast Lead in Gaza as a classic war of conquest. For further reading see Subcomandante Marcos, "Gaza Will Survive," *Counterpunch*, February 1, 2009, https://www.counterpunch.org/2009/02/01/gaza-will-survive/. The original text was delivered during a public Zapatista gathering that took place in Chiapas on January 5, 2009, under the title "Fourth Wind: A Dignified Organized Rage."

2. Comandante Tacho, "Inauguration of the First Exchange of Indigenous Peoples of Mexico with Zapatista Peoples," *The Enlace Zapatista Archive*, August 5, 2014, https://enlacezapatista.ezln.org.mx/2014/08/05/inauguration-of-the-first

-exchange-of-indigenous-peoples-of-mexico-with-zapatista-peoples/. The words "massacre" and "Palestinian" are both written in capital letters in the original text. The emphasis of "death and "destruction" is mine.

3. The Captain, "Sorry for the Blow, Lad," *The Enlace Zapatista Archive*, November 9, 2023, https://enlacezapatista.ezln.org.mx/2023/11/09/fifth-part-sorry-for-the-blow-lad/.

4. MEE Staff, "Mexico Seeks to Join South Africa's Genocide Case Against Israel at ICJ," *Middle East Eye*, May 28, 2024, https://www.middleeasteye.net/news/mexico-seeks-join-south-africa-genocide-case-against-israel-icj.

5. See Atef Abu Saif, *The Drone Eats with Me: A Gaza Diary* (Beacon, 2016).

6. Ross Domoney, Antonis Vradis, and Waleed Samer, "'Like a Mini Gaza': IDF Raid on Nur Shams Causes Worst West Bank Destruction in Decades," *The Real News Network,* May 7, 2024, ews.com/like-a-mini-gaza-idf-raid-on-nur-shams-causes-worst-west-bank-destruction-in-decades.

7. "Palestinian Activist Ahed Tamimi Freed Under Israel-Hamas Truce," *Al-Jazeera*, November 30, 2023, https://www.aljazeera.com/program/newsfeed/2023/11/30/palestinian-activist-ahed-tamimi-freed-under-israel-hamas-truce.

8. "120 Academics Condemn Israel's Arrest of Palestinian Professor Opposed to Genocide," *The Middle East Monitor,* April 19, 2024, https://www.middleeastmonitor.com/20240419-120-academics-condemn-israels-arrest-of-palestinian-professor-opposed-to-genocide/.

Bibliography

Abdou, Ibrahim Mahfouz, and Refqa Abu-Remaileh. "A Literary *Nahda* Interrupted: Pre-Nakba Palestinian Literature as *Adab Maqalat*." *Journal of Palestine Studies* 51, no. 3 (2022): 23–43

Abū, Ṣāliḥ Sayf al-Dīn. *Al-Ḥaraka al-Adabīya al-ʿArabīya fī Isrāʾīl: Ẓuhūruhā wa-Taṭawwuruhā min khilāl al-Mulḥaq al-Thaqāfī li-Jarīdat al-Ittiḥād bayna al-Sanawāt 1948–2000*. Majmaʿ al-Lugha al-ʿArabīya, 2010.

Abu-Hanna, Hanna [Ḥannā Abū Ḥannā]. "Al-ʾArḍ wa-al-Lugha." *al-Ṣanāra*, March 29, 1990, 10.

Abu-Hanna, Hanna, et al. "Ḥannā Abū Ḥannā: Riḥlat al-Adab wa-al-Siyāsa wa-al-Muqāwama." *Journal of Palestine Studies*, no. 105 (2016): 92–109.

Abu-Remaileh, Refqa. "Country of Words: Palestinian Literature in the Digital Age of the Refugee." *Journal of Arabic Literature* 52, no. 1–2 (2021): 68–96.

Abu Shama, Hashem. "The Palestinian City, the Song, and Settler Colonial Gentrification: On 'Better than Berlin' by Faraj Suleiman and Majd Kayyal." *Jadaliyya*, January 12, 2021. https://www.jadaliyya.com/Details/42216.

Abu Sitta, Salman. *Atlas of Palestine, 1917–1966*. Palestine Land Society, 2010.

Abu Sitta, Salman. *Mapping My Return: A Palestinian Memoir*. American University of Cairo, 2016.

Agsous, Sadia. *Derrière l'hébreu, l'arabe: Le roman palestinien en hébreu*. Classiques Garnier, 2022.

Aguilar Gil, Yásnaya Elena. *Ää: Manifiestos sobre la diversidad lingüística*. Ensayo. Tabla Rasa Libros y Ediciones. Almadía Ediciones, 2023.

Aguilar Gil, Yásnaya Elena, Gloria Anzaldúa, and Ruperta Bautista. *Lo lingüístico es político*. 3rd ed. Ediciones OnA, 2020.

Akash, Munir [Munīr ʿAkash]. *Dawla Filasṭīniyya li-l-Hunūd al-Ḥumr*. Riyāḍ al-Rayyis lil-Kutub wa-al-Nashr, 2015.

al-ʿArabī al-Jadīd. "Munīr ʿAkash: Al-Filasṭīniyyūn laysaū Hunūdan Ḥumran." August 18, 2015. https://www.alaraby.co.uk/منير-العكش-الفلسطينيون-ليسوا-هنودًا-0-حمرًا. Accessed May 24, 2025.

Al Jazeera Mubasher. "ʾAwal Panorama Tuḥākī Majzarat Kufur Qāsem." https://www.youtube.com/watch?v=dlBU4j6A1fE.

AlAmmar, Layla. "'Cached Memories': Spatiotemporal (Dis)ruptures and Postmemorial Absence in *Palestine + 100*." *MOSF Journal of Science Fiction* 4, no. 2 (2021): 65–76.

Albaladejo, Anna, ed. *La risa olvidada de la madre: 10 años de Fortaleza de la Mujer Maya (Fomma)*. La Burbuja, 2005.

Alim.org. "Compare Surah 8. Al-Anfal, Ayah 63." https://www.alim.org/quran/compare/surah/8/63/.

Allen, Chadwick. *Trans-Indigenous Methodologies for Global Native Literary Studies*. University of Minnesota Press, 2012.

Amara, Muhammad. *Arabic in Israel: Language, Identity and Conflict*. Routledge Studies in Language and Identity. Routledge, 2018.

ʾAmāra, Muḥammad. *Lughati Huwiyyatī: Naḥwa Siyāsa Lughawiyya Shumūliyya Muwājahat Taḥaddiyāt al-Lugha al-ʿArabiyya fī Isrāʾīl*. Dār al-Hudá, 2020.

Amer, Ramy. Interview by Amal Eqeiq, October 26, 2022.

Anzaldúa, Gloria. *Borderlands: The New Mestiza/La Frontera*. Aunt Lute Books, 1987.

Apter, Emily. "Translation at the Checkpoint." *Journal of Postcolonial Writing* 50, no. 1 (2014): 56–74.

Arias, Arturo. *Recovering Lost Footprints: Contemporary Maya Narratives*, vol. 2. State University of New York Press, 2017.

Art in Defense of Humanism, AIDOH. "The Pillar of Shame in Mexico City." News release, April 24, 1999. http://www.aidoh.dk/news_releases/pos/mexico/ukposmexnews03.htm.

"Arte contemporáneo maya y zoque de Chiapas." Edited by Galería MUY. Galería MUY, 2020.

Asad, Muhammad. *The Message of the Qur'an*. Dar Al-Andalus, 1980.

Asmar, Fouzi [Fawzī al-Asmar]. *To Be an Arab in Israel*. 2nd ed. Reprint Series no. 8. Institute for Palestine Studies, 1978.

Austin Henry, Robert. "Global Palestine: International Solidarity and the Cuban Connection." *Journal of Holy Land and Palestine Studies* 18, no. 2 (2019): 239–62.

ʿAwaḍ Aḥmad Rafiq, Mundhir ʿĀmir, Liyāna Badr, and Zakariyyā Muḥammad. "Imīl Ḥabībī: Al-Ḥiwār al-Akhīr—Anā Māniʿat al-Ṣawāʿiq al-Filasṭīnīya." *Majallat Mashārif* 9 (1996): 12–27.

Awayed-Bishara, Muzna. "*Sumud* Pedagogy as Linguistic Citizenship: Palestinian Youth in Israel Against Imposed Subjectivities." *Language in Society* (2023): 1–23.

Azem, Ibtisam [Ibtisām ʿĀzim]. *Sāriq al-Nawm: Gharīb Ḥayfāwī*. Manshūrāt al-Jamal, 2011.

Azem, Mustapha. Interview by Amal Eqeiq, January 28, 2017.

Babb, Florence E. *The Tourism Encounter: Fashioning Latin American Nations and Histories*. Stanford University Press, 2011.

Baeza, Cecilia. "Palestinians and Latin America's Indigenous Peoples: Coexistence, Convergence, Solidarity." *Middle East Report*, no. 274 (2015): 34–37.

Bal, Mieke, Jonathan V. Crewe, and Leo Spitzer, eds. *Acts of Memory: Cultural Recall in the Present*. Dartmouth College Press, 1999.

Baldy, Cutcha Risling, and Melanie K. Yazzie, eds. "Introduction: Indigenous Peoples and the Politics of Water." *Decolonization: Indigeneity, Education & Society* 7, no. 1 (2018): 1–18.

Barakat, Rana. "How to Read a Massacre in Palestine: Indigenous History as a Methodology of Liberation." *Al-Muntaqa* 5, no. 2 (September/October 2022): 41.

Bautista Vázquez, Ruperta. *Xchamel Ch'ulel: El Telar del Alma*. Editorial Pluralia, 2013.

Bellinghausen, Hermann. *Acteal: Crimen de Estado*. Los Nuestros. La Jornada Ediciones, 2008.

Betan, Xun. "Jme'tik ta bats'i k'op / La madre luna Tsotsil." In *Insurrección de las palabras: Poetas contemporáneos en lenguas mexicanas*, edited by Hermann Bellinghausen, 294. Fondo de Cultura Económica 2023.

Betan, Xun. "Semillas de esperanza / Seeds of Hope," "Flores para el corazón / Flowers for the Heart." Translated by Sean S. Sell. *North Dakota Quarterly* 86, no. 3/4 (2019): 218–22.

Bissonnette, Andréanne, and Élisabeth Vallet, eds. *Borders and Border Walls: In-Security, Symbolism, Vulnerabilities*. Routledge, 2021.

Blatman, Naama, and Areej Sabbagh-Khoury. "The Presence of the Absence: Indigenous Palestinian Urbanism in Israel." *International Journal of Urban and Regional Research* 47, no. 1 (2023): 119–28.

Bolom Pale, Manuel. "Didáctica de la resistencia desde el Lekil Kuxlejal del Pueblo Originario y la educación intercultural en contextos educativos pluriculturales." In *Razos del tiempo: Hacia una escuela sustentable e intercultural*, edited by Felipe Reyes Escutia and Carmen Yolanda Quintero Reyes, 99–125. Secretaría de Educación de Chiapas y UNACH, 2017.

Bonder, Julian. "On Memory, Trauma, Public Space, Monuments, and Memorials." *Places* 21, no. 1 (2009): 62–69.

Bonfil Batalla, Guillermo. *México Profundo: Reclaiming a Civilization*. Translated by Philip Adams Dennis. University of Texas Press, 1996.

Brustad, Kristen. "The Question of Language." In *The Cambridge Companion to Modern Arab Culture*, edited by Dwight Fletcher Reynolds, 19–35. Cambridge University Press, 2015.

Burdette, Hannah. *Revealing Rebellion in Abiayala: The Insurgent Poetics of Contemporary Indigenous Literature*. University of Arizona Press, 2023.

Bustani, Butrus al- [Buṭrus al-Bustānī]. *The Clarion of Syria: A Patriot's Call Against the Civil War of 1860*. Translated by Jens Hanssen and Hicham Safieddine. University of California Press, 2019. doi:10.1525/luminos.67.

Byrd, Jodi A., Alyosha Goldstein, Jodi Melamed, and Chandan Reddy. "Predatory Value: Economies of Dispossession and Disturbed Relationalities." *Social Text* 36, no. 2 (2018): 1–18.

Camacho Padilla, Fernando, and Jessica Stites Mor. "Presence and Visibility in Cuban Anticolonial Solidarity: Palestine in OSPAAAL's Photography and Poster Art." In *Palestine in the World: International Solidarity with the Palestinian Liberation Movement*, edited by Sorcha Thomson and Pelle Valentin Olsen, 167–96. I. B. Tauris, 2023. https://doi.org/10.5040/9780755647026.ch-007.

Casanova, Pascale. *The World Republic of Letters*. Translated by M. B. DeBevoise. Harvard University Press, 2004.

Castellanos, M. Bianet. "Introduction: Settler Colonialism in Latin America." *American Quarterly* 69, no. 4 (2017): 777–81. https://www.jstor.org/stable/26794695.

Chacón, Gloria Elizabeth. *Indigenous Cosmolectics: Kab'awil and the Making of Maya and Zapotec Literatures*. University of North Carolina Press, 2018.

Chechev, Ibrahim. WhatsApp message to the author. March 5, 2023.

Chikinib, ta. "Conversatorio 'Kojtikinbetik xch'ulel li jk'optike-Reconozcamos la esencia de nuestra lengua.'" December 5, 2022. https://chikinib.wixsite.com/zinacantan/post/conversatorio-kojtikinbetik-xch-ulel-li-jk-optike-reconozcamos-la-esencia-de-nuestra-lengua.

Cohen, Abner. *Arab Border-Villages in Israel: A Study of Continuity and Change in Social Organization*. Manchester University Press, 1965.

Cortés-Galán, Aracely. *El papel de Israel en la militarización de México*. Stop the Wall and Para Leer en Libertad AC, 2019.

Cubells, Lola. "La Justicia del Corazón: Sabiduría tseltal-maya sobre la vida buena." *El Salto* (blog), October 9, 2018. https://www.elsaltodiario.com/el-rumor-de-las-multitudes/la-justicia-del-corazon-sabiduria-tseltal-maya-sobre-la-vida-buena.

Cuevas, Sandra Cañas. "The Politics of Conversion to Islam in Southern Mexico." In *Islam and the Americas*, edited by Aisha Khan, 163–85. University Press of Florida, 2015.

Darwish, Mahmoud [Maḥmūd Darwīsh]. "Azhār al-Damm." In *Dīwān Maḥmūd Darwīsh*, 523–40. Dār al-ʻAwda, 1971.

Darwish, Mahmoud. *In the Presence of Absence*. Translated by Sinan Antoon. 1st Archipelago Books ed. Archipelago Books, 2011.

Darwish, Mahmoud. *Journal of an Ordinary Grief*. Translated by Ibrahim Muhawi. 1st Archipelago Books ed. Archipelago Books, 2010.

Darwish, Mahmoud. *Memory for Forgetfulness: August, Beirut, 1982*. Translated and introduced by Ibrahim Muhawi, with a new foreword by Sinan Antoon. University of California Press, 2013.

Dawson, Alexander S. *Indian and Nation in Revolutionary Mexico*. University of Arizona Press, 2004.

Dawson, Brittany, and Gabriel Schivone. "Interview with Gabriel Schivone: U.S. Borderlands, Israel's Latest Surveillance Technology Laboratory." *Journal of Palestine Studies* 47, no. 4 (2018): 57–68.

Deleuze, Gilles, and Félix Guattari. *What Is Philosophy?* Translated by Hugh Tomlinson and Graham Burchell III. European Perspectives. Columbia University Press, 1994.

Desille, Amandine, and Yara Sa'di-Ibraheem. "'It's a Matter of Life or Death': Jewish Migration and Dispossession of Palestinians in Acre." *Urban Planning* 6, no. 2 (2021): 32–42. https://doi.org/10.17645/up.v6i2.3676.

Díaz López, Óscar. *Smelolal sts'ibael bats'i k'op tsotsil: Norma de escritura de la lengua tsotsil.* Instituto Nacional de Lenguas Indígenas [INALI], 2011.

Doha Historical Dictionary of Arabic. "Al-'Ulfa." Accessed April 8, 2025. https://www.dohadictionary.org/dictionary/%D8%A7%D9%84%D8%A3%D9%84%D9%81%D8%A9.

Dyg'Nojoch. Interview by Amal Eqeiq, June 25, 2023.

Eber, Christine, and "Antonia." *The Journey of a Tzotzil-Maya Woman of Chiapas, Mexico: Pass Well over the Earth.* University of Texas Press, 2011.

Ebileeni, Maurice. *Being There, Being Here: Palestinian Writings in the World.* Syracuse University Press, 2022.

Eqeiq, Amal. "From Haifa to Ramallah (and Back): New/Old Palestinian Literary Topography." *Journal of Palestine Studies* 48, no. 3 (2019): 26–42.

Eqeiq, Amal. "Literary Historical Intersections: Indigenous Ethnography and Rewriting History from Mexico to Palestine." In *Routledge Companion to World Literature and World History,* edited by May Hawas, 122–34. Routledge, 2018.

Eqeiq, Amal. "Of Borders and Limits: Comparative Indigeneity in Mexico and Palestine." *Jadaliyya*, August 27, 2018. https://www.jadaliyya.com/Details/37898.

Eqeiq, Amal. "Writing the Indigenous: Contemporary Mayan Literature in Chiapas, Mexico and Palestinian Literature in Israel." ProQuest Dissertations, 2013.

Escobar, Arturo. *Pluriversal Politics: The Real and the Possible.* Duke University Press, 2020.

Frischmann, Donald H. "New Mayan Theatre in Chiapas: Anthropology, Literacy, and Social Drama." In *Negotiating Performance: Gender, Sexuality, and Theatricality in Latin/o America,* edited by Diana Taylor and Juan Villegas, 213–38. Duke University Press, 1994.

Furani, Khaled. *Silencing the Sea: Secular Rhythms in Palestinian Poetry.* Stanford University Press, 2012.

Garduño García, Moisés. "Resonancias del zapatismo mexicano y la resistencia palestina: Dos ejemplos de autonomía en el Sur Global." *Espiral (Guadalajara)* 23, no. 65 (2016): 125–63.

Ghalayini, Basma, ed. *Palestine +100: Stories from a Century After the Catastrophe.* Comma, 2019.

Ghanayim, Mahmud. *The Quest for a Lost Identity: Palestinian Fiction in Israel.* Harrassowitz, 2008.

Ghanim, Honaida. "Israel's Nation-State Law: Hierarchized Citizenship and Jewish Supremacy." *Critical Times* 4, no. 3 (2021): 565–76.

Ghanim, Honaida. "Once upon a Border: The Secret Lives of Resistance—the Case of the Palestinian Village of Al-Marja, 1949–1967." *Biography* 37, no. 2 (2014): 476–504.

Ghazali, Imam al- [Imām al-Ghazālī]. *The Duties of Brotherhood in Islam*. Translated by Muhtar Holland. Kube, 2012.

Guabli, Brahim El. "(Re)Invention of Tradition, Subversive Memory, and Morocco's Re-Amazighization: From Erasure of Imazighen to the Performance of Tifinagh in Public Life." *Expressions maghrébines* 19, no. 1 (2020): 143–68.

Guabli, Brahim El. "Where Is Amazigh Studies?" *Africa Is a Country*, May 8, 2023. https://africasacountry.com/2023/05/where-is-amazigh-studies.

Habibi, Emile [Imīl Ḥabībī]. *Al-Mutashāʾil: al-Waqāʾiʿ al-Gharība fī Ikhtifāʾ Saʿīd abī al-Naḥs*. al-Ṭabʿah 2, 1974. Published in English as *The Secret Life of Saeed, the Ill-Fated Pessoptimist*, translated by Salma Khadra Jayyusi and Trevor Le Gassick. Vantage, 1982.

Habibi, Emile. "Kufur Qāsim: Al-Majzara—al-Sīyāsa." *Majallat Mashārif* (1995): 94–116.

Halaby, Samia. *Drawing the Kafr Qasem Massacre*. Schilt, 2016.

Hart, Maria Ramona. "'The Gifts of Enemies': The Acteal Massacre, Sociedad Civil Las Abejas and Mexico's Ejército Zapatista de Liberación Nacional and Humanitarian and Development Aid During the Low-Intensity War, 1997–1999." ProQuest Dissertations, 2020.

Hass, Amira. "To Expel Palestinians Efficiently, Learn Arabic." *Haaretz*, June 6, 2023.

Haug, Sebastian, Jacqueline Braveboy-Wagner, and Günther Maihold. "The 'Global South' in the Study of World Politics: Examining a Meta Category." *Third World Quarterly* 42, no. 9 (2021): 1923–44. https://doi.org/10.1080/01436597.2021.1948831.

Helawy, Sheikha [Shaykha Ḥulaywī]. "The Braid." Translated by Aicha Yassin. *World Literature Today* 95, no. 3 (2021): 41–42.

Hernández Castillo, Rosalva Aída, ed. *La otra palabra: Mujeres y violencia en Chiapas, antes y después de Acteal*. CIESAS, 2008.

Hernández Castillo, Rosalva Aída. "'Putting Heart' into History and Memory: Dialogues with Maya-Tseltal Philosopher, Xuno López Intzin." *Memory Studies* 13, no. 5 (2020): 805–19.

Higgins, Nick, dir. *A Massacre Foretold*. First Run/Icarus Films, 2008.

Hirales Morán, Gustavo A. *Camino a Acteal*. Rayuela Editores, 1998.

Hochberg, Gil Z. *In Spite of Partition: Jews, Arabs, and the Limits of Separatist Imagination*. Princeton University Press, 2007.

Hoffman, Adina. *My Happiness Bears No Relation to Happiness: A Poet's Life in the Palestinian Century*. Yale University Press, 2009.

Ibn Hazm, Ali ibn Ahmad [ʿAlī Ibn Aḥmad Ibn Ḥazm]. *The Ring of the Dove: A Treatise on the Art and Practice of Arab Love*. Translated by Arthur John Arberry. Luzac, 1953.

IsraelArabic (@IsraelArabic). "Al-Lugha al-ʿArabiyya fī Isrāʾīl." Twitter, December 18, 2022, 2:56 AM. https://twitter.com/IsraelArabic.

Jamal, Amal. *Arab Minority Nationalism in Israel: The Politics of Indigeneity*. Routledge, 2014.
Jammal, Aḥmad al-. "Ḥulaywī, Shaykha: Lahjatī al-Badawiyya Ghuyyibat ʿan al-Adab al-Filstīnī." *Independent Arabia*, January 23, 2023.
Jarrar, Khaled. *Khaled's Ladder*. Film, 2016. https://www.culturunners.com/films/khaleds-ladder. Accessed May 20, 2025.
Johnson, Jimmy, and Linda Quiquivix. "Israel and Mexico Swap Notes on Abusing Rights." *Electronic Intifada*, May 21, 2013. https://electronicintifada.net/content/israel-and-mexico-swap-notes-abusing-rights/12475.
Joseph, G. M., and Timothy J. Henderson. *The Mexico Reader: History, Culture, Politics*. Duke University Press, 2002.
Kanafani, Ghassan [Ghassān Kanafānī]. *Resistance Literature in Occupied Palestine 1948–1966*. Rimal, 2013.
Kari, James, and Jeff Leer. "Review of *The Navajo Language: A Grammar and Colloquial Dictionary*." *International Journal of American Linguistics* 50, no. 1 (1984): 124–30. http://www.jstor.org/stable/1265203.
Karkabi, Nadeem. "How and Why Haifa Has Become the 'Palestinian Cultural Capital' in Israel." *City & Community* 17, no. 4 (2018): 1168–88.
Kashua, Sayed. "Advanced Hebrew with an Arabic Accent." Interview by Matt Seaton. *New York Review of Books*, August 14, 2021. https://www.nybooks.com/online/2021/08/14/advanced-hebrew-with-an-arabic-accent/.
Kashua, Sayed. "My Palestinian Diaspora." *New York Review of Books*, August 7, 2021. https://www.nybooks.com/online/2021/08/07/my-palestinian-diaspora/.
Kayyal, Majd [Majd Kayyāl]. *al-Mawt fī Ḥayfā: Al-Mawt Qaṣaṣ Kathīra wa-al-Mawt Riwāya Wāḥida*. Al-Ahliyya li-l-Nashr wa-al-Tawzīʿ, 2019.
Khleif, Waleed, and Susan Slyomovics. "Palestinian Remembrance Days and Plans: Kafr Qasim, Fact and Echo." In *Modernism and the Middle East: Architecture and Politics in the Twentieth Century*, edited by Sandy Isenstadt and Kishwar Rizvi, 186–217. University of Washington Press, 2011.
King, Linda. "Learning Through the Soul: Concepts Relating to Learning and Knowledge in the Mayan Cultures of Mexico." *International Review of Education* 45, no. 3/4 (1999): 367–70.
Lambert, Léopold. "Decentering the U.S." *Funambulist*, April 2022.
Laughlin, Robert M., and John Beard Haviland. *The Great Tzotzil Dictionary of Santo Domingo Zinacantán with Grammatical Analysis and Historical Commentary*. 3 vols. Smithsonian Institution Press, 1988.
LeVine, Mark. "The 'New-Old Jaffa': Tourism, Gentrification, and the Battle for Tel-Aviv's Arab Neighbourhood." In *Consuming Tradition, Manufacturing Heritage: Global Norms and Urban Forms in the Age of Tourism*, edited by Nezar AlSayyad, 240–72. Routledge, 2001.
LeVine, Mark. *Why They Don't Hate Us: Lifting the Veil on the Axis of Evil*. Oneworld, 2005.
Levy, Lital. *Poetic Trespass: Writing Between Hebrew and Arabic in Israel/Palestine*. Princeton University Press, 2014.

Lewis, Stephen E. *Rethinking Mexican Indigenismo: The INI's Coordinating Center in Highland Chiapas and the Fate of a Utopian Project*. University of New Mexico Press, 2018.

Lockman, Zachary. *Comrades and Enemies: Arab and Jewish Workers in Palestine, 1906–1948*. University of California Press, 1996.

Lonetree, Amy. *Decolonizing Museums: Representing Native America in National and Tribal Museums*. University of North Carolina Press, 2012.

López de la Torre, Carlos Fernando. "The Cuban Poster and Palestine: Solidarity and Third Worldism in Images." Paper presented at the Middle East Studies Association Annual Meeting, San Antonio, TX, November 17, 2018.

Magnusson, Andrew D. "Ethnic and Religious Minorities." In *The Cambridge Companion to Modern Arab Culture*, edited by Dwight Fletcher Reynolds, 36–53. Cambridge University Press, 2015.

Makhoul, Manar H. *Palestinian Citizens in Israel: A History Through Fiction, 1948–2010*. Edinburgh University Press, 2020.

Manna, Adel. *Nakba and Survival: The Story of Palestinians Who Remained in Haifa and the Galilee, 1948–1956*. University of California Press, 2022.

Marcos, Subcomandante Insurgente. *Our Word Is Our Weapon: Selected Writings*. Edited by Juana Ponce de León. Seven Stories, 2001.

Marcos, Sylvia, and Linda Quiquivix. "Chiapas and Palestine, Together and Side by Side." *NACLA Report on the Americas* 56, no. 4 (2024): 442–47. https://doi.org/10.1080/10714839.2024.2427986.

Martínez, Javier Castellanos. "El escritor indígena." *Ojarasca*, July 2013, 3.

Martínez González, Rocío Noemí. *Totik, Metik, Kanal: Dos años de Acteal*. Centro de Información y Análisis de Chiapas, 2000.

Masalha, Nur. *The Palestine Nakba: Decolonising History, Narrating the Subaltern, Reclaiming Memory*. Zed Books, 2021.

Meari, Lena. "Reading Che in Colonized Palestine: On Analyzing and Drawing Inspiration from Revolutionary Latin American Texts." *NACLA Report on the Americas* 50, no. 1 (2018): 49–55.

Mendel, Yonatan. *The Creation of Israeli Arabic: Security and Politics in Arabic Studies in Israel*. Palgrave Macmillan, 2016.

Mendel, Yonatan, and Abeer AlNajjar, eds. *Language, Politics and Society in the Middle East: Essays in Honour of Yasir Suleiman*. Edinburgh University Press, 2018.

Mendoza, Gardenia. "The Sinaloa and Jalisco Cartels Wage an Intense Battle in Chiapas Territory." Translated by *Schools for Chiapas*, April 20, 2023. https://schoolsforchiapas.org/the-sinaloa-and-jalisco-cartels-wage-an-intense-battle-in-chiapas-territory/.

Mignolo, Walter D. *Local Histories/Global Designs: Coloniality, Subaltern Knowledges, and Border Thinking*. Princeton Studies in Culture/Power/History. Princeton University Press, 2000.

Mignolo, Walter D. *The Politics of Decolonial Investigations*. Duke University Press, 2021.

Million, Dian. "Intense Dreaming: Theories, Narratives, and Our Search for Home." *American Indian Quarterly* 35, no. 3 (2011): 313–33. https://doi.org/10.1353/aiq.2011.a447049.

Morales López, Micaela. *Raíces de la ceiba: Literatura indígena de Chiapas*. Universidad Autónoma Metropolitana, 2004.

Moreton-Robinson, Aileen. *The White Possessive: Property, Power, and Indigenous Sovereignty*. University of Minnesota Press, 2015.

Morris, Benny. *Israel's Border Wars, 1949–1956: Arab Infiltration, Israeli Retaliation, and the Countdown to the Suez War*. Rev. ed. Oxford University Press, 1997.

Murre-van den Berg, H. L., Karène Sanchez-Summerer, and Tijmen C. Baarda, eds. *Arabic and Its Alternatives: Religious Minorities and Their Languages in the Emerging Nation States of the Middle East (1920–1950)*. Brill, 2020.

Nash, June C. *Mayan Visions: The Quest for Autonomy in an Age of Globalization*. Routledge, 2001.

Nashef, Ismail. *A Language of One's Own: Literary Arabic, the Palestinians and Israel*. Edinburgh University Press, 2023.

Nassar, Maha. *Brothers Apart: Palestinian Citizens of Israel and the Arab World*. Stanford University Press, 2017.

Navarro, Luis Hernández. "Acteal: Impunidad y memoria." *El Cotidiano*, no. 172 (March–April 2012): 99–115.

Ngũgĩ wa Thiong'o. *The Language of Languages: Reflections on Translation*. Seagull Books, 2023.

Olwan, Dana M. "On Assumptive Solidarities in Comparative Settler Colonialisms." *Feral Feminisms*, no. 2 (Winter 2013): 89–102.

Orbach, Danny. "Black Flag at a Crossroads: The Kafr Qasim Political Trial (1957–58)." *International Journal of Middle East Studies* 45, no. 3 (2013): 491–511.

Palacios, Rita M. "Maya Literature." In *Oxford Research Encyclopedia of Literature*. Oxford University Press, 2022.

Pappé, Ilan. *The Forgotten Palestinians: A History of the Palestinians in Israel*. Yale University Press, 2011.

Past, Ámbar, Xalik Guzmán Bakbolom, and Xpetra Ernándes. *Incantations: Songs, Spells and Images by Mayan Women*. Translated by Ámbar Past. Cinco Puntos, 2005.

PEN International. "Writing the Future in Indigenous Languages." July 11, 2019. https://www.pen-international.org/news/kl7hgawijzo3vvftq8iehuw60olukn.

Peñate Montejo, Juana Karen. *Isoñil ja'al: Agua que llueve*. Consejo Estatal para las Culturas y las Artes de Chiapas, 2013.

Pérez Moreno, María Patricia. *Corazón: Una forma de ser-estar-hacer-sentir-pensar de los tseltaletik de Bachajón, Chiapas, México*. Ediciones Abya-Yala, 2014.

Pérez Tsu, Mariana. "A Tzotzil Chronicle of the Zapatista Uprising." In *The Mexico Reader: History, Culture, Politics*, edited by Gilbert M. Joseph and Timothy J. Henderson, 655–69. Duke University Press, 2002.

Pinderhughes, Charles. "Toward a New Theory of Internal Colonialism." *Socialism and Democracy* 25, no. 1 (2011): 235–56. https://doi.org/10.1080/08854300.2011.559702.

Pratt, Mary Louise. "Arts of the Contact Zone." *Profession* (1991): 33–40.

Pratt, Mary Louise. *Planetary Longings*. Duke University Press, 2022.

Pukuj, Manu. "Vovijel." In *Snichimal Vayuchil: Experimental Poetry in Bats'i K'op*, edited and translated by Paul M. Worley, 11–14. University of North Dakota, 2018.

Quijano, Aníbal. "El 'Movimiento indígena' y las cuestiones pendientes en América Latina." *Argumentos (México, D.F.)* 19, no. 50 (2006): 51–77.

Quintanilla, Leslie, and Jennifer Mogannam. "Borders Are Obsolete: Relations Beyond the 'Borderlands' of Palestine and US-Mexico." *American Quarterly* 67, no. 4 (2015): 1039–46. https://doi.org/10.1353/aq.2015.0066.

Quiquivix, Linda. *Palestine 1492: A Report Back*. Wild Ox Books, 2024.

Rabasa, José. *Without History: Subaltern Studies, the Zapatista Insurgency, and the Specter of History*. University of Pittsburgh Press, 2010.

Rendall, Steven, trans. "The Translator's Task, Walter Benjamin (Translation)." *TTR* 10, no. 2 (1997): 151–65.

Reyes-Escutia, Felipe. "The Living Interculturality of Chiapas to Recreate the Modern University Towards Sustainability Horizons." In *Sustainable Development Research and Practice in Mexico and Selected Latin American Countries*, edited by Walter Leal Filho, Ricardo Noyola-Cherpitel, Pedro Medellín-Milán, and Valeria Ruiz Vargas, 39–51. Springer International, 2018.

Reyes-Escutia, Felipe, and Carmen Yolanda Quintero Reyes, eds. *Trazos del tiempo: Hacia una escuela sustentable e intercultural*. Secretaría de Educación de Chiapas y UNACH, 2017.

Robinson, Shira N. *Citizen Strangers: Palestinians and the Birth of Israel's Liberal Settler State*. Stanford University Press, 2020.

Robinson, Shira N. "Commemoration Under Fire: Palestinian Responses to the 1956 Kafr Qasim Massacre." In *Memory and Violence in the Middle East and North Africa*, edited by Ussama Samir Makdisi and Paul A. Silverstein, 103–32. Indiana University Press, 2006.

Rodríguez-Mejía, Fredy, and James D. Sexton. "Depiction of Animals in the Popol Vuh and Current Mayan Folktales." *Latin American Indian Literatures Journal* 26, no. 1 (2010): 1–26.

Rohana, Shadi. "Latin America in the Palestinian Journal *Al-Karmel*." *Middle East Studies Association Annual Meeting*, November 17, 2018, San Antonio, TX, conference paper.

Rolef, Sheila Hattis, trans. "Basic-Law: Israel—the Nation State of the Jewish People." Edited by The Knesset, 2018.

Ruiz, Mikel. *Ch'ayemal nich'nabiletik / Los hijos errantes / The Errant Children: A Trilingual Edition*. Translated by Sean S. Sell. SUNY Series, Trans-Indigenous Decolonial Critiques. State University of New York Press, 2023.

Ruiz, Mikel. "La literatura en tsotsil (1996–2017)." In *Enciclopedia de la literatura en México*, 2019.
Rus, Jan, and Gaspar Morquecho Escamilla. "The Urban Indigenous Movement and Elite Accommodation in San Cristóbal, Chiapas, 1975–2008: Tenemos que vivir nuestros años / 'We Have to Live in Our Own Times.'" In *Enduring Reform: Progressive Activism and Private Sector Responses in Latin America's Democracies*, edited by Jeffrey W. Rubin and Vivienne Bennett, 81–112. University of Pittsburgh Press, 2015.
Rus, Jan, and Diane L. Rus. "The Taller Tzotzil of Chiapas, Mexico: A Native Language Publishing Project, 1985–2002." In *Decolonizing Native Histories: Collaboration, Knowledge, and Language in the Americas*, edited by Florencia E. Mallon, 144–74. Duke University Press, 2012.
Sacco, Joe. *Footnotes in Gaza*. Metropolitan Books, 2009.
Salaita, Steven. *The Holy Land in Transit: Colonialism and the Quest for Canaan*. Syracuse University Press, 2006.
Salaita, Steven. *Inter/Nationalism: Decolonizing Native America and Palestine*. University of Minnesota Press, 2016.
Sánchez, Rosaura, and Beatrice Pita. "Rethinking Settler Colonialism." *American Quarterly* 66, no. 4 (2014): 1039–55. https://doi.org/10.1353/aq.2014.0065.
Santana E., María Eugenia. "El buen vivir, miradas desde dentro." *Revista pueblos y fronteras digital* 10, no. 19 (2015): 171–98.
Satouri, Ouissem, Dhia Ben Naser, and Gabriel Marchand. *Somos Musulmanes*. Film. France, 2019.
Schavelzon, Salvador. *Plurinacionalidad y Vivir Bien / Buen Vivir: Dos conceptos leídos desde Bolivia y Ecuador post-constituyentes*. CLACSO, 2015.
Seikaly, Sherene. *Men of Capital: Scarcity and Economy in Mandate Palestine*. Stanford University Press, 2016.
Selim, Samah. "Nation and Translation in the Middle East: Histories, Canons, Hegemonies." *Translator (Manchester, England)* 15, no. 1 (2009): 1–13.
Sell, Sean S. "The Chiapas Jaguar as Symbol of Maya Resintencia—Resistance and Intention." *Latin Americanist* 65, no. 1 (2021): 105–22.
Shalhoub-Kevorkian, Nadera, and Himmat Zoabi [Nādira Shalḥūb-Kevorkian and Himmat Zuʿbī]. "Al-Nafī fī al-Waṭan wa-al-Numū ilā al-Judhūr." *Majallat al-Dirasat al-Filastiniyya*, no. 93 (2013): 50–65.
Shammas, Anton [Antūn Shammās]. "Can the Bilingual Speak?" *Markaz Review*, May 15, 2022. https://themarkaz.org/can-the-bilingual-speak-thoughts-on-the-arabic-hebrew-mind/.
Shidyaq, Ahmad Faris al [Aḥmad Fāris al- Shidyāq]. *Leg over Leg, or, The Turtle in the Tree Concerning the Fāriyāq*. Edited and translated by Humphrey Davies. New York University Press, 2015.
Shih, Shu-mei. "Comparison as Relation." In *Comparison: Theories, Approaches, Uses*, edited by Rita Felski and Susan Stanford Friedman, 79–98. Johns Hopkins University Press, 2013.

Shohat, Ella. *On the Arab-Jew, Palestine, and Other Displacements: Selected Writings*. Pluto, 2017.

Simpson, Audra. *Mohawk Interruptus: Political Life Across the Borders of Settler States*. Duke University Press, 2014.

Simpson, Leanne Betasamosake. *As We Have Always Done: Indigenous Freedom Through Radical Resistance*. University of Minnesota Press, 2017.

Slyomovics, Susan. *The Object of Memory: Arab and Jew Narrate the Palestinian Village*. University of Pennsylvania Press, 1998.

Smith, Linda Tuhiwai. *Decolonizing Methodologies: Research and Indigenous Peoples*. 2nd ed. Zed Books, 2012.

Snichimal Vayuchil. Translated by Paul M. Worley. Digital Press at the University of North Dakota, 2018.

Sodaro, Amy. *Exhibiting Atrocity: Memorial Museums and the Politics of Past Violence*. Rutgers University Press, 2018.

Sommer, Doris. *Proceed with Caution, When Engaged by Minority Writing in the Americas*. Harvard University Press, 1999.

Sommers, Joseph. "El ciclo de Chiapas: Nueva corriente literaria." *Cuadernos Americanos* 133, no. 2 (1964): 246–61.

Sorek, Tamir. *The Optimist: A Social Biography of Tawfiq Zayyad*. Stanford University Press, 2020.

Sorek, Tamir. *Palestinian Commemoration in Israel: Calendars, Monuments, and Martyrs*. Stanford University Press, 2015.

Stahler-Sholk, Richard. "Massacre in Chiapas." *Latin American Perspectives* 25, no. 4 (1998): 63–75.

Steele, Cynthia. "Power, Gender, and Canon Formation in Mexico." *Studies in 20th & 21st Century Literature* 20, no. 1 (1996). http://dx.doi.org/10.4148/2334-4415.1381.

Stephen, Lynn. "The First Anniversary of the Acteal Massacre in Chiapas." *Cultural Survival Quarterly* 23, no. 1 (1999): 27–29.

Stites Mor, Jessica. "Rendering Armed Struggle: OSPAAAL, Cuban Poster Art, and South-South Solidarity at the United Nations." *Jahrbuch für Geschichte Lateinamerikas* 56 (2019): 42–65.

Suleiman, Camelia. *The Politics of Arabic in Israel: A Sociolinguistic Analysis*. Edinburgh University Press, 2017.

Suleiman, Yasir. *Arabic in the Fray: Language Ideology and Cultural Politics*. Edinburgh University Press, 2013.

Suleiman, Yasir. "A Language in Conflict: Arabic in Israel and Palestine." *Journal of Sociolinguistics* 24, no. 3 (2020): 388–402.

Taha, Helwa Saleem. Interview by Amal Eqeiq, February 21, 2021.

Tarica, Estelle. *The Inner Life of Mestizo Nationalism*. University of Minnesota Press, 2008.

Tavanti, Marco. *Las Abejas: Pacifist Resistance and Syncretic Identities in a Globalizing Chiapas*. Taylor & Francis, 2002.

Taylor, Analisa. *Indigeneity in the Mexican Cultural Imagination: Thresholds of Belonging*. University of Arizona Press, 2009.
Tedlock, Dennis. *2000 Years of Mayan Literature*. University of California Press, 2010.
Tuck, Eve, and K. Wayne Yang. "Decolonization Is Not a Metaphor." *Decolonization: Indigeneity, Education & Society* 1, no. 1 (2012): 1–40.
Tynan, Lauren. "What Is Relationality? Indigenous Knowledges, Practices and Responsibilities with Kin." *Cultural Geographies* 28, no. 4 (2021): 597–610. https://doi.org/10.1177/14744740211029287.
van den Berghe, Pierre L. *The Quest for the Other: Ethnic Tourism in San Cristóbal, Mexico*. University of Washington Press, 1994.
Vázquez López, Mariano Reynaldo. *Nichim vayichetik / Orquídea de sueños*. Tsotsil/Spanish ed. Unidad de Escritores Mayas-Zoques, 2006.
Vogt, Evon Z. *Fieldwork Among the Maya: Reflections on the Harvard Chiapas Project*. University of New Mexico Press, 1994.
Wade, Peter. "Afro-Indigenous Interactions, Relations, and Comparisons." In *Afro-Latin American Studies: An Introduction*, edited by Alejandro de la Fuente and George Reid Andrews, 92–129. Cambridge University Press, 2018.
Wildcat, Matt, and Daniel Voth. "Indigenous Relationality: Definitions and Methods." *AlterNative: An International Journal of Indigenous Peoples* 19, no. 2 (2023): 475–83.
Williams, Paul Harvey. *Memorial Museums: The Global Rush to Commemorate Atrocities*. Berg, 2007.
Wolfe, Patrick. "Settler Colonialism and the Elimination of the Native." *Journal of Genocide Research* 8, no. 4 (2006): 387–409. https://doi.org/10.1080/14623520601056240.
Worley, Paul M. *Telling and Being Told: Storytelling and Cultural Control in Contemporary Yucatec Maya Literatures*. University of Arizona Press, 2013.
Worley, Paul M., and Ellen Jones. "'Tequio Literario': Translating Indigenous Literature as Communal Labor." In *The Routledge Handbook of Latin American Literary Translation*, edited by Delfina Cabrera and Denise Kripper. Taylor & Francis, 2023.
Worley, Paul M., and Rita M. Palacios. *Unwriting Maya Literature: Ts'íib as Recorded Knowledge*. University of Arizona Press, 2019.
Xie, Ming. *Conditions of Comparison: Reflections on Comparative Intercultural Inquiry*. Bloomsbury, 2015.
Yeshurun, Helit. "Exile Is So Strong Within Me, I May Bring It to the Land." *Journal of Palestine Studies* 42, no. 1 (2012): 46–70.
Youssef, Mary. *Minorities in the Contemporary Egyptian Novel*. Edinburgh University Press, 2018.
Yucatán Magazine. "Mayan Train Project Ignites Anger Among Zapatistas." January 1, 2019. https://yucatanmagazine.com/mayan-train-project-ignites-anger-among-zapatistas/.

Zayyad, Tawfiq [Tawfīq Zayyād]. *ʿAn al-Adab wa-al-Ādāb al-Shaʿbī fī Filasṭīn.* Dār al-ʿAwdah, 1970.

Zayyad, Tawfiq. *Dīwān Tawfīq Zayyād.* Dār al-ʿAwdah, 2000.

Zureik, Elia T. *The Palestinians in Israel: A Study in Internal Colonialism.* Routledge & K. Paul, 1979.

Index

Abdullah, Nusair, 35
Abu-Hanna, Hanna, 78–79, 82, 85
Abu-Remaileh, Refqa, 23–24, 73
Abu Sitta, Salman, 105
Abya Yala, 44, 183n24
Acteal (village), Chiapas, 118; as border village, 124–30; commemorative practices in, 122–23; human rights organizations in, 134, 137; Indigenous massacre in, 120–21, 128–37, 208n69; Indigenous resistance in, 121–22; murals in, 142; settler colonialism in, 126; *Sociedad Civil Las Abejas* and, 119, 127–28, 133–34, 136–37; state surveillance in, 150–51; transport to, 119; Tseltal use in, 126; Tsotsil language use in, 126–27
activism. *See* feminist activism; Indigenous activism; Palestinian activism
Adab al-Iltizām (Literature of Commitment), 179
affinity (*'ulfa*): in Arabic language, 26; between Arabic/Tsotsil languages, 22–30; bilingual model of, 24–25; as characteristic of Muslim conduct, 27–28; conceptual framework and scope of, 4, 7, 18; emotional connotations of, 22; equality and, 47; al-Ghazali on, 27–28; in Global South, 165–66; methodological approach to, 14–18; organic development of, 4; in Quran, 26; relationality and, 8, 48–50; solidarity and, 26; *ṣumūd* and, 151; supernatural elements of, 28–29; verb forms of, 26–27
Aguilar Gil, Yásnaya Elena, 31
Ahmadiyya Muslims, 36
Ak'abal, Humberto, 104

Akash, Munir, 182n14
AlAmmar, Layla, 112
Ali, Yusuf, 27, 186n14
Allen, Chadwick, 7
Amara, Muhammad, 75
Amazigh, 23
Amer, Ramy, 150–51
Amer, Rose, 155–56
American Indian languages, 24
Amin, Samir, 5
anticolonialism: Global South and, 23; in Latin America, 10; in Palestine, 10; Zapatista uprising and, 1
anti-globalization, Zapatista uprising and, 1
Antoon, Sinan, 106
Anzaldúa, Gloria, 25, 106, 115–117
Apartheid Wall (*al-Jidār*), 179; in murals, 3; in occupied Bethlehem, 19, 165; symbolism of, 19
Apter, Emily, 40–41
Arab Americans, murals by, 2–3
Arabesques (Shammas), 79
Arabic language: affinity concept in, 26, 50; affinity with Tsotsil language, 22–30, 50, 55–56, 197n45; Classical, 81; colloquial (*'amiyya*), 81; as endangered language, 16; erasure of, 56, 80–90, 200n101; *fuṣḥa*, 81–82; geographical boundaries of, 93; Hebrew Zionists use of, 74; Indigenous languages in relationship with, 189n49; linguistic erasure of, 73–80; militarization of, 77–78; as model of authenticity, 74; modernization of, 29; Modern Standard Arabic, 81; as official language, 76,

225

Arabic language *(continued)*
  92–93; preservation of, 80–90; racialization of speakers, 77–78; in rap music, 21–22; relationality in, 43; religious connection with Tsotsil, 35–36; Spanish language as mediator with Tsotsil, 33–34; Tsotsil bilingualism with, 6, 50; *'ulfa* in, 31–32
Arab Writer's Union, 77
Aragón Reyes, Alberto, 184n1
'Araidi, Na'im, 79
Arias, Arturo, 84, 101, 195n14
Asad, Muhammad, 186n14
Ashkenazim, as Jewish cultural group, 75, 77
El-Asmar, Fouzi, 77
Atlas of Palestine, 1917–1966 (Abu Sitta), 105
Aubry, Andrés, 57–58
awakening. See *Nahda*
Azem, Ibtisam, 95, 106–110, 114
Azem, Mustapha, 125

Baeza, Cecilia, 6
Baldly, Cutcha Risling, 49
Barakat, Rana, 144
Bariento, Pedro, 195n14
Basic Law: Israel as the Nation-State of the Jewish People (2018), 76
"Bats'i k'op" ("Tsotsil") (Vázquez López), 67–68
Bats'i k'op (Tsotsil language), 51, 84; and *Bats'il k'op* (Tseltal), 33
Bautista Vázquez, Ruperta, 62, 65–66, 138, 208n69
Bay Area World Without Walls Coalition, 2
BDS. See Boycott, Divestment, and Sanctions movement
Ben-Gurion, David, 132
Benjamin, Walter, 39–40
Berghe, Pierre van den, 99
Betan, Xun, 16, 56, 102, 187n29; "Flowers for the Heart," 69–73; "Mother Moon," 69–70; Tsotsil language and, 32, 42–43
Bethlehem, Israel, occupation of, 19, 165
Bible, Tsotsil translation of, 32, 41–42
bilingualism: affinity and, 24–25; Arabic language and, 6; in education, 62; fragmentary, 53; in Mayan literature, 11, 56, 193n6; in Palestinian literature, 11, 56; Tsotsil and, 6, 50, 53
Blatman, Naama, 106
Bolom Pale, Manuel, 45–46
Bonfil Batalla, Guillermo, 59–60
The Book of Disappearance (Azem), 112
borders, borderlands and: Anzaldúa on, 115–117; checkpoint metaphor and, counter-border space and, 41; Green Line and, 120, 203n1; for Israel, 203n1; in Mayan literature, 115–118; in Palestinian literature, 115–118; settler colonialism and, 116–117; *ṣumūd* and, 118; *'ulfa* and, 40–41, 116–117; between U.S. and Mexico, 40–41
Boycott, Divestment, and Sanctions movement (BDS), 159
Buenvivir concept, 44–45
Burdette, Hannah, 64–65
Burstein, John, 58
al-Bustani, Butrus, 29

Canova, Jane, 138
Casanova, Pascale, 12
Casas, Bartolomé de las, 127
Caso, María Lombardo de, 195n20
Castellanos, Rosario, 60–62, 195n20
Castellanos Martínez, Javier, 62–63
Castro, Carlo Antonio, 62, 195n20
El Centro Indigena de Capacitación Integral (CIdeCi) (UNITIERRA), 5
Chacón, Gloria Elizabeth, 11, 59, 193n6
Chamula Muslims, in San Cristóbal, 5; Tsotsil use by, 37
Chávez Pavón, Gustavo, 19, 160, 165, 184n1
Chechev, Ibrahim (Imam), 32–33, 42
Chechev, Marcos Abdel Hafeeth, 188n41
checkpoint, metaphor, 40–41. See also *Maḥasīm*
Chiapas state, Mexico: La Escuelita Zapatista in, 34; indigeneity in, 91; *indigenismo* and, 60; *indigenista* literary movement in, 60; modernization of, 101–2; Muslim community in, 37; New Chiapanecan School, 44; political similarities to Palestine, 1; settler colonialism in, 90; solidarity with Palestine, 21–25; *To Exist Is to Resist* mural, 20, 50; Tsotsil in, 90
Chicano/a people: materiality of borders for, 116; murals by, 2–3
Cho'l (Indigenous language), 52
CIdeCi. See *El Centro Indigena de Capacitación Integral*
The Civil Society of Bees. See *Sociedad Civil Las Abejas*
Classical Arabic, 81
Clement, Jennifer, 64
colloquial Arabic. See Arabic language
colonialism: Spanish, 95; trans-Indigenous approach to, 7; Tsotsil erasure by, 31. See also settler colonialism
communalism, 44

INDEX

connection between similar things. See *ko'olajel*
Conquista (Spanish conquest of the Americas), 180; historical context for, 10
Cooperson, Michael, 30
Cortázar, Julio, 9
coyote smuggler. See *pollero*
critical comparativity, 43–44
Cruz Cruz, Petrona de la, 96–97
Cuba, OSPAAAL in, 9
Cubells, Lola, 46
Cutipa-Zorn, Gavriel, 2

Darwish, Mahmoud, 6, 16, 56, 81, 131, 205n29; Palestinian Liberation Organization and, 80; resistance poetry of, 78, 88–90, 145–46; in Resistance Poets movement, 87–88; on *'ulfa*, 30
David, Humphrey T., 30
Davies, Humphrey, 24
de-Arabization, of Palestine, 73–75, 78–79
decolonialism, decolonization and: border crossing and, 40; Global South and, 23; radical relationality and, 49; relationality and, 49; Zapatistas and, 64–65
Decolonizing Methodologies (Smith), 192n73
Deleuze, Gilles, 43
deterritorialization, indigeneity and, 56
dialogical thinking, 25
Díaz, Julio César, 134
Dori, Latif, 131
Duarte, Carlota, 58
Dyg'Nojoch, 149–51

Ejército Zapatista de Liberación Nacional (Zapatista Army of National Liberation, EZLN), 136–37
Eqeiq, Amal, 181n4, 184n1, 185n3, 200n1, 208n71
equality, affinity and, 47
erasure, eradication and: of Arabic language, 56; colonialism as influence on, 31; of Tsotsil, 31, 56
La Escuelita Zapatista (The Little School), 34
ethnic cleansing, genocide and: in Gaza, 157–66; of Mayan culture, 195n13; of Palestinians, 7–8
EZLN. See *Ejército Zapatista de Liberación Nacional*

Fanon, Frantz, 11–12
feminist activism: Amer and 155–56; Cubells and, 46; López and, 155–56; Shalhoub-Kevorkian and, 114, 165; Tamimi and, 5, 165
feminist movements: Arab feminism, 110; Indigenous feminism, 49; La FOMMA and, 95–98
First Intifada, 107
Fedzilla, 21
"Flowers for the Heart" (Betan), 69–73
La FOMMA, 100, 102, 105; in feminist movement, 95–98; *Las risas de Pascuala*, 98–99; San Cristóbal and, 95–99
47Soul, 21
freedom, 45
Freire, Paulo, 25, 57
Frischman, Donald, 57

Gabriel, Dahan, 132–33
García Márquez, Gabriel, 9
Gaza, Palestine: artist activism in support of, 159; Boycott, Divestment, and Sanctions movement, 159; Chiapas Palestine Action and, 159; genocide in, 157–66, 198n76; Zapatistas solidarity with, 157–66
Ghalayini, Basma, 111–112
Ghanayim, Mahmud, 198n69
Ghanim, Honaida, 204n10, 198n62
al-Ghazali, Abu Hamed, 27–28
al-Ghazi, Abu Ishaq, 83
Ginsburg, Mitch, 183n28
Glaschiøt, Jens, 137
Glissant, Édouard, 48
global intifada, 1
Global North: knowledge production, 24–25; neoliberal capitalism in, 10. *See also specific countries; specific regions*
Global South, 8; affinities in, 165–66; anticolonialism and, 23; decolonialism and, 23; Indigenous subalternization in, 23; political landscape of, 10; racialization in, 23; settler colonialism in, 158. *See also specific countries; specific regions*
González Casanova, Pablo, 3
The Great Tzotzil Dictionary of Santo Domingo Zinacantán (Haviland and Laughlin), 41–42, 57, 187n28, 189n51
Green Line: border of, 120, 203n1; Historic Palestine and, 4; Kafr Qasem village and, 124; The Triangle and, 4, 161–62. *See also* Armistice Line
Gritón, Antonio, 160
El-Guabli, Brahim, 185n6, 189n49,
Guatemala, 134
Guattari, Félix, 43

Habibi, Emile, 81–82, 107, 115, 130–31
Haifa (Historic Palestine), Israel, 107–111, 114–115; racial segregation in, 112; settler colonialism in, 113; urbanization of, 105–6
Haj Yehia, Raoof, 204n6
Halaby, Samia, 144
Hart, Maria H., 128
Hass, Amira, 75
Haviland, John Beard, 32, 41–42, 57, 187n28, 189n51, 194n8
Hebrew language, use of: in Israel, 74, 80–81; Language War and, 74; in Palestinian literature, 80
Hebrew Zionists, 74
Helawy, Sheikha, 16, 95, 110–111, 114–115
Herrera, Juan Felipe, 138
al-Himyari, Marthad al-Khayr bin Yankaf, 186n17
Historic Palestine: Green Line and, 4; Judaization of maps of, 75; Language War in, 74; *Nakba* and, 162–65; partition of, 8; territorial erasure of, 80–81
humanism, *'ulfa* and, 29–30
"*Hunā bāqūn*" ("Here We Shall Remain") (Zayyad), 85–87
al-Husayni, Abed Al-Qadir, 185n3
Hussein, Rashid, 78, 80

Ibn al-Qaysarani, 82–83
Ibn Hazm, Ali ibn Ahmad, 28–29
ICC. *See* International Criminal Court
ICJ. *See* International Court of Justice
Idle No More Movement, 9
INALI. *See Instituto Nacional de Lenguas Indígenas*
Incantations (Past), 65
Inda, Angélica, 58
indigeneity: Amazigh and, 23; in Chiapas, 91; deterritorialization and, 56; *mestizaje* and, 3–4; settler colonialism and, 106
indigenismo, 60
indigenista literary movement, 59–62
Indigenous activism: in Israel, 4; in music, 21–22; transnational networks for, 2
Indigenous languages: Arabic language in relationship with, 189n49; contact zones and, 34; demands of, 31; de-Othering of, 31; erasure of, 59; International Year of Indigenous Languages, 91; in Mayan literature, 52; translation of, 32–33, 104. *See also* Tseltal; Tsotsil
Indigenous literature: in Chiapas, 60; *indigenista* literary movement, 59–62. *See also* Mayan literature; *tequio literario*

Indigenous peoples: Otherness of, 34; right to self-determination for, 1. *See also* Mayans; *specific people*
Indigenous studies, 7; terminology challenges in, 13–14
Instituto Nacional de Lenguas Indígenas (National Indigenous Languages Institute, INALI), 44
interculturalism, 44
International Court of Justice (ICJ), 157, 160–61
International Criminal Court (ICC), 160
International Solidarity Movement (ISM), 139–40
Intifāda (uprising), 179
Intifada, in Palestine (1987): First Intifada, 107; global intifada and, 1; Second Intifada, 162–63; Zapatista uprising compared to, 1
al-Isfahani, Abu al-Faraj, 27
ISM. *See* International Solidarity Movement
Israel: Basic Law: Israel as the Nation-State of the Jewish People, 76; borders for, 203n1; creation as exclusively Jewish state, 50, 193n5; Hebrew use in, 74, 80–81; Indigenous resistance in, 4; occupied Bethlehem, 19; Rhodes Ceasefire Agreement, 124; settler colonialism in, 3–4, 198n62; June 1967 War and, 81, 83. *See also* Historic Palestine; Palestine; The Triangle; *specific cities*

"*al-Jadīla*" ("The Braid"), (Helawy), 95, 110–111
Jarrar, Khaled, 20–21
Jayyusi, Salma Khadra, 107
al-Jidār (Apartheid Wall), 179. *See also* Apartheid Wall
"*Jme'tik ta bats'i k'op*" ("Mother Moon") (Betan), 69–70
Johnson, Jimmy, 129
Jones, Ellen, 32–33, 187n31
Juan Pérez Jolote (Pozas), 60–61, 180
Juárez Espinosa, Isabel, 96–97
June 1967 War, 81, 83

Kafr Qasem (village), Palestine, 119, 208n76; as border village, 124–30; commemorative practices in, 122–23; familial networks in, 123; Green Line and, 124; Indigenous massacre in, 120–21, 130–37, 141, 143–44; Indigenous resistance in, 130–37; massacres in, 120–21, 130–37, 141, 143–44, 155; murals in, 146–47; The Panorama and, 143–46, 146–47, 148; rural infrastructure

of, 122–23; state surveillance in, 150–51; urbanization of, 144–45
Kanafani, Ghassan, 83, 109, 115
Karkoutly, Burhan, 185n3
al-Karmel (journal), 9, 183n2
Kashua, Sayed, 11, 80, 183n28, 183n30, 193n6
kaxlan (derogatory term for mestizos/as), 180
Kayyal, Majd, 16, 95, 111–113, 114–115
Khaled's Ladder (Jarrar), 20–21
Khalidi, Tarif, 186n14
Khan Younes massacre, 208–9n76
Khatibi, Abdelkebir, 25
Khattab, Mustafa, 186n14
Khleif, Waleed, 204n6, 209n77
Khoury, Elias, 24
knowledge production, in Global North, 24–25
ko'olajel (connection between similar things), 42–44
kuffiyeh (Palestinian scarf), 2, 5, 19–20, 160
Kushelevsky, Shabtay, 75
kuxlej (to exist, sustenance), 38–44; methodological approach to, 14–18
kuxlejal (life, or "life-existence") 44; methodological approach to, 14–18

ladino/as: domination over Mayans by, 8, 96–98; racial segregation by, 117; racism by, 96–98, 103–4; in San Cristóbal, 96–105. See also Mayans, as people
Lamber, Léopold, 185n11
Landa, Diego de, 58
Language War, 74
Lassele, Ferdinand, 74
Latin America: anticolonial movement in, 10; liberation movement in, 10. See also specific countries; specific topics
Latino/a culture, iconography for, 22
Laughlin, Robert M., 32, 41–42, 57, 187n28, 189n51, 194n8
Lebanese Civil War, 29
Lebanon, newspapers in, 111
Le Gassick, Trevor, 107
LeVine, Mark, 1
Levy, Lital, 74, 79
liberation movements: in Latin America, 10; in Palestine, 10. See also Indigenous activism; Mayan activism; Palestinian activism; Zapatista uprising; Zapatistas
literatura indigenista, 180
Literature of Commitment. See *Adab al-Iltizām*
The Little School. See *La Escuelita Zapatista*
Lonetree, Amy, 151
López, María Vázques, 155–56

López Gonzáles, Juan, 51, 53–54
López Intzin, Xuno, 46–47
López Obrador, Andrés, 91

Mahasim (checkpoint), 179
Mahfouz, Ibrahim, 73
Majzara massacre, 179
Makhoul, Manar, 83, 114
Malinki, Shmuel, 130
Mansour, Shadia, 21
Marcos, Sylvia, 1
Marín, Luis, 84
Martí, José, 187n29
martyrs. See *Shuhadā'*
Masalha, Nur, 73–74, 133
Masalha, Salman, 79
Massarwah, Mariam, 54–55
matanza (slaughter), 180
al-Mawt fī Ḥayfā (Death in Haifa) (Kayyal), 95, 111–114
Mayan activism, Mayan rebels and, 1. See also Zapatista uprising; Zapatistas
Mayan Awakening, 58
Mayan literature: affinity with Palestinian literature, 7–8; bilingualism in, 11, 56, 193n6; borders as theme in, 115–118; contemporary traditions of, 65–73; human-environmental interactions in, 205n24; *indigenista* literary movement and, 59–60; land as theme in, 154–55; political redemption of, 65–73; *El Taller Tzotzil*, 25, 57; *tequio literario* and, 33; in Tsotsil language, 53, 57–73; UNEMAZ and, 51–55
Mayans, as people: *Chilam Balam*, 31; cultural genocide of, 195n13; *ladino/as* dominant over, 8, 96–98, 103–4; literacy for, 59; mestizos/as as dominant over, 8; Originative Peoples, 62, 66; poetry for, 70–71; *Popol Vuh* for, 31; racial segregation for, 117; second-class citizenship of, 9–10; solidarity with Palestinians, 23–25, 46. See also Mayan literature; Tsotsil
Mayan Train project, 91
Melara Navio, Abdel Ghani, 33
Mendel, Yonatan, 76
Mendoza, Carlos, 129
Mendoza Lopez, Jose Bartolomé, 32, 37, 42, 51
Mesoamerica, as conceptual term, 13–14. See also Latin America; Mexico
mestizaje: indigeneity and, 3–4; national imaginary of, 50
mestizos/as, Mayans dominated by, 8; *kaxlan*, 180. See also *ladino/as*

Mexico: national whitening project in, 3; Revolution in 1910, 59–60; settler colonialism in, 3; Trump Wall, 20; U.S. border with, 20–21. *See also* Chiapas state; Indigenous peoples; *specific topics*
Mignolo, Walter, 25, 48–49
Million, Dian, 154
Ming Xie, 43
mirroring, in murals, 3
Mizrahim, as Jewish cultural group, 75
Modern Standard Arabic (MSA), 81
Molina Urbina, Juan Erasto, 184n1
Montemayor, Carlos, 58
Moraga, Cherrie, 25
Moreton-Robinson, Aileen, 118
Morquecho Escamilla, Gaspar, 96
MSA. *See* Modern Standard Arabic
Muhawi, Ibrahim, 198n67, 205n29, 206n42
multiculturalism, 64
murals, artworks and: in Acteal village, 142; Apartheid Wall in, 3; by Arab Americans, 2–3; by Chicano/a people, 2–3; contact motifs in, 3; in Kafr Qasem village, 146–47; mirroring in, 3; by Muslim Americans, 2–3; by Palestinians, 2–3; *ṣumūd* themes in, 137–42, 144–51; Zapatistas and, 158
El muro (U.S. fence wall), 180
music, songs and, activism through, 21–22
Muslim Americans, murals by, 2–3
Muslims: affinity as characteristic of, 27–28; Ahmadiyya Muslims, 36; in Chiapas, 37. *See also* Chamula Muslims; Muslim Americans
Mustawṭana (Zionist colony), 179
Muʾammar, Tawfiq, 83

Nafez, Omm, 208–9n76. *See also* Khan Younes massacre
Nahda (awakening/renaissance), 73
Nakba (catastrophe), 73, 105, 179; Historic Palestine and, 162–65
Nash, June, 204n21
Nashef, Ismail, 75, 83–84
Nassar, Maha, 80
National Indigenous Languages Institute. *See Instituto Nacional de Lenguas Indígenas*
nationalism, Indigenous peoples as icon of, 59–60
Native Americans, 182n14
neoliberalism: in Global North, 10; Zapatista uprising as response to, 1
New Chiapanecan School, 44
New Materialism, 48

Occupied West Bank, in Palestine, 55, 75, 138
Oficio de tinieblas (Castellanos), 61
Olwan, Dana M., 8–9
On the Duties of Brotherhood, 28
Organization of Solidarity with the Peoples of Asia, Africa, and Latin America (OSPAAAL), 9
Originative Peoples, Mayans as, 62, 66
Oslo Peace Accords, 179
OSPAAAL. *See* Organization of Solidarity with the Peoples of Asia, Africa, and Latin America
Othering, Otherness and, of Indigenous peoples, 34

Palacios, Rita M., 13, 45
Palestine: anticolonial movement in, 10; Apartheid Wall as symbol of, 19; Armistice Line in, 125; under British Mandate, 76; colonial fragmentation of, 106; de-Arabization of, 73–75, 78–79; division of, 76; educational system in, 54; erasure of, 73–80; First Intifada, 107; global recognition as independent state, 164; as global symbol of resistance, 163–64; International Solidarity Movement in, 139–40; Judaization of, 81, 96; in 1948, 25; Occupied West Bank in, 55, 75, 138; Palestinian Liberation Organization, 80; political similarities to Chiapas, 1; re-mapping of, 95; settler colonial policy in, 81; solidarity with Chiapas, 21–25; steadfastness in development of, 2; The Triangle in, 4; in Tsotsil language, 38–39. *See also* Gaza; Palestinians; The Triangle; *specific topics*
Palestine 1492 (Quiquivix), 35
Palestinian activism, through music, 21–22
Palestinian Liberation Organization (PLO), 80
Palestinian literature: affinity with Mayan literature, 7–8; bilingualism in, 11, 56; borders as theme in, 115–118; in Hebrew, 80; land as theme in, 154–55; *Nahda* and, 73; perplexity novels, 114; in post-*Nakba* era, 24, 144
Palestinian Revolution, 9
Palestinians: checkpoint metaphor for, 40–41; clothing and attire for, 2; ethnic cleansing of, 7–8; as Indigenous national minority, 114; *kuffiyeh* for, 2, 5, 19–20, 160; murals by, 2–3; *Nakba*, 73, 105, 162–65, 179; solidarity with Mayans, 23–25
Pan-Arabism, 80
Pappé, Ilan, 133

Past, Ámbar, 5, 58, 65, 188n40
Paz, Octavio, 138
Peñate Montejo, Juana Karen, 138, 208n69
People's Conference on Climate Change and the Rights of Mother Earth (2010), 44
Pérez, Maria Patricia, 190n59
perplexity novels, 114
pessoptimism, 107–8
PLO. *See* Palestinian Liberation Organization
pluriversality, 44, 48
poetry, poetics and: for Mayans, 70–71; resistance, 78, 84–90; Resistance Poets movement, 87–88; in Tsotsil, 65–66, 68–73; Zionist, 77
pollero (coyote smuggler), 180
Popol Vuh (Book of Creation), 31
Pozas, Ricardo, 60–61, 180, 195n20
Pratt, Mary Louise, 34
Pukuj, Manu, 16, 95–98, 102–4

al-Qasim, Samih, 179
Quijano, Aníbal, 59
Quiquivix, Linda, 1, 34–35, 129
Quran: affinity in, 26; in Classical Arabic, 81; Spanish translation of, 33; *'ulfa* in, 26–27

Rabasa, José, 129, 134, 206n56
Rabinovich, Silvana, 10
racial segregation. *See* segregation
racism: against Palestinians, 25, 86, 93, 108–110; La FOMMA and, 95–98; in Israeli education system, 75–77; by *ladino/as* against Mayan women, 96–98, 103–4; in San Cristóbal/Jobel, 102, 105; social-scientific, 73. *See also* borders; de-Arabization, of Palestine; segregation, racial; settler colonialism
radical relationality, 49
Al-Ramli, Kashjem, 82
Raz, Adam, 133
relationality: affinity and, 8, 48–50; decolonization and, 49; New Materialism and, 48; radical, 49; *ṣumūd* and, 50; transformative nature of, 8; in Tsotsil, 43–44; *'ulfa* and, 41–47
religion, *'ulfa* and, 30
renaissance. See *Nahda*
resistance movements: in Acteal village, 121–22; in Israel, 4; in Kafr Qasem, 130–37; Palestine as global symbol of, 163–64; poetry and, 78, 84–90; Resistance Poets movement, 87–88. *See also* Zapatista uprising
resistance poetry, 78, 84–90

Resistance Poets movement, 87–88
Reyes-Escutia, Felipe, 44
Rhodes Ceasefire Agreement, 124
right to self-determination: of Indigenous peoples, 1; Mayan rebels and, 1; for Palestinians, 6
Las risas de Pascuala (La FOMMA), 98–99
Rivas, Eduardo, 160
Robinson N., Shira, 132, 206n34
Rodríguez, Aldo, 159
Rohana, Shadi, 10, 35
Rosenthal, Ruvik, 133
Rubín, Ramón, 195n20
Ruiz, Mikel, 16, 95–98, 100, 196n40
Ruiz, Samuel, 127
rural areas: Kafr Qasem village infrastructure, 122–23; rural-urban divide in San Cristóbal, 96–105, 200n7
Rus, Diane L., 58
Rus, Jan, 58, 63, 96

Sabbagh-Khoury, Areej, 106
Sabra and Shatila massacre, 134, 206–7n56
El-Sa'doni, Abdullah, 208–9n76. *See also* Khan Younes massacre
Said, Edward, 5, 12
Salaita, Steven, 7
San Cristóbal/Jobel, Chiapas, Mexico: Chamula Muslim community in, 5, 37; La FOMMA and, 95–99; ladino/as in, 96–105; racial exclusion of Mayans in, 102, 105; rural-urban divide in, 96–105, 200n7; Zapatista uprising of 1994 in, 96, 99–100
Santana Echeagaray, María Eugenia, 45
"*Sāriq al-Nawm:Gharib Ḥayfāwi*" (The sleep thief) (Azem), 95,106–110
Sarsur, Wadi' Muhammad, 130
Second Intifada, 162–63
segregation, racial: Apartheid Wall as symbol of, 19; in Haifa, 112; by ladinos, 117; for Mayans, 117
Selim, Samah, 40
Sell, Sean S., 100
settler colonialism: in Acteal village, 126; Apartheid Wall as symbol of, 19; borders and, 116–117; in Chiapas, 90; in Global South, 158; in Haifa, 113; indigeneity and, 106; in Israel, 3–4, 198n62; in Mexico, 3; in Palestine, 81, 90; racialized, 161; *ṣumūd* and, 154–55; tenets of, 4; by Zionists, 1, 39, 162, 198n62
Shalhoub-Kevorkian, Nadera, 114, 165
Shamdi, Yishhar, 130
Shammas, Anton, 11, 79, 193n6

al-Shidyaq, Faris, 29–30
Shohat, Ella Habiba, 77
Shu'arā' al-muqāwama. See Resistance Poets movement
Shuhadā' (martyrs), 179
Shu-mei Shih, 48
Sikseck, Ayman, 80
Simpson, Audra, 117
Simpson, Leanne Betasamosake, 95, 104
Siqueiros, David, 185n3
slaughter. See *matanza*
Slymovics, Susan, 84, 204n6, 209n77
Smith, Linda Tuhiwai, 192n73
Snow, Jess X., 2
social Darwinism, 73
social-scientific racism, 73
Sociedad Civil Las Abejas (The Civil Society of Bees), 119, 127–28, 133–34, 136–37
Sodardo, Amy, 121
Sojob, Maria, 200n7
solidarity, 44; affinity and, 26
Sommer, Doris, 104
Sommers, Joseph, 195n20
Sorek, Tamir, 204n6
Spanish, as language: as mediator language between Arabic and Tsotsil, 33–34; in rap music, 21–22; Tsotsil bilingualism with, 55
Sommers, Joseph, 195n20
steadfastness. See *ṣumūd*
Steele, Cynthia, 61
Suleiman, Camelia, 75
Suleiman, Faraj, 111
Suleiman, Yasir, 75
ṣumūd (steadfastness), 16, 179; affinity and, 151; border crossing and, 118; murals and, 137–42, 144–51; political vision of, 44; relationality and, 50; settler colonialism and, 154–55; Zayyad and, 87

El Taller Tzotzil (The Tsotsil Workshop), 25, 57
Tamimi, Ahed, 165
Tarica, Estelle, 195n21
Tavanti, Marco, 128
Taylor, Analisa, 195n24
Teatro Guignol, 61
Tedlock, Dennis, 59
Tel Aviv, Israel, 109–110
tequio literario, 33, 187n31; *'ulfa* and, 38–39
testimonio, 180
Third World, political geography of, 22
Third Worldism, 9
Tojolabal (Indigenous language), 52
Tonalmeyotl, Martín, 64
Tote-Abuelo, (Sojob), 200n7

To Exist is to Resist (mural), 20, 50
to link. See *vincularidad*
translational identity, 41
The Triangle, 4, 124, 161–62
Trump, Donald, Trump Wall and, 20
Tseltal (Indigenous language), 25, 46–47, 190n59; in Acteal village, 126; Zapatistas and, 66
Tsotsil (Indigenous language): in Acteal village, 126–27; affinity concept in, 26, 50; affinity with Arabic language, 22–30, 50, 55–56, 197n45; Arabic bilingualism with, 6, 50; Betan and, 32, 42–43; bilingualism and, 6, 50, 53; among Chamula Muslims, 37; Chamulas and, 35–36; in Chiapas, 90; code-switching with, 32; colonial erasure of, 31; as endangered language, 16; erasure of, 31, 56; "Flowers for the Heart" and, 69–73; geographical boundaries of, 93; literary revitalization of, 57–65; in Mayan literature, 53, 57–73; "Mother Moon" and, 69–70; Palestine and, 38–39; in poetry, 65–66, 68–73; reclamation of, 31, 66; relationality in, 43–44; religious connection with Arabic language, 35–36; scope of, 31; Spanish bilingualism with, 55; *El Taller Tzotzil*, 25; territorialization of, 31; translation of Bible in, 32, 41–42; *'ulfa* in, 31–47; UNEMAZ and, 51–55, 66; urban use of, 54; Zapatistas and, 66
The Tsotsil Workshop. See *El Taller Tzotzil*
Tsu, Marián Peres, 134–35
Tubi, Tawfiq, 131
Tuck, Eve, 95
Tynan, Lauren, 8

'ulfa (Arabic): affective attributes of, 25–30; in Arabic language, 31–32, 39–40; borderlands and, 40–41, 116–117; conceptual framework for, 4, 29, 186n17; Darwish on, 30; humanism and, 29–30; *ko'olajel* and, 42–44; nonreligious elements of, 28; in Quran, 26–27; relationality and, 41–47; religion and, 30; solidarity of, 6; *tequio literario* and, 38; in Tsotsil, 31–47
UN. See United Nations
Unidad de Escritores Mayas-Zoques (UNEMAZ), 51–55, 66
United Nations (UN): Genocide Convention, 161; International Year of Indigenous Languages, 91
United States (U.S.): American Indian languages in, 24; imperialism of, 48; Mexico border with, 20–21

UNITIERRA. See *El Centro Indigena de Capacitación Integral*
universalism, Arab, 30
uprising. See *Intifāḍa*
urban areas, urbanization and: of Haifa, 105–6; of Kafr Qasem, 144–45; rural-urban divide in San Cristóbal, 96–105, 200n7; Tsotsil use in, 54
U.S. *See* United States

Vázquez Gómez, María, 135
Vázquez López, Mariano Reynaldo, 16, 56, 67–68, 196n40
Vidal-Naquet, Pierre, 206n56
Vilner, Meir, 131
vincularidad (to link), 48–49
Vogt, Evon Z., 57
Voth, Daniel, 8
"*Vovijel*" (Pukuj), 102–4

Wahbi, Hassan, 40
Wildcat, Matt, 8
Wilde, Oscar, 74
Wolfe, Patrick, 4
Words of the True Peoples, 58
Worley, Paul M., 32–33, 45, 187n31

Yang, K. Wayne, 95
Yassin, Aicha, 110–111
Yawmiyyāt al-Ḥuzn al-ʿĀdī (*Journal of an Ordinary Grief*), (Darwish), 78, 88–90

Yazzie, Melanie K., 49
Younan, Munib, 184n1

al-Zamashkhari, Mahmoud ibn Omar, 27
Zapata, Emiliano, 180, 185n3. *See also* Zapatistas
Zapatismo, 180. *See also* Zapatista uprising
Zapatista Army of National Liberation. See *Ejército Zapatista de Liberación Nacional*
Zapatista uprising (1994): as anticolonialist, 1; anti-globalization and, 1; global intifada and, 1; neolilberalism and, 1; Palestinian Intifada compared to, 1; as postmodern revolution, 1; in San Cristóbal, 96, 99–100
Zapatistas, 180; Chiapas Palestine Action and, 159; clothing and attire for, 2; decolonial movement and, 64–65; EZLN and, 123, 129, 136–37; Gaza Genocide and, 157–66; murals and, 158; Tsotsil and, 66
Zayyad, Tawfiq, 16, 56, 81–82; resistance poetry of, 78, 84–87; *ṣumūd* poetry, 87
Zedillo Ponce de León, Ernesto, 137
Zepeda, Eraclio, 195n20
Zionism, Zionists and: Hebrew, 74; historical context for, 10; literacy mode of, 83; poetry for, 77; settler colonialism and, 1, 39, 162, 198n62
Zoabi, Himmat, 114
Zoque (Indigenous language), 52
Zureik, Elia, 3

Amal Eqeiq is Associate Professor of Arabic Studies and Comparative Literature at Williams College.

www.ingramcontent.com/pod-product-compliance
Lightning Source LLC
Chambersburg PA
CBHW041227070526
44584CB00006B/322